CLASSIC FASHION PATTERNS

of the 20th century

Anne Tyrrell

Mayfair Fashions

JAEGER

The new shooting Floor opens July 20th.

JAEGER HOUSE, 204, REGENT ST., W.1. TEL. REG. 4050

CLASSIC FASHION PATTERNS

of the 20th century

Anne Tyrrell

BATSFORD

ACKNOWLEDGMENTS

I would like to express my thanks to the following for their guidance and assistance in the preparation of this book: The British Museum Newspaper Library, Colindale, London; Miss Diana Condell and staff of the Imperial War Museum, London; The Costume and Fashion Research Centre, Bath; The Gallery of English Costume, Platt Hall, Manchester; The Hayward Gallery, London; Mrs Dorothy Hedges; Miss Anita Horrocks and staff of the County Museum of Hereford and Worcester, Hartlebury and The Victoria & Albert Museum, London. I should also like to thank International Thomson Publishing Ltd, who have permitted the adaptation of sketches and pattern details from *Tailor and Cutter* magazine, once the world's foremost authority on bespoke tailoring, and which was incorporated into *Men's Wear*, the UK's only weekly publication for the men's clothing trade.

It is impossible to acknowledge all the personal contributions from which this book has benefited. I am greatly indebted to those who have given or lent photographs, fashion journals and clothes.

In addition, I would like to add my warm thanks to my mother, who so carefully typed the manuscript; to my father for his diligence in checking the text and illustrations; and to my husband for his constant support and hard work in lettering and presentation of the patterns. This book owes a great deal to their interest, guidance and criticism. I acknowledge their valuable contribution with sincere thanks.

*** To David ***

First published in the United Kingdom in 1986 under the title *Changing Trends in Fashion*
This edition published in the United Kingdom in 2010 by
Batsford
10 Southcombe Street
London W14 0RA

An imprint of Anova Books Company Ltd

ISBN: 9781906388515

A CIP catalogue record for this book is available from the British Library.

15 14 13 12 11 10 09 08 09
10 9 8 7 6 5 4 3 2 1

Reproduction by Dot Gradations Ltd, UK
Printed and bound by 1010 Printing International Ltd, China

This book can be ordered direct from the publisher at the website: www.anovabooks.com, or try your local bookshop.

Page 1: Gentleman in morning coat, 1913.

Page 2: 1930s hunting dress by Jaeger.

Contents

Introduction

The drawings on the following pages illustrate the main fashion trends for each year under study. They have been compiled from selected garments, patterns, photographs and fashion articles in contemporary newspapers and magazines.

The aim of the book is to provide the reader with a clear picture of the changing trends in fashion during the 20th century up to, and including, the 1960s, and an in-depth study of the evolution of pattern cutting. A major feature is a selection of scaled patterns, presented in chronological order, which will prove invaluable to the theatrical costume designer, cutter, student of fashion and actor alike. The patterns given are representative of each period, and care has been taken to follow pattern construction techniques appropriate to the time.

In any book of this type, selection is necessary, and many interesting details have to be omitted. However, an extensive bibliography and sources of additional information are supplied, which may lead the reader to further research.

The costumes chosen are those that are felt to be most important or most characteristic of the time, and they have been categorized for the sake of clarity and convenience. Costumes are mostly those of the upper middle classes, but the very essence of fashion during the 20th century is its more democratic nature and therefore, as during the 1950s, teenage fashion is included. No fashion study can ignore the influence that youth begins to exert on major fashion trends.

Fashion is a strange phenomenon, and one which reflects and adds to a total 'spirit of the time', and an attempt has been made to capture this spirit in the illustrations of each period. Each era begins with a detailed introduction which examines the contrasts, distinctions and similarities that exist in 20th century fashions in relation to social, economic and technological changes within society.

The 20th century witnesses the birth of 'fashion', as we are familiar with the term today. Technological developments in mass-production, introduction of new fibres, improved methods of transport and distribution, the expansion of the mass media with greater circulation of newspapers and magazines – providing as they did greater advertising opportunities – all interacted, as fashion became a universal, powerful, commercial interest. The availability of cheaper fabrics gave added momentum to the progress of ready-to-wear and inevitably to department and chain stores. It is the period of the 'retail revolution', in which road transport and rationalization of outlets made possible the concentration of distribution in a few large centres, and spread the concept of multiple chain stores selling the products of large, wholesale organizations. The rise of the boutique in the 1960s also served to increase the availability of fashion and to accelerate pace and change.

The role of the great fashion houses began to diminish and there was a move from the monopoly which Society and Paris had enjoyed. These still furnished an indispensable foundation, but were supplemented by further very varied elements to which the cinema, the stage, the world of sport and motoring, the role of women within society, youth and the arrival of the pop scene, all supplied contributions.

Interest centres mainly on female dress, which witnesses far more rapid and drastic changes than male fashion. During the 20th century there have been no major changes in the style of the male lounge suit, and standardization set in, accelerated by mass-production. Prior to 1939 there were specific rules for correct attire on certain occasions, although we are aware of a change in outlook beginning in the inter-war period. Informality became the overriding influence dominating male dress, and major changes were seen only in lapel shapes, number of buttons and length and width of trousers. Feminine dress, likewise, followed a more casual trend; by contrasting the styles of the early 1900s with following fashions, it can be seen that the period before World War I witnessed an interesting transitional stage from early constriction to ease and informality. The war years and feminist movements throughout the 20th century have made important contributions to the cut of female dress.

Whatever steps mankind may take, fashion is always in search of new and revolutionary trends. We have seen that fashion reflects the predominant mood of contemporary life; we can only speculate what form the cut of our clothes will take in future years as lifestyles and attitudes continue to change.

INFORMATION ON PATTERNS

All patterns are ⅕ scale. A grid of 0.5cm squares is provided to assist in enlarging to full-size: one 0.5cm square is equal to 2.5cm. More detailed instructions on enlarging are given in the following section. Some general points:

1 A seam allowance of 6mm (¼in) is included in male patterns, except at fronts and collar edges, since this is the most usual form of presentation in men's tailoring.
2 Seam allowances are not included for women's garments.
3 All patterns are cut without hem allowances, vents, plackets and facings.
4 Grain lines and pattern instructions are included on all pattern pieces. All grain lines are parallel to the edge of the page unless otherwise marked.
5 All patterns are based on a UK size 10–12 (US size 6–8), based on the following standard measurements:

WOMEN

BUST	88cm (34½in)
WAIST	66cm (26in)
HIPS	93cm (36½in)
BACK WAIST LENGTH	
(NAPE TO WAIST):	39.5cm (15½in)
HEIGHT	165–170cm (5ft 5in–5ft 7in)

MEN

CHEST	100cm (39in)
WAIST	82cm (32¼in)
INSIDE LEG	81cm (32in)
NECK (COLLAR SIZE):	40cm (16in)
HEIGHT	170–178cm (5ft 7in–5ft 10in)

Any deviation from the above is clearly indicated in individual pattern notes.

Specific instructions on the making up of garments are not included; additional information and hints on construction are provided in the accompanying text where relevant.

Listing of suitable fabrics and colours becomes increasingly difficult as each year progresses due to the wider variety available. Only the most popular are therefore mentioned.

The patterns follow the basic principles of pattern cutting appropriate to the period. For the most part, men's and ladies' tailored styles have been taken from surviving garments and contemporary tailoring books and magazine articles. Alterations may be required in some instances to retain the correct proportions appropriate to the era, and in relation to the wearer. It should be stressed that tailored clothes for both men and women require skilful cutting and manipulation of the fabric through stretching, shrinking, easing, padding, interfacing and inner construction details, to achieve perfect fit and balance. It is not recommended that the inexperienced attempt such styles without expert advice and assistance.

It is advisable to cut all costumes directly from measurements taken from the wearer's figure, over the appropriate foundation garments. This is of particular importance with the intricate construction at the turn of the century and tightly fitting or bias-cut styles. The patterns are provided as a basis on which to build further adaptations to suit the requirements of the particular costume, and in relation to the figure of the person for whom the garment is intended.

Undergarments change simultaneously with fashion – indeed, they are essential to it – and must be selected with the same consideration and attention to detail as the outer garments. A dress from the 1920s, however carefully constructed, will lack the feeling and colour of the times if it is dressed on a modern figure. The clothes must be worn as they were worn, if a truthful representation of the fashionable figure is to be achieved. Details of underclothes and accessories are provided throughout the text.

INSTRUCTIONS ON ENLARGING PATTERNS

1 Trace the appropriate garment pattern using stout tracing paper.
2 Position the tracing paper over the grid provided and secure with paper clips or any other form of temporary fixing (Figure 1).
3 A new grid should be drawn up with squares five times the size of the squares on the grid provided (i.e. 2.5cm), as shown opposite. The pattern can then be redrawn to full scale, using the squaring method. It is advisable to work with only one pattern piece at a time (Figure 2).

The use of a metric pattern cutting board or metric pattern paper will make this task easier.

NB: To enlarge using imperial measurements, trace the pattern on to a grid of ¼in squares. The pattern may then be enlarged to full scale, using the method outlined above and a grid of 1¼in squares.

Figure 1

Figure 2

Decade 1900–1909

VERLAG DER BAZAR-ACTIEN-GESELLSCHAFT, BERLIN

JUNI

1904

The turn of the century witnessed the passing of the Victorian age with the death of Queen Victoria in 1901. In the same year Marconi developed radio telegraphy and sent the first wireless signal across the Atlantic, the first electric tram cars ran in Britain, and two years later the Wright Brothers made the world's first powered flight – all memorable events and forerunners of a century of change and innovation.

The turn of the century, then, neatly marks the end of the Victorian era; fashion did not change overnight but significant movements did occur with the coming of the Edwardian age. Female fashion, with its flamboyant, extravagant character, adhered to strict rules of dress which placed it well out of reach of all but select high society. Male costume likewise remained tied to convention, with the cut and quality of fabric formulating the essential detail. Paris dictated the new modes and remained unrivalled in the influence it exerted. The very cut and detail of women's clothes defied successful imitation, and dressmaking with its many empiecements made mass-production in any form impossible. The importance of the overworked and underpaid dressmaker remained paramount. By its very nature fashion demanded time and money, and was not yet established as a right of the masses; it remained exclusively a luxury and a status symbol.

Edwardian fashions were all expensive, elaborate and ultra-feminine, relying on numerous undergarments to shape the silhouette. A bell-shaped skirt trailing the ground rustled with the movements of the wearer, achieving the desired shape by the combination of many petticoats, flounced and frilled above the hem. Remaining smooth over the hips, such petticoats rivalled the outer costume with trimmings of ribbon and lace, the final layer of coloured silk correctly revealed as an important fashion feature as the lady walked. The bell-shaped skirt, often remaining longer behind, heightened the effect of the

S-shape silhouette which favoured the figure of the mature, well-built woman. The corset as the foundation of the mode supported the stomach from below, the front of the bodice being made absolutely straight by a rigid whalebone structure. All fullness was thrust forward and upward into the stomach and chest, emphasizing a waspish waist and large hips, and creating a curvaceous and unnatural bend at the back of the body. As James Laver, writing in 1937, suggested: 'the general effect was as if the female body had been cut in two at the waist and the pieces put together again after the upper portion had been pushed several inches forward'.

The size of the bust was further emphasized by the pouching blouse, embellished with tucks, frills, braids and laces, which hung over the corseted waistline, and appeared rather like an overhanging cliff. Boning in foundation garments, and in the dress, moulded, or more accurately, contorted the figure to its essential rounded line. Stiffened supports incorporated in the bodice also controlled the high neckline of the blouse, compelling women to stand with the head inclined slightly upwards. The stance balanced the top-heavy bust and supported wide-brimmed hats worn far forward on the head, projecting almost as far as the bust line. During the day, a lady's clothing covered her from head to toe, with *décolletage* reserved for the evening gown and falling low to reveal a large expanse of bosom, and sometimes, the shoulders.

The efforts which the morning dress ritual inevitably entailed may seem to us in retrospect quite exhausting, and require us to consider the spirit of the age and the purpose to which these energies were directed: that is, an outward display of rank and position in society. We may become even more intrigued when we understand that the fashionable lady adopted several modes throughout the day according to occasion, time and place. These might include breakfast and matinée gowns, walking dresses, travelling coats, sports suits, frilly tea gowns, and luxurious ball and dinner gowns. The list is by no means exhaustive, and each change of clothing possessed an entirely different character inextricably linked with custom according to the hour of the day.

Men's dress, too, was governed by the law of the hour, which necessitated a change of costume maybe three to four times a day. Men's formal wear at the turn of the century included a frock or morning coat with silk top hat, for morning – as the name implies – or business wear, worn usually with striped trousers and contrast waistcoat. A lounge suit or Norfolk jacket provided a more practical alternative for informal or sports events, and men always changed for dinner, even in their own homes, a dress coat or the increasingly popular dinner jacket completing the correct evening attire. Rigid high collars echoed those of their female counterparts, trousers were narrower than previous fashion and without turn-ups, except for country and sport. A sharp crease in the trouser leg also became a more common sight with the introduction of the trouser press in the final years of the 19th century.

Until World War I men's clothes remained tied to strict conventions with little loosening of existing rules of etiquette. However, signs of change were present, which led to small, but significant movements towards a less formal mode of dress. Edward VII exerted a great influence on men's fashion by the care and interest he so obviously took in his own appearance. He occasionally wore the lounge suit, which was establishing itself as the standard male day dress, instead of the frock or morning coat. The frock coat, however, still remained correct for formal and city wear. The lounge suit would usually be worn with matching striped or checked trousers, contrast waistcoat, high collar, bow tie, boots and soft felt hat, and was favoured by younger gentlemen. In summer a boater-style straw hat might be worn, and there began a vogue for lighter fabrics and colours, a trend even more significant in female dress, which chose not to confine the use of cream, eau-de-nil, and pastel blues and greens to the summer months alone – a reaction perhaps to the unrelieved dark, sombre colours of the Victorian age.

Above: Advertisement for Viyella, showing day and night wear.

Opposite: Fashion plate showing elegant day dresses for women and young ladies.

Women, too, like the younger men with their increased activity and interest in sport, looked to adopt an alternative costume. A new generation of women had taken up clerical or shop work, typewriting or telephone operating, and middle-class girls had abandoned leisurely home life to train for professions. Domestic service as the traditional occupation of the working-class woman began to decrease steadily from 1900 with the introduction of gas fires, plumbing and new forms of heating and lighting in wealthier homes. The tailor-made suit for travelling and walking fitted the needs of the 'New Woman' and was one of the first fashions initiated in the British Isles. The outfit consisted of a full ankle-length skirt, blouse or masculine collar and tie, worn with a straw boater, or – for more special occasions – a wide-brimmed hat. The silhouette remained the same as for the main fashion trend, with a wide, stiffened belt tightly encircling the corseted waist. The basic suit could be adapted for cycling, golf or tennis, with the jacket usually discarded for the latter. There was also a separate costume for motoring, but this became almost divorced from fashion, bowing to separate rules and requirements. However, true comfort was not yet established, and dusty roads led to the adoption of voluminous dust coats by men and women alike. For women flat caps, secured by veils, and sometimes enclosing the head completely, protected the complexion of the fair English rose. By the end of the decade private car ownership had increased, aided by Henry Ford's mass-production techniques from 1903. Significantly, many road surfaces were to be tarred and a Road Highways Act of 1903 required registration of motor vehicles and restricted the speed limit to 20 miles per hour.

Above: 1906 illustration showing a muslin frock.

The more active female began to question her role in society on a social and political level. In 1903 Emmeline Pankhurst formed the Women's Social and Political Union to demand votes for women; this became increasingly militant when demonstrations alone failed to have any impact. In 1908 suffragettes chained themselves to the railings at 10 Downing Street and 280,000 attended a demonstration at Hyde Park.

Women were demanding changes to their traditional role and during the 1900s much was beginning to be achieved in developments at other levels of society. The Liberal government introduced a number of reforms which brought an improved standard of living to ordinary people. The Education Act of 1902 established free elementary education to the age of 13, and in 1907 school meals were set up in British schools. In 1909 an Old Age Pension was given to all over seventy with an income of less than ten shillings a week. Better washing facilities, cleansing powders, antiseptics, toothpaste and soaps brought higher levels of hygiene, and new devices such as the phonograph, vacuum cleaner and electric washing machine, from 1907, although they had little impact at the time, promised an easier existence. Improvements in public transport with the first motor buses, electric trams and trains, provided mobility and increased freedom of movement.

The latter half of the decade also brought subtle changes to the cut of female dress, which from 1908 saw the extreme of the fashion modified, and the effective straightening of the female silhouette. The bust became less pronounced and skirts narrowed at the hem. Hats remained large, however, and gradually continued to increase in width.

A positive and forward-looking age, the Edwardian era staged the final scenes of fashion dictated solely by society. In the year that closed the decade a hundredweight of suffragist leaflets were scattered over London from a balloon and Bleriot flew the English Channel. We can now view the age in the wider context of the 20th century, and are aware that although pursuing a slow course, the signs of progress indicated undercurrents of the wave of change that was to affect British fashion and society in ensuing years.

1901

WOMEN

PREDOMINANT FASHION FEATURES

Silhouette softer, lighter and more feminine in contrast to rigid Victorian fashions. Straight-fronted corsets provide the essential hour-glass figure, flattening below the waist and accentuating the bust and hips. Bell-shaped skirts grow progressively tighter over the hips, trailing the ground and usually longer at the back, with the exception of the walking or sports skirt, which just clears the ground. Fussily trimmed corsage with blouse pouching over waist and high neckline. For full evening dress the neckline is cut low, either squared or rounded, the full, trailing skirt often made of diaphanous, flimsy fabrics over a silk or satin foundation.

FABRICS Softer and lighter in character; alpaca, mohair, lawn, fine velvets, silks, fine facecloth, chiffon, faille. Universal use of lace, and lace trimmings. Dust coats and sportswear are made from gabardine, heavy wools and tweeds.

COLOURS Pale pinks, blues, peach, eau-de-nil.

UNDERGARMENTS Straight-fronted whalebone corset, laced at the back with stocking suspenders attached. Silk replacing linen for luxurious underwear (lingerie). Chemise or vest of fine linen, muslin, batiste or lawn, worn under the corset. Camisoles or corset-covers shaped to the waist in batiste or fine muslin, worn under the blouse. Petticoats are essential to bell-shape effect of the skirt, with frills and flounces at the hem. They are sometimes buttoned to lower edge of corset.

FOOTWEAR Pointed or round-toed shoes, high-laced shoes for winter wear, leather, suede or kid. Black, beige or bronze court shoes with Louis heel for evening.

STOCKINGS Black ribbed lisle or cashmere for winter. White stockings are worn with white shoes for summer. Stockings often have lace insertion for evening.

HAIR Drawn on to the top of the head over pads. Hair softly waved with additional fullness at sides and dressed high and full. For evening, hair decorated with ornamental combs, flowers, feathers and false hair pieces.

HATS Always worn. Small and high, lavishly trimmed with feathers, flowers, birds, lace, ribbons and buckles, and worn straight on the head. Toques and straw boaters are popular. Hats secured with decorated and jewelled metal hatpins.

ACCESSORIES Short gloves of black leather or suede for day wear. Full-length gloves in soft kid or silk for evening with long button fastening. Small leather bags for day, embroidered silk or beadwork for evening, with metal chain. Small fans of lace, embroidered or painted silk; feather fans popular for evening. Parasols and umbrellas of lace, silk or moiré. Rings, clip earrings, bracelets and neckbands to enhance the low evening *décolletage*.

MOVEMENT Upright poise with head held high above stiffened neckline. Upper carriage thrust forward and shoulders down. Skirt lifted with the fingers at one side while walking, with the hand resting on backward thrust of the hip, displaying the lower edge of the petticoat.

DETAILS OF ILLUSTRATED PATTERNS

Lady's afternoon dress consisting of a separate bodice and skirt. The bell-shaped skirt trails the ground, being longer at the back than the front, and fits smoothly over the hips. The blousing of the front bodice is very pronounced, and undersleeves are gathered into a cuff. The overbodice meets at the centre front with bell-shaped, set-in sleeves and turn-back roll collar, extending over the sleevehead and to shoulder-bone at back bodice.

Far left: Tunic dress with a chevron design, accordian pleated ruffles and double ruffle decoration.

Left: Advertisement for whale bone corsets.

Right: Drawing of a lady's afternoon dress (for the pattern see pages 16–17).

FABRICS Dress and bodice are worn in alpaca, crêpe and lightweight woollen materials. Bodice blouse front and sleeve ends are made from silk crêpe de Chine, jap silk and nun's veiling. Heavy cotton fabric for underbodice. Heavier silk fabric used for front bodice foundation.

COLOURS Soft subdued tones – powder blue, pink, pale grey, eau-de-nil. Front bodice uses ivory, pink or sky blue.

DECORATION Bodice collar and sleeves are faced in silk taffeta in a deeper tone than the main fabric and edged with pleated taffeta frills. Matching frills are also applied above the hemline of the skirt with taffeta strappings. The bloused bodice front is pin-tucked across its entire width with ivory insertion lace and small frills at centre front. Narrow black velvet ribbon edges the high tucked collar and cuffs. A neck jabot of ivory lace completes the outfit.

HAT Straw hat with upturned brim, decorated lavishly on the underside and crown with various artificial flowers and petersham ribbon.

NOTES ON CONSTRUCTION OF GARMENTS

Make up the underbodice of heavy cotton fabric; this fastens edge to edge at the centre front. The bloused front bodice panel is tucked along lines indicated, then mounted on to front bodice foundation of heavier silk. The raw edges of bodice and foundation are joined at the lower edge, gathered and bound with 2.5cm (1in) wide taffeta crossway strips.

The entire front panel is stitched to the underbodice on the right side and fastens with hooks and eyes at the left (the position is indicated by dotted line on the underbodice pattern), concealing the foundation. The collar is tucked along the lines indicated, stiffened and boned, fastening at the left shoulder seam.

Construct the main bodice separately, the collar cut in one with the front and faced in taffeta. The lower edge of the front bodice is pleated and gathered in to the lower bodice panel to give a pouched effect; this then fastens at the centre front.

Sleeves are faced in taffeta at the lower edge. Sleeve ends of ivory silk are attached to the sleeves under the faced section.

Position of boning on bodice seams is indicated by heavier black lines. The bodice is attached to the skirt with hooks and eyes at centre back.

The skirt is sewn to a narrow waistband with concealed placket in right-front seam. The petticoat is cut on the same lines as the skirt.

MEN

PREDOMINANT FASHION FEATURES

Menswear remains tied to strict conventions. Lounge suits increasingly worn as practical alternative for day or informal wear, fronts of jacket occasionally rounded. Short, pointed lapels with the jacket cut slightly longer and shaped to the waist. Worn with waistcoats of contrasting colour and fabric. Trouser legs are narrow with a crease down the front, slightly wider with morning coat. Trousers sometimes feature turn-ups for country or sportswear.

FABRICS Fine worsted suitings – alpaca, flannel, mohair.

COLOURS Soft blues and greys, small checks and stripes, pale grey for summer wear.

UNDERGARMENTS, UNDERWEAR AND SOCKS As 1902.

FOOTWEAR Boots – two-tone with cloth tops; round-toed, lace-up Oxford-style shoes in black or brown calfskin or patent leather. Tan or white buckskin for summer. Light-coloured spats fastening with buttons and buttonholes.

HATS Always worn outdoors. Silk top hat with morning or frock coat. Bowler hats for city and business wear. Trilby in soft felt, velour or straw, and straw boaters for summer.

HAIR Short with centre parting, smoothed lavishly with hair creams and oils.

ACCESSORIES As 1902.

MOVEMENT Straight and dignified poise with head held proud due to high collar. Stance determined by formality of occasion.

DETAILS OF ILLUSTRATED PATTERNS

Double-breasted frock coat with three buttons on each side and button stands. Lapels are faced in silk, with buttonholes parallel to the top lapel. An outside breast pocket may be present (not illustrated). The coat has a waist seam and centre vent at the back with two hip buttons at the top. The straight sleeves are slit at the cuff, fastening with three buttons. The frock coat is usually worn open, revealing single-breasted waistcoat with collar and lapels. Double-breasted waistcoats are also popular with frock coats. Black-and-white striped trousers.

FABRIC Wool gabardine, worsted or barathea.

COLOUR Black.

HAT Silk top hat.

NOTES ON CONSTRUCTION OF GARMENTS

Face lapels with ribbed silk fabric, as illustrated. Adapt waistcoat pattern from 1906–1907.

Right: Drawing of frock coat (for the pattern see page 17).

COLLAR

CB

COLLAR

A

BODICE
FRONT
cut 2

Fold

A

UNDER-BODICE
FRONT
cut 2

SKIRT

BACK
— — — SIDE BACK
—·—·— SIDE FRONT

cut 2 of each

A

BODICE
FRONT
FOUNDATION
cut 2

CF fold

JABOT
cut 2

CF

BLOUSED BODICE FRONT cut 2

A

CF

BODICE
SLEEVE
cut 2

UNDERSLEEVE CUFF   cut 2

CF fold

SKIRT
FRONT
cut 1 on fold

Gather

Gather

Opening

BODICE
SLEEVE END
cut 2

FROCK COAT
BACK
cut 2

CB

FROCK COAT
SIDE BACK
cut 2

FROCK COAT
FRONT
cut 2

FROCK COAT
FRONT BAND
cut 2

CB fold

FROCK COAT
COLLAR
cut 2
on fold

TROUSERS

BACK cut 2

FRONT cut 2

FROCK COAT
SKIRT
cut 2

BODICE
LOWER PANEL
cut 2

CF

BODICE
SIDE BACK
cut 2

BODICE
BACK
cut 1 on fold

BODICE
PANEL cut 2

CB fold

FROCK COAT
FRONT SLEEVE
cut 2

FROCK COAT
BACK SLEEVE
cut 2

1902

WOMEN

PREDOMINANT FASHION FEATURES

'It was the age of the 'fine' woman, of the mature and well-rounded contour and every fashion of the period might actually have been designed to set her off to advantage and to handicap the young girl' (Laver, *Taste and Fashion*).

All fashion expensive, elaborate and ultra feminine. 'S-shape', Gibson Girl silhouette – straight front; full, heavy, protruding bust; hips pushed backwards.

Pouching blouse exaggerated, deep lace, embroidered yokes, higher necklines, boned to just under the ears. Skirts continue to tighten over the hips.

New corselet skirt, boned and extended above the waistline, usually worn with shorter bolero.

FABRICS Similar to previous fashion. For day wear, velveteen, velvets, silk, organdie, gauze, muslin, gingham, net, serge, alpaca, taffeta, tussore, cashmere, satin, linen, batiste. For evening and tea gowns, frothy lace, chiffon faille, Breton net, ninon, voile, crêpe de Chine and mousseline de soie are all worn.

COLOURS Pale, delicate shades, eau-de-nil, shades of green and blue, soft greys, browns, navy for tailor-mades. White and pastels for evening. Blouses usually white or ecru. Velveteens come in greens, emerald, sage green; reds – tulip, geranium and poppy. Cream serge for country, also grey, fawn, and pale blues.

DECORATION Embroidered and hand-painted fabrics; ubiquitous use of lace – guipure, Cluny, Brussels. Ornamental strappings and stitching, dull metallic buttons, gold and silver braids, ribbon velvet, ruched and pleated silks. Blouses heavily tucked, with lace insertion.

UNDERGARMENTS Straight-fronted corset with long metal stays and hook fastening gives long, sloping bust-line, the bend of the narrow waist accentuated at the back above smoothly curving hips. Empire corset, short above the waist and just covering the bust. Suspenders are attached to the corset, replacing garters. Bust-improvers add emphasis for the less well endowed. Chemise and camisole are worn as previous fashion. Many petticoats, flounced and decorated at the lower edge, continue to support the bell-shaped silhouette. The top petticoat (underslip) in brighter colours – pink, green, peach and luxurious fabrics – taffeta, satin, glacé silk, moirette, rustling with the movements of the wearer.

SHOES AND STOCKINGS Similar to previous fashion.

HATS Slightly larger, with small crowns, tilted with the brim upturned and decorated, as in the previous year. Lavishly trimmed, tricorne shapes and toques remain popular. Fur hats and trimming for winter.

HAIR As previous fashion, with hair fuller at the sides.

ACCESSORIES Similar to previous fashion; round muffs and fur stoles in fox or sable for winter wear. Increasing amount of jewellery worn.

MOVEMENT Poise determined by rigidity of corset and high neck stays, as previously. Head thrown back to balance carriage of body. Movement is further restricted by tightness of skirt over the hips. Petticoats 'swish' with movement.

VERLAG DER BAZAR-ACTIEN-GESELLSCHAFT, BERLIN

JULI
1902

Left: Fashion plate showing two dress designs from 1902.

Right: Drawing of walking skirt and bolero jacket (for the pattern see pages 20–21).

DETAILS OF ILLUSTRATED PATTERNS

Floor-length walking skirt and matching bolero jacket. The skirt extends above the natural waistline, with decorative front panel, and is attached to a silk foundation, boned at the waist and pleated at lower edge. There are four panels, flaring from slim hips. The panelled jacket meets at centre front, with high-rolling shawl collar and three-quarter-length sleeves, gathered tightly at the sleevehead. A cream, silk blouse, with high boned collar and button front, completes the outfit (pattern not supplied).

FABRIC Facecloth.

COLOURS Pale apple green.

DECORATION Panel seams of jacket and skirt are trimmed with a very fine black silk piping. Heavy metal buttons and rouleau loops are applied between curves of these seams. Cuffs and collar are faced with pleated black silk taffeta and cream hopsack fabric, separated by a line of top fabric and piping. The shaped top panel of the skirt is edged with black piping and top-stitched to the skirt; it is decorated with mock gold braid buttonholes.

HAT Straw hat with shallow crown perched well forward on head. Lavishly decorated with artificial flowers and grosgrain ribbon.

NOTES ON CONSTRUCTION OF GARMENTS

The bolero should fit the figure snugly with all seams boned for 10–14cm (4–5½in) from lower edges.

Sleeves are strapped with self-fabric from centre of sleevehead and tucked into shaped facing at lower edge.

Skirt waist is boned for 10cm (4in), or use wide-boned petersham ribbon to face top edge.

Petticoats cut on same lines as skirt; add extra flouncing and pleating at lower edge to support skirt hem.

MEN

PREDOMINANT FASHION FEATURES

Similar to previous year. Lounge suits with slightly longer jackets.

Overcoats – calf-length chesterfield style remains popular, either single-breasted with fly front, or double-breasted, slightly waisted with back vent, and with collars, and sometimes cuffs, faced in velvet. Ulsters, raglans and caped overcoats continue to be worn.

FABRICS Alpaca, grey flannel, narrow-striped fabrics for summer lounge suits.

COLOURS As previous fashion.

SHIRTS All shirts tunic-style. Coloured shirts acceptable for day wear, with linen front and cuffs, white or coloured to match the shirt. Detachable rigid collars, 8cm (3¼in) in height, of white linen or celluloid (for poorer classes). Wing collars (with the points turned down) are worn with evening dress. Polo or double collar popular for day wear.

UNDERGARMENTS Undervest and long pants of knitted wool, wool and silk mix or cotton for summer. Combinations and shorter 'drawers', ending just below the knee, are also worn.

FOOTWEAR Similar to previous fashion.

SOCKS Reaching to mid-calf and held up with suspenders.

HATS Similar to previous fashion. Straw panama styles popular for summer, and stiff felt Homburg styles with indented crown and curled brim.

HAIR As previous fashion.

ACCESSORIES A variety of necktie styles are worn, silk bow ties popular, white with evening dress suit or tails. Fancy Ascot cravat with morning suit. Plain, striped or spotted ties worn with lounge suits. Suede, leather or kid gloves always worn outdoors. White kid or buckskin gloves for evening wear. White handkerchief worn in breast pocket, for decoration. Umbrella or walking stick. Collar studs and cuff links made to match in mother-of-pearl or onyx. For evening wear, links match studs on dress shirt.

DETAILS OF ILLUSTRATED PATTERN

Double-breasted close-fitting chesterfield overcoat with four-button fastening. The lapels are soft rolling, with buttonhole on each side and upper collar of velvet. The close-fitting skirt has centre-back vent and slanted welt pocket at hip. Two-piece straight sleeves are slit at the cuff with four-button fastening. Worn with striped trousers.

FABRICS AND COLOURS Oxford and medium grey cheviots and velours, black-and-white feather designs.

HAT Silk top hat.

NOTES ON CONSTRUCTION OF GARMENT

Use trouser pattern from 1901; adapt waistcoat pattern from 1906–1907.

Right: Drawing of chesterfield overcoat (for the pattern see page 21).

CB

SKIRT
BACK
cut 2

Gather

TUCK

BOLERO
SLEEVE
cut 2

TUCK

SKIRT
FRONT
cut 2

A

CF

BOLERO
CUFF   cut 2

A

CF

SKIRT FRONT PANEL

Ease

CHESTERFIELD
BACK
cut 2

CB

vent

CHESTERFIELD
FRONT
cut 2

CHESTERFIELD
FRONT SLEEVE
cut 2

CHESTERFIELD
BACK SLEEVE
cut 2

CB fold

CHESTERFIELD
COLLAR
cut 2 on fold

BOLERO
FRONT
cut 2

CB

CB fold

BOLERO
BACK
cut 1 on fold

BOLERO
SIDE FRONT
cut 2

BOLERO
SIDE BACK
cut 1 on fold

CB fold

1906–1907

WOMEN

PREDOMINANT FASHION FEATURES

Boleros and skirts remain popular, with full sleeves, semi-gigot style to wrist. Corselet skirts extend well above natural waistline. Walking, sports skirt 5cm (2in) from ground.

Bust less exaggerated and blouses no longer pouched, with straighter front, remaining highly decorated with tucks, embroidery and lace. Empire line, with raised waist effects. Evening dresses cut with low *décolletage* at front and back.

Afternoon or tea gowns are made in one piece in princess or Empire style. Skirts are pleated, gathered or flounced. Ribbon sashes at the waist. Tailor-mades continue in popularity with wider shoulders, and closer-cut sleeves from 1907. Three-quarter-length sleeves popular.

FABRICS Woollen checks, fine herringbone, serge and facecloth for tailor-mades. For afternoon wear, summer linens, heavy lace, muslin, chiffon, tussore, alpacas and shantung are worn; striped fabrics popular. Undergarments are worn in cambric, lawn, batiste, glacé silk, moirette and nainsook.

COLOURS Black, white and pastel shades.

DECORATION Tassels on stoles, jackets and evening wear; velvet pompoms in black and brown; velvets, fur, feathers, embroidery. Crochet lace is in vogue throughout 1907.

UNDERGARMENTS Underclothes slim down; Empire line, princess-style petticoats with higher waist and straighter skirts. Narrow ribbon, lace trim and insertion lace. Corsets shorten above waist, longer below.

FOOTWEAR As previous fashion.

HATS Becoming wider, still lavishly trimmed, fuller crowns and brims, worn tilted forward or to one side (right) with face veils. Tweed hats or caps for sports and countrywear.

HAIR Coiffure similar to previous style although fuller and more puffed. Permanent Marcel waving is popular.

ACCESSORIES Gloves are worn gauntlet style for outdoor wear. Evening gloves are long, to the elbow, in light kid or buckskin, or silk; feather boas and fans. Large fur muffs and stoles are worn in winter. Accessories are generally larger.

MOVEMENT Poise more natural but remaining rigid with front carriage thrust less far forward. Head still held high above boned collar and to balance the wider hat.

DETAILS OF ILLUSTRATED PATTERNS

The outfit consists of a long, belted Norfolk jacket with full-length two-piece sleeves, pleated into sleevehead and narrow at the wrist with shaped cuff. Front and back jacket are strapped with crossway self-fabric, remaining unstitched at waist-level to act as belt carriers. The jacket is single-breasted with high lapel opening, the upper collar faced in silk or velvet.

The gored skirt just clears the ground, with inverted pleats at the base of each seam. Seams are strapped with shaped self-fabric.

The outfit is worn with stiff masculine collar and tie and large tweed peaked cap.

FABRIC AND COLOURS Checked tweed or plain serge in subtle browns and greens.

Left: Bolero bodice with bell-shaped skirt.

Right: Drawing of Norfolk jacket with gored skirt (for the pattern see page 24).

NOTES ON CONSTRUCTION OF GARMENTS

Cut 2.5cm (1in) wide strips of bias fabric to cover jacket seams – position of strappings is indicated by broken lines. Straps are left free over the waistline for belt loops.

Bone all jacket seams, breaking at the waistline.

Attach the skirt to a 5cm (2in) waistband, with concealed placket in left-front seam. The skirt should fit the waist and hips smoothly. The petticoat is cut on the same lines as the skirt, with additional flouncing to support the weight at the lower edge and allow for easy movement. Add pleat extension to all skirt seams as illustrated on skirt front.

Broken lines indicate position and pattern of self-fabric decoration, cut on bias of fabric.

MEN

PREDOMINANT FASHION FEATURES

Lounge suits are generally worn in place of frock coat during the day, except by older gentlemen – the proportions remain similar to previous fashion. A soft-fronted white shirt replaces starched front for business, and coloured for less formal occasions, with the collar remaining white and rigid. Dress shirt fronts are often tucked.

Double-breasted, straight-cut reefer jackets or lounge jackets are worn as informal or sportswear. Tweed sports jackets worn with flannels or matching trousers or knickerbockers.

Norfolk jackets with separate or attached belt and box pleats, popular for shooting and golf. Knitted jumpers, cardigans or waistcoats might also be worn, and breeches or knickerbockers.

FABRICS English wools for overcoats and suits. Trousers are made from vicunas, serge, worsted. Overcoats made from Melton cloth. Tweeds, herringbones for sports jackets. Shirts constructed mainly from Zephyr and Oxford.

COLOURS Grey or brown shades of twill, check or stripe. Heathers and soft browns, small checks with coloured thread forming overcheck in great evidence. Relief from grey, in favour during the first part of the decade. Wide herringbone or feather designs, striped or overchecked with bright coloured twist threads. Grey with slight tinges of blue.

UNDERGARMENTS All shirts tunic-style. Soft-fronted shirt fronts as noted above. Collar height shortened from 7.5cm (3in) to 5cm (2in). Flannel shirt with linen polo, or stand collar for sports. Underwear in previous style.

SOCKS As previous fashion. Patterned in checks or stripes with knickerbockers or breeches.

FOOTWEAR As 1901. Short garter-spats for town and country – usually light grey or fawn, buttoning at one side and fastening under instep with buckle and strap.

HATS For day wear as previous modes. Tweed hats, deerstalkers and pleated caps for sports.

HAIR Side-parting becoming more usual than centre-parting.

ACCESSORIES Similar to previous fashion; walking sticks.

MOVEMENT Movement and posture determined by formality of occasion and clothes. Rules of etiquette in fashion become less rigid.

DETAILS OF ILLUSTRATED PATTERNS

Norfolk jacket with high lapel opening, attached belt and box pleats to waist level at front and back. The jacket skirt is close-fitting with large, expanding flapped pockets and centre-back vent. Two-piece sleeves are slit at the cuff with one-button fastening.

Knee-length knickerbockers are in matching fabric and fasten under the knee with strap and button. They are looser in fit than breeches.

The outfit is worn with peaked cap, long woollen stockings, boots and short gaiters.

FABRIC Checked brown tweed.

NOTES ON CONSTRUCTION OF GARMENTS

Broken line on front jacket indicates position of pleat. Expand the pattern 8cm (3in) to allow for 4cm (1½in) box pleat, as on jacket back.

Construct pockets with additional 2.5cm (1in) pleats at outside edges to allow for pocket expansion.

Left: Gentleman in knickerbockers, ready for a game of golf.

Right: Drawing of Nofolk jacket with knee-length knickerbockers (for the pattern see page 25).

JACKET
BACK
cut 1 on fold

CF fold

JACKET
SIDE BACK
cut 2

SKIRT

PLEAT UNDERLAY   cut 7

SKIRT
BACK AND SIDES
cut 6

Add pleat extension

JACKET
FRONT
cut 2

CB

JACKET
COLLAR
cut 2

JACKET
SLEEVE CUFF
cut 2

CB fold

JACKET   cut 1 on fold
BELT

CF

SKIRT
FRONT
cut 1 on fold

CF fold

JACKET
BACK SLEEVE
cut 2

JACKET
FRONT SLEEVE
cut 2

CB fold

BACK YOKE

NORFOLK
JACKET
BACK
cut 1 on fold

CB fold

NORFOLK
JACKET
BACK SKIRT
cut 1 on fold

CB fold

NORFOLK
JACKET
FRONT
cut 2

CB fold

NORFOLK JACKET
COLLAR cut 2 on fold

KNICKERBOCKERS
--- BACK cut 2
— FRONT cut 2

CB

NORFOLK JACKET KNEE BAND cut 2

NORFOLK JACKET BELT cut 1 on fold

CB

WAISTCOAT
BACK
cut 2

NORFOLK JACKET
SLEEVE FRONT
cut 2

NORFOLK JACKET
SLEEVE BACK
cut 2

WAISTCOAT
FRONT
cut 2

1908

WOMEN

PREDOMINANT FASHION FEATURES

Change in line, with the extreme of Edwardian fashion modified; bust and waist are less exaggerated, with a closer-fitting tubular silhouette. Collar remains stiff and higher than in previous modes. Empire or *Directoire* line affects all fashion. *Décolletage* remains low for evening wear, squarer and with the shoulders covered, and usually consisting of transparent fabrics, partially lined. Outdoors, longer coats are worn over the slimmer skirt. Jackets lengthen generally with the bolero jacket, popular since the turn of the century, no longer worn. Coats or jackets and skirts often differ in both fabric and colour. The Redingote, a long, Empire-line coat is popular.

FABRICS Crêpe de Chine, shantung and georgette. Striped fabrics are seen everywhere. Undergarments in fine linen, muslin, batiste, lawn are worn.

COLOURS Evidence of renewed interest in colour – yellow, peach, blue, brown and pastels. Tea gowns are worn in greens, lavender, warm greys or orange.

DECORATION Ruching for lighter tea gowns and evening dresses, chiffon flowers and embroidery. Braids, strappings and decorative buttons are popular. Tassels on stoles, jackets and evening wear. Feather trimmings on hats.

UNDERGARMENTS As skirts narrow at the hem petticoats slim down, losing their fullness and 'rustling' qualities. Trimmings and decoration are still restricted to the lower edge. Empire style continues. Chemises are worn in Empire style, with narrow shoulders and wide neckline, cut close to figure. Skirt knickers replace combinations.
Corsets even shorter above the waist and longer below, 51–64cm (20–25in) in length. Ribbon corset – 3–4 widths of satin ribbon 5cm (2in) wide, lightly boned at the sides, front fastening, back lacing, for sport and general wear. Petticoats and corsets sometimes combined.

FOOTWEAR High boots to the knees, either buttoned or laced, with higher Louis heels.

STOCKINGS No major changes.

HATS Generally flatter in the crown, with significantly wider brims. Trimming remains lavish, restricted to the crown and top of the hat, rather than under the brim.
'An extremely wide hat always seems to have the effect of narrowing the width of the skirt, as if there were some natural law that forbids the feminine figure to be wide at both ends at once' (Laver, *Taste and Fashion*).

HAIR Middle parting with coiffure widened at the sides, and hair styled more to the back of the head than on the crown, to accommodate larger millinery fashions.
Marcel waving is popular.

ACCESSORIES Generally large – fur muffs, stoles. Evening gloves are worn long, to the elbows.

MOVEMENT Similar to previous year.

DETAILS OF ILLUSTRATED PATTERN

Directoire evening dress with draped bodice and low, square-cut neckline. The skirt is straighter than styles of the early 1900s and less fussily trimmed. A wide velvet sash accentuates the high waistline. The dress fastens at the centre back with placket and hook-and-eye closure. Double sleeves of transparent net and chiffon are gathered into velvet ribbon shoulder straps.

FABRICS Bodice and skirt composed of layers of satin, net and chiffon over a firmer silk foundation.

COLOURS Black, ivory, midnight blue.

DECORATION Dress bodice of draped black net is covered with tiny pearl beads, which also decorate the net overskirt, combined with

Left: *Decolleté* gowns, worn with scandalously transparent fabrics over the chest, conform to the fashion for high collars.

Right: Drawing of the *Directoire* evening dress (for the pattern see page 28).

silver embroidery above hemline. Pearl trimming edges the neckline and black velvet sash, which is finished with silver embroidery and tassels. A silver and pearl buckle under the bust accentuates the raised waistline.

ACCESSORIES Silver and lace fan with silver tassel trim; long kid gloves; wide silver and pearl choker and hair bandeau of velvet and pearls. The hair may also be decorated with trailing flowers, ribbons, combs or feathers.

NOTES ON CONSTRUCTION OF GARMENT

Construct bodice foundation of firm silk and bone all seams as indicated by darker lines on pattern. The foundation meets edge to edge at centre back with hook-and-eye closure. It is entirely covered by a draped overbodice of two layers of net and chiffon, gathered and held in position with pearls and invisible stitching at side seams. An overlap is required on the right side of the overbodice only, to conceal back fastening. The upper edge is trimmed with velvet ribbon and pearls, in the same fashion as the upper sleeve edge.

Make up sleeve and oversleeve separately, each consisting of a layer of net and chiffon, and ease, as one, into shoulder band of velvet trim.

The overskirt of two layers of net and chiffon is gathered on to the skirt foundation of firmer silk and joined to the bodice, leaving a short opening at centre back. The waist seam is concealed by the velvet belt and the latter secured at centre back. The position of the belt is indicated by dotted lines on bodice pattern.

Pleat ends of sash along broken lines indicated on pattern, before applying to underside of belt at centre front.

MEN

PREDOMINANT FASHION FEATURES

No significant changes from previous year in style or fabrics. Bottom button of waistcoat with lounge jacket usually left undone, a trend which continues throughout the 20th century. Collarless styles become more frequent, with opening cut lower.

FABRICS Viyella – new unshrinkable flannel for shirts.

COLOUR Shades of green popular for shirts, but still with white linen collar.

SHIRTS AND UNDERGARMENTS For full evening dress, white shirt with high wing collar, starched dress front in piqué or marcella, pleated front, 23–25cm (9–10in) wide. Square cuff. Viyella shirts, slightly shaped at waist. Less high collar continues. Rounded cuffs. Soft-fronted flannel or cambric shirts in summer. Length of stiff-fronted business shirt reduced. Undervest is worn in natural-coloured wool, wool and silk mix or cellular cotton in summer, with long or short sleeves.

Drawers or pants are worn in similar fabric to undervest, with button front and tape loops at waist for braces. Pants are worn to ankle or mid-calf; drawers to just below or above the knee.

HATS Previous modes continue. Popular styles: bowler – hard felt hat with bowl crown and narrow brim, curled upwards for city or business. The Homburg – a stiff felt hat with indented crown and silk-bound brim – is worn with lounge suits. The Trilby is similar to the Homburg in softer felt with no trim on brim.

HAIR As previous year.

FOOTWEAR As 1901.

ACCESSORIES As previous year. Evening dress shirt worn with white tie, 1–3 mother-of-pearl studs and links.

DETAILS OF ILLUSTRATED PATTERNS

Full evening dress consisting of a black tail coat and trousers worn with a white waistcoat.

The coat has square-cut fronts with closely fitting, knee-length tails cut in one with the lower forepart. The collar is stepped, and the lapels faced with silk. Two-piece sleeves are slit at the wrist with three-button fastening and silk piping set into mock cuff seam. The coat is always worn open.

Trousers are slightly narrower in the leg than for contemporary daytime fashions and trimmed with silk braid on outer leg seams.

The single-breasted waistcoat of white piqué with low-cut, curved lapels fastens at centre front with four pearl buttons, with cuff links and shirt studs to match.

White dress shirt with starched front, high stiff collar and white bow tie. Black tie correct only with dinner jacket, which might be worn with soft-pleated shirt front.

FABRICS AND COLOURS Black wool worsted. White piqué.

SHOES AND SOCKS Black patent-leather shoes with rounded toes and ribbon bow decoration; black silk lisle socks.

NOTES ON CONSTRUCTION OF GARMENTS

Tail coat and trousers should fit closely to the figure – expert cutting and construction are essential to achieve correct proportion and balance.

Make up waistcoat back in cheaper lining fabric with strap and buckle, to enable closer fit at waistline.

Right: Drawing of full man's evening dress (for the pattern see page 29).

CB

TAIL COAT
BACK
cut 2

TAIL COAT
SIDE BACK
cut 2

TAIL COAT
FRONT
cut 2

TAIL COAT
SKIRT
cut 2

TROUSERS

———— BACK
.... FRONT
cut 2

CB fold

TAIL COAT
COLLAR
cut 2
on fold

CB

WAISTCOAT
BACK
cut 2

WAISTCOAT
FRONT
cut 2

TAIL COAT
SLEEVE FRONT
cut 2

TAIL COAT
SLEEVE BACK
cut 2

Decade 1910–1919

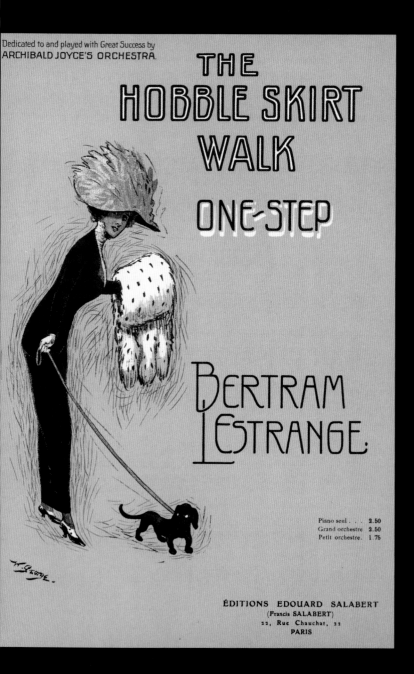

Dedicated to and played with Great Success by
ARCHIBALD JOYCE'S ORCHESTRA.

THE HOBBLE SKIRT WALK ONE-STEP

BERTRAM LESTRANGE

Piano seul 2.50
Grand orchestre 2.50
Petit orchestre. 1.75

ÉDITIONS EDOUARD SALABERT
(Francis SALABERT)
22, Rue Chauchat, 22
PARIS

1910 witnessed the passing of the Edwardian age, with the death in May of King Edward VII. The new reign of George V, which was to last until 1936, was to be troubled with world war with its unprecedented loss of life, and unemployment on a destructive scale; alongside this, improved technology and the rise of new industry led Britain ever forward. Fashion was to form part of that industry.

Between 1910 and 1914 many new fashions were introduced, their effect stifled by the declaration of war. Many of the fashions of postwar Britain have been entirely credited to the impact which war itself had on society. We will see that war did have far-reaching effects, but must not distort the true picture by ignoring movements immediately prior to it.

1910 was an important and reactionary year in the history of fashion, which witnessed a fundamental change in the female line. The silhouette straightened out completely and women moved from the S- to the I-shape. Skirts narrowed to the extent that they appeared to hug the ankles, the waist slackened, and the bust resumed a normal proportion. The line was essentially tubular, and far removed from the full-flowing skirts of the previous decade. The fashions were inspired by oriental art and, more importantly, by the French designer Paul Poiret and the *Ballet Russe*, which toured Europe with a show of vivid and revolutionary costume. The ballet was a riot of colour, with orange, cerise, blues and golds combined in oriental designs. The immediate mode that arose from these fresh influences was the 'harem' skirt, which became the hobble of 1911. The skirt was aptly named, for the narrow hem restricted the movements of the wearer to the extent that the lady could only hobble, or, at least, walk with tiny steps. Many Punch cartoons focused on this intriguing and amusing mode, which was considered the height of femininity at the time. A slit was later introduced to give greater freedom, sometimes extending as high as knee level, necessitated particularly by the craze for ragtime dancing towards the middle of the decade. With the narrow skirt, hats remained large and became flatter and wider, reaching the extreme of the fashion by 1912. Every theatre had its notice requesting ladies to

The effect of the tubular look was often heightened by the vogue for using the same fabric throughout the dress, replacing the more usual blouse and skirt. However, the tailored suit, which had been so popular, remained in a looser form, with the walking skirt shortened to just above the ankle, and vibrant colours replaced the traditional blue serge. Over the tubular dress from 1912 a tunic or drape became popular, often combining the use of rich and plain fabrics, or gold for evening wear. Colour in fashion was thus made possible. The tunic line, and more precisely the 'lampshade tunic', which flared out over the clinging dress, became the uniform of fashion until 1914.

With the start of the new look necklines had remained high, but by 1913 the fussy corsage was replaced by the V-shape. The abandonment of the high-necked blouse or bodice brought sharp comment and criticism, which is surprising when we look back at the low *décolletage* of the Edwardian evening gown.

Fashions of the day favoured the younger, slimmer figure, the closer-fitting, sheath-like dress inevitably leading to a fundamental change in the line and embellishment of undergarments. Numerous petticoats became obsolete, for beneath the tight skirt a tubular slip hugged the hips and finished above the ankle. It was no longer considered exciting to show your petticoat, or daring to display an ankle when lifting your skirt to cross a street. The corset retained its straight front but was worn far lower on the female figure, often extending as low as the knees and losing height above. As the corset was now short above the waist, a cache-corset often replaced the camisole, which might be boned to give additional support to the large figure. New ribbon straps are surely indicative of the lighter character of lingerie.

By 1914 the male silhouette had changed to the line it was to follow, with slight alterations, throughout the 20th century. Indeed, the formal male suit has changed very little, although other fashions introduced alongside it can hardly be considered as standardized. Between 1910 and 1914 there were no startling changes. Jackets were generally cut looser and straighter, and trousers wider, sometimes with pleats from the waistband. Since the trousers remained narrow at the hem, this created a kind of peg-top effect. Knitted cardigans were introduced for golf, and shoes were preferred to boots for sports and informal dress by the younger set. For summer a blazer might be worn with flannel trousers, although this was not always considered to be in the best of taste. Moustaches and high collars remained fashionable. With the declaration of war in 1914 the majority of men adopted a uniform.

For women, ostentatious fashion and unnaturally tight corseting appeared to be things of the past. However, the new fashions, freer and healthier, can hardly be attributed to the new woman's search for emancipation, for the fashion of the day restricted the female in a different way, by constricting the legs. Peaceable means had failed to win attention for the cause of women's suffrage. Women smashed windows and chained themselves to railings in order to be imprisoned and gain recognition. In prison the suffragettes continued their cause with hunger-strikes, and in 1912 the movement claimed its first martyr when Emily Davison threw herself in front of the King's horse on Derby Day.

By the outbreak of war the movement seemed no nearer to realizing its aims, and the suffragettes rechannelled their agitation into encouraging women to take part in the national effort. This undoubtedly played an important part in enabling women to exploit opportunities opened to them by war. In May 1915, the shortage of munitions led to the setting up of a special Ministry of Munitions, while a shortage of soldiers

Above: A young man wears a half-length double-breasted overcoat and a bowler hat in the snow.

Opposite: A musical poster from 1909 shows a woman in a fashionable hobble skirt.

led in January 1916 to the conscription of single men, and in May to universal male conscription. The enforced withdrawal of men from the domestic front provided the critical impetus towards full-scale employment of women in all types of jobs.

Expansion of job opportunity was a central phenomenon of women's war work, and, as will become obvious, was fundamental to the changes which took place in fashion, not so much as regards the more obvious aspects of economy and utility in dress, but in relation to a wider view of women's role in society and preconceptions of their capabilities. Few of the women who took up new types of employment during the war, whether as WAACs (Women's Army Auxiliary Corps), conductresses, munitionettes, or land workers, were consciously working for women's rights. Yet simply by doing new jobs and doing them well, they achieved a great deal.

Above: Two ladies, wearing a pink hobble skirt and a purple gored skirt, take a walk in the park.

On a purely simplistic level, women's war work illustrated the necessity of adopting functional clothing, at least during working hours. There can be no doubt that in this respect the war was largely responsible for the disappearance of the corset – that is, in the form of a rigid whalebone structure. Before 1914 covered steel had begun to replace whalebone, and a vulcanized rubber foundation garment was introduced with no boning; this was worn universally during the war.

The predominant tunic line of 1914 provided a convenient means to move away from the impractical fashions of the day. The tunic had been considerably lengthened before the war, standing away from the figure over the narrow skirt. The skirt was discarded and the tunic lengthened, resulting in a rather flared skirt which reached below the calf. Worn with high-laced boots, this became the overriding fashion of the war. The fashion world remained dormant over the war years, for a demonstration of wealth was not in keeping with the times. Strategically placed posters were a constant reminder that 'to dress extravagantly in war-time is more than bad form: it is unpatriotic'. Economy was the watchword of the day, with petrol rationing in June 1917 and ration cards issued for meat, sugar, butter and other foodstuffs in 1918. The government set up the Women's Land Army to gain optimum use from our agricultural resources, the recruits assuming a uniform of breeches, smocks and gumboots. A khaki uniform styled on contemporary dress was adopted by the WAACs, formed in 1916. British women joined the armed forces for the first time in history, and although uninvolved in active service, further proved their capabilities and simultaneously strengthened their cause. Women not only demonstrated their adaptability, but, more importantly, were earning on their own account, and thus gained a measure of economic and social freedom. In consequence there was more money available to spend on personal appearance. The average woman was still a long way from social and financial independence, but in the absence of men the war had removed some of the more tiresome constraints. It was during the war that the age-old tradition of the chaperone died. As the *Daily Mail* commented in 1915: 'The war-time business girl is to be seen any night dining out alone ... Formerly she would never have had her evening meal out unless in the company of a man-friend. But now with money and without men she is more and more beginning to dine out.'

War work not only brought women greater economic and social freedom; it also led to the questioning of their political role. As the time approached for a general election it became more difficult to defend denial of the vote to men with restricted or no voting right before 1914, who were now at the front. The same, said the suffragettes, should apply to the army of female patriots.

It was the consideration of the problems of votes for men which inevitably brought the question of votes for women into full view. The Representation of the People Act, 1918, included women over thirty as well as all males over twenty-one, the age bar on women being on the grounds of their numerical majority in the population. Although the Franchise Reform Act did mark a significant step forwards in the political history of women, the impact of the Act was limited, for it did not enfranchise the younger woman, who, as Graves and Hodges remark, had 'done the hardest and most thankless war work'. With the increased freedom the war had given these women, the fight for political emancipation seemed to recede and assume a secondary importance.

The political and legal story of women's rights is relatively straightforward, with important developments being achieved during this and the following decade. After the General Election of December 1918, when the mainly Conservative coalition government under Lloyd George took office, the Government brought in a Sex Disqualification Act which opened nearly all the public offices and professions to women. It also made clear that there was, in law, no barrier to their full membership of the ancient universities of Oxford and Cambridge. Various other measures of emancipation followed in the 1920s.

In the years immediately following the war there were many cross-currents, as if fashion were unsure whether to continue from 1914 or begin again with renewed vigour. The barrel line of 1918 displayed the shortest skirt, 15–20cm (6–8in) from the ground, yet in becoming narrower towards the hem exhibited pre-war characteristics. Other fashions resulted directly from the war: the British Warm and the trenchcoat, practical overcoats for men and women alike. The tubular figure, which was to become the foundation of the 1920s, originated towards the end of this decade. Women's undergarments now consisted of a shapeless camisole bra and girdle or hip-belt, the bra compressing rather than supporting the breasts. The youthful line predominated; 'Never has the skirt been so youthful and irresponsible in charater,' noted *Vogue* in 1919.

Dancing was a particularly popular pastime in the period immediately following World War I, and is often seen as part of the reaction against the restrictions it imposed. Yet, like many other features associated with the high-life of post-war Britain, it was established in the early war years. Dancing gained popularity during the war with troops on leave, and by the end of 1919 many new dance clubs and halls were opened. By the beginning of 1920 jazz was well established, and the dancing mania was a familiar topic in press articles and women's journals.

The type of dancing involved a new closeness and since it called for increased movement inevitably demanded greater freedom of dress. As Vogue commented: 'Now a long skirt and a minuet may go comfortably together, but the dancers of the moment decline with scorn to contemplate any unjust impediments in the shape of superfluous length. And so, of course, nothing was left to the skirt, but to conform.'

In brief, the early years of the decade might be seen as a transitional period, as fashion became less ostentatious and less staid. By 1919, fashion had set the course it was to follow for the next decade. Young men and women who had experienced the harsh realities of war looked forward to enjoying a lighter side of life. The war experience offered a unique opportunity for bringing about changes in the structure of society, evident on a number of levels; not least it precipitated a society in which women were to gain importance socially and economically. Similarly, it provided the essential impetus which accelerated the acceptance of new fashions. The many developments of the war, as will become obvious, not even those directly associated

Women's and Misses' Ready-to-Wear Tailored Suits
Fall & Winter 1912-1913

Sample Book No. 80
Sears, Roebuck and Co.
Chicago

Above: Advertisement for tailored suits, showing a hobble skirt worn with a wrap-over jacket.

1911

WOMEN

PREDOMINANT FASHION FEATURES

The waistline continues to rise and the skirt narrows progressively, achieving a straight, tubular silhouette, advancing quickly towards the hobble skirt. The trend reaches its extreme at first in evening wear, with the legs shackled either with additional bands of fabric or by drawing in the existing skirt hem at the lower edge or at any point below the knee. Skirt length reaches the instep. Harem skirt, short-lived fashion of full divided skirt drawn in at ankles; worn with overdress – forerunner of the tunic line.

Dresses are now more usually constructed in one piece rather than the previous bodice and skirt, heightening the straight-line effect. Skirts are plainer in comparison to lavish decorations of previous decade. One-piece dresses for summer feature looser bodices with Magyar or kimono sleeves.

A more masculine trend is observable in tailor-mades, with the new longer jacket, plainer, more fitted sleeves with cuffs, loose-waisted and with the walking skirt shortened to the ankle. Other forms include the wrapover, knee-length tunic, fastening at one side, and the Zouave (bolero) jacket and Empire skirt.

Necklines remain high for day wear, lower and often rounded for evening.

FABRICS Velvet, crêpe, georgette, shantung, satins. Linens for summer frocks. Woollen facecloth, broadcloth and serge for tailor-mades, commonly striped, worn with Oxford and zephyr shirting fabrics, traditionally masculine. Undergarments are made in lighter fabrics: muslin, nainsook, cambric, lawn, batiste, crêpe de Chine. Fine black-and-white stripes or checks.

COLOURS Soft colours: pinks, peach, apricot, silver grey and snuff browns.

DECORATION Elaborate braiding and strapping, large decorative buttons. Tassels on evening wear, stoles and to edge jackets. Wide belts and sashes, frequently with tasselled ends.

UNDERGARMENTS Slimmer petticoats necessitated by tubular skirt, narrowing towards the ankles. Princess petticoats remain popular, retaining light flouncing at lower edge, and broderie anglaise and ribbon trim. Corsets less heavily boned, longer over the hips and shorter above the waist, creating slim hips and freeing the waist and bust to some extent. Cache-corset (corset cover) might be boned to give additional support to the fuller figure, often laced at the back. Hobble gaiters made of braid worn below the knees prevent the lady from taking too long a stride.

FOOTWEAR Boots worn in winter reaching to mid-calf – two-tone with gabardine, kid, or suede tops in light colours. Heels higher and curved or straight. Coloured gaiters buttoned over patent leather, pointed shoes. Shoes fastened with instep strap, low vamps and court styles.

STOCKINGS Black for day wear in lisle or cotton; coloured silk for evening. Most fashionable to match the dress with which they are worn.

HATS Reach greatest width, creating a top-heavy effect. Exotic trimmings begin to move upwards with decorative satin flowers, wide ribbons and ostrich plumes. The crown is full, fitting lower on the head. High toques (brimless hats) with large satin rosettes.

HAIR Coiffure increasingly simplified and flatter on the crown and sides with centre or side parting. Hair swept backwards, coiled or braided towards the back of the head.

ACCESSORIES All large. Long, broad stoles in fur or black satin, tasselled ends. Velvet, suede or tapestry handbags with clasp or flap closure and long cord straps. Day gloves wrist length. Longer jewelled hatpins with butt to protect sharp point. Long bead necklaces.

Left: A white fox-fur stole was a must-have accessory in 1911.

Right: Drawing of jacket and corselet skirt (for the pattern see page 36).

MOVEMENT Restricted by narrowness of skirt at ankle, causing women to move with tiny steps – to hobble. The body assumes an upright position with the head held high to balance the large hat.

DETAILS OF ILLUSTRATED PATTERNS

Straight-line costume consisting of double-breasted, panelled jacket with low eight-button fastening, set on decorative contrast braiding. Broad lapels are also edged with contrast braid, and set-in sleeves narrow at the wrist with mock button fastening. This decoration is also employed in centre-back panel.

The ankle-length corselet skirt extends above the natural waistline and is constructed in six panels, with the lower side skirt pleated to the hemline. Button and braid trimming unifies the skirt and jacket.

Lace blouse with high, stiffened collar, centre-back fastening and jabot front.

FABRICS Fine woollen tweed or facecloth.
COLOURS Grey and white or soft browns.
HAT Large-brimmed hat lavishly trimmed with black lace, grosgrain ribbon and ostrich feathers.

NOTES ON CONSTRUCTION OF GARMENTS

Pad the jacket softly over the chest and shoulders and stiffen the collar, front and cuffs. Trim lapel edges with flat silk braid.

For the skirt, construct a concealed placket at left side seam. Bone all seams for 19cm (7½in) from top. Expand the lower side skirt panel to form horizontal pleats to hemline. To make a petticoat, adapt the foundation skirts from the skirt pattern.

MEN

PREDOMINANT FASHION FEATURES

Three-piece lounge suit increasingly popular for day wear. Frock and morning coats still worn by older gentlemen, harking back to the Edwardian era. Trousers reach to the instep, or ankle length when worn with turn-ups. Overcoats are similar to previous fashions, with chesterfields, ulsters and raglan all popular. Loose-fitting single-breasted sack coat to mid-calf. During the evening, dinner jackets, tail coats and dress coats are worn with a white piqué waistcoat, or occasionally black waistcoat with black dinner jacket. Trousers match jackets, with no turn-ups, and with braiding on outer leg seam.

FABRICS AND COLOURS Similar to previous decade – flannel, worsted suitings, coarser tweeds, herringbones for sport and country. Finely striped shirting fabrics.
SHIRTS AND UNDERGARMENTS Shirts continue to be classed as undergarments, never exposed when ladies are present,

except for the specially prepared front. Starched front of formal white shirt shortened significantly, worn with wing or double collar, now approximately 5cm (2in) in height. Striped shirts popular with white linen collars and cuffs. Dress shirt worn with full evening dress, with pleated front and wing collar most common; square cuffs. Vests with long or short sleeves, drawers, pants and combinations.
FOOTWEAR Shoes more usual than boots for younger gentleman. Light-coloured cloth or suede spats. Socks are lighter in weight, made of thinner wools and cotton.
HATS Similar to previous decade.
HAIR Side-parting remains popular, slightly fuller and brushed back from the hairline. Short clipped or walrus moustaches, waxed for stiffness.
ACCESSORIES Similar to previous decade, tightly rolled umbrellas and walking sticks.

DETAILS OF ILLUSTRATED PATTERNS

Single-breasted morning coat with fronts cut well away from the stomach and tails ending at the knee. The waist is cut on the short side with medium skirt room over the hips. Low lapels roll from two-button fastening, with notched collar and buttonhole on left lapel. Two-piece sleeves are finished with turn-back cuff and slit fastening with three buttons. Cuffs and coat edges are braided or ribbon bound. Back vents with pleats end at the waist with buttons. Pockets may be included in the pleats as well as a breast pocket and inside ticket pocket.

The single-breasted waistcoat may match the coat, or be made in contrast fabric. For the back of the waistcoat, use the back waistcoat pattern from 1908 (see page 29).

The outfit is most frequently worn with striped trousers, without turn-ups.

FABRICS Wool worsted.
COLOURS Shades of grey – dark for more formal occasions and winter, light for summer.
SHIRT Soft-fronted tunic-style shirt with starched wing collar and cuffs.
SHOES Black leather Oxford shoes with light-coloured spats.
HATS Top hat correct with morning coat.
ACCESSORIES Four-in-hand or Ascot tie. Handkerchief in breast pocket for decoration only.

NOTES ON CONSTRUCTION OF GARMENT

Use back waistcoat pattern from 1908.

Right: Drawing of morning coat and waistcoat (for the pattern see page 37).

CB fold

JACKET
BACK
cut 1
on fold

JACKET
SIDE BACK
cut 2

JACKET
SIDE FRONT
cut 2

JACKET
FRONT
cut 2

SKIRT
—— SIDE FRONT
••••• SIDE BACK
cut 2

SKIRT
FRONT
AND
BACK

JACKET
COLLAR

JACKET
SLEEVE FRONT
cut 2

JACKET
SLEEVE BACK
cut 2

A

SKIRT
LOWER SIDE PANEL
cut 2

CF

CB

MORNING COAT
BACK
cut 2

COAT
SIDE BACK
cut 2

MORNING COAT
FRONT
cut 2

COAT
SKIRT
cut 2

TROUSERS
—— BACK cut 2
•••• FRONT cut 2

COAT
COLLAR
cut 2 on fold

WAISTCOAT
FRONT
cut 2

MORNING
COAT
SLEEVE BACK
cut 2

MORNING COAT
SLEEVE BACK
cut 2

1914

WOMEN

PREDOMINANT FASHION FEATURES

Pre-war hobble skirt, narrow to the ankle, incorporating side slits or buttons which might be left undone. Peg-top – i.e. with fullness at the waist – worn with cut-away coats.

Tailor-mades are short-waisted with Magyar or kimono sleeves cut in one with the bodice, evidence of a looser fit. The vogue for wrapover styles, buttoning to the left, continues. The tailor-made is sometimes worn with fancy waistcoat of brocade or moiré silk.

Tunic styles predominate. Necklines drop dramatically with the new V- or U-shapes and softer flat or roll collars.

All blouses feature the new open front with large limp or Medici collar (standing high at the back of the neck), and stand-up frills of tulle to edge a plain neckline.

Afternoon and evening dresses commonly feature overdraping tunics, combining rich and plain fabrics, and skirt split almost to the knee for dancing. *Décolletage* at the back of dancing dresses is extreme, cut to the waist at times.

From 1915, due largely to the impact of war, skirts become fuller and shorter, approximately 20cm (8in) from the ground. This is partly achieved by abolishing the underskirt and retaining the tunic, which had become fuller and longer prior to 1914 – the 'lampshade tunic'.

Skirts become progressively shorter during the war – 25cm (10in) from the ground in 1917; they are worn with calf-length laced boots and dark-coloured cotton or wool stockings, white in summer. Jackets are looser, cut in military style with large patch pockets. Hair is drawn into a loose bun at the back of the neck.

FABRICS Crêpe de Chine, chiffon, georgette, brocades and firm satins. The vogue for striped fabrics continues. Evening wear is worn in plain or embroidered brocades, satins, silk, tulle, lace, charmeuse or marquisette. Serge, broadcloth and hopsack are used for tailor-mades. Undergarments worn in crêpe de Chine, cambric, broderie anglaise or ninon. Underskirts in satin, taffeta or moirette.

COLOURS Brighter colours are worn: cerise, orange, yellow, bright blue and emerald. Coloured underskirts are worn in scarlet, navy, purple and blue.

DECORATION Fur and velvet trimmings on cuffs, collars, pockets and jacket edges. Ribbon, embroidery, decorative buttons on sides and hem of skirts and jackets. Much draping of fabrics. Bead fringing, tassels, satin sashes with large bows and flowers for evening.

UNDERGARMENTS 'Princess' petticoats in Empire style continue, tubular and flounced or pleated from the knee. Hobble petticoats grip the knees. Waist-length petticoats (underskirts). Harem-style petticoats for dancing consist of two wide legs, fastened with button and loop to one side of the split skirt. Rubber-coated steel or celluloid replacing whalebone to stiffen corsets, which continue short above the waist and long below. Camisoles with fine ribbon straps. French knickers with wider frilled legs or *Directoire* knickers, drawn into bands at the knee. Modesty vests fill in low V-neckline.

FOOTWEAR Shoes laced or buckled, with higher, straighter heels, pointed toes and bar-and-button closure. Stitching decoration, buckles, ribbon bows and punched designs on court shoes. Elastic used to achieve higher, closer fit. Coloured shoes, matching the outfit, are fashionable. For dancing, satin slippers with pretty ribbon ties are worn.

STOCKINGS Similar to previous fashion.

HATS Smaller, with higher crowns and narrower brims popular in turban style with single-plume trim, wired vertically or backwards. High toques, berets, tam o'shanters in straw, velvet and furs.

Left: Tailor-made outfit with draped skirt, waistcoat and jacket by couture house Redfern.

Right: Drawing of tunic-style jacket and cutaway skirt (for the pattern see page 40).

HAIR Dressed higher on the crown with soft curls falling on to the face. For evening, hair decorated with wired feather decorations fastened to velvet or jewelled bandeaux.

ACCESSORIES Gloves are worn long to the elbow for day or evening wear with short sleeves and gathered from the wrist upwards for evening – in kid, buckskin and silk in light colours; white for evening. Large black fox muffs and stoles. New dyes for other furs; coney and sealskin increase their use in fashion. Asian influence brings fringed silk sunshades and silk fans in bright colours.

MOVEMENT Walking restricted due to with of skirts at ankle.

DETAILS OF ILLUSTRATED PATTERNS

Finger-length tunic-style jacket with V-neckline, cutaway skirt and button and rouleau trim at centre-front fastening. The jacket is gathered at the sides and held in at raised waistline with attached three-quarter belt. Raglan sleeves fit at elbow, flaring at wrist with pleated inset, finished with button and rouleau loop.

Side-fastening ankle-length hobble skirt narrows towards the hemline, with two unstitched pleats at centre-front seam for draped effect.

The blouse (pattern not provided) has full-length kimono sleeve, fitting tightly from elbow to cuff. Medici collar with low V-opening and pearl button fastening.

Toque of stiffened faille is worn straight on head and decorated with single wired ostrich plume and jewelled trim.

NOTES ON CONSTRUCTION OF GARMENTS

Jacket – slit jacket front from A to B and gather upper section to fit; stitch with narrow seam. Cover seam with belt, attach with single button at each end and catch at side seams.

Narrow hem and accordion-pleat sleeve inset along broken lines indicated on pattern; a seam allowance of 1cm (⅜in) is recommended. Slit jacket sleeve from C to D and attach inset using 1cm (⅜in) tapered seam (dotted line). Finish with button and rouleau loop trim.

Skirt – add placket at left side seam for opening.

MEN

PREDOMINANT FASHION FEATURES

Major change is in cut of trousers, worn clean-fitting about the waist with ample ease over the seat, created by pleating from the waistband, from which the legs taper to more or less peg-top form. Average size for knee and bottom 48cm (19in) and 40cm (16in) respectively, with deep turn-ups. Trousers made with waistbands eliminate the need for braces.

Jackets to lounge suits also more generously cut, with wider shoulders and deep-cut armhole. Single-breasted lounge jackets more usual.

FABRICS As previous fashion, black-and-white check very popular, and black-and-white check silk neckwear.

COLOURS Grey browns, soft browns, snuff and tobacco, subdued greens for sports and country; black and white.

SHIRTS AND UNDERGARMENTS Soft-fronted, coloured tunic shirt with soft, detachable collar, sometimes matching, provides practical alternative for more casual wear, especially in summer. Collar height continues to decrease. Underwear similar to previous fashion.

SHOES Similar to previous fashion.

SOCKS Similar to previous fashion.

HATS Previous styles continue; slightly wider brims.

HAIR Similar to previous fashion.

ACCESSORIES Similar to previous fashion.

MOVEMENT More relaxed poise in comparison to Edwardian era. Heads held less rigidly with lower collars.

DETAILS OF ILLUSTRATED PATTERNS

Single-breasted lounge suit with three-button fastening, squared lapels and curved lower edges. Two-piece sleeves slit at the wrist with three-buttons and slit cuff. Flap pockets at hip level and left breast pocket. The jacket is cut with centre-back seam and vent and with ample length to cover the seat.

Peg-top trousers, pleated into front waistband, with ample ease over the hips and upper thighs, narrowing to the instep with turn-ups. Sharp centre crease.

The waistcoat is single-breasted with a V-opening and six-button fastening; the last button is usually worn undone. There are two welt pockets at waist level and a breast pocket at left side only. For the back of the waistcoat, use the back waistcoat pattern from 1908 (see page 29).

FABRICS Tweed.

COLOURS Black or grey and white.

SHIRT Tunic-style shirt with detachable starched square cuffs and polo collar.

SHOES Black leather Oxford shoes with light-coloured felt spats.

HAT Felt Homburg.

ACCESSORIES Four-in-hand tie; handkerchief in breast pocket with double points showing; grey buckskin gloves, gauntlet style.

NOTES ON CONSTRUCTION OF GARMENTS

Use back waistcoat pattern from 1908. Add vent to centre back of jacket.

Right: Drawing of lounge suit (for the pattern see page 41).

LOUNGE JACKET
BACK
cut 2

CB

LOUNGE JACKET
FRONT
cut 2

CB fold

COLLAR

pleat   pleat

TROUSERS

——— FRONT

• • • • • BACK

cut 2

JACKET
SLEEVE FRONT
cut 2

JACKET
SLEEVE BACK
cut 2

WAISTCOAT
FRONT
cut 2

TROUSERS   cut 2 on fold
WAISTBAND

CB fold

1918

WOMEN

PREDOMINANT FASHION FEATURES

With the end of the war skirts lengthen once again, 15–20cm (6–8in) from the ground. The barrel line, curving towards the skirt hem, is reminiscent of the pre-war hobble skirt. The most significant feature is the absence of the 'figure'; the waistline is not emphasized, is usually high and never pulled in tightly. Garments are loose and easy-fitting. 'The silhouette... is not sternly masculine, it is boyish. Indeed with straight, waistless garments for day wear, slim women look more like their own sons than anything else' (*Women's Wear Fashion*, November 1918).

Ready-to-wear begins to emerge more forcibly after the war with the coat-frock, the first real ready-to-wear garment, which had been adapted as a practical alternative to the coat and skirt during the war; V- or square neck. Long pleats and outside pockets are characteristic.

Costume coats worn with plain, narrow skirt and waistcoat. Blouses loose-fitting with deep V-neckline, often pouched into the skirt waistband. Jerseys worn over the skirt. Sailor collars are also popular.

Outdoor garments – overcoats follow barrel line. British Warm and trenchcoat adapted for civilian use from war-time, loose-fitting with deep collar, revers, large pockets and belt.

FABRICS Gabardine, Melton cloth for overcoats. Artifical silk, wool or silk stockinette for jerseys. Bedford cord suitings, check suitings and overcheck tweeds.

COLOURS Soft and subdued maize, soft greys, fawn, cream, black, navy and white. Brighter colours such as rose pink or saxe blue are worn in the evening.

DECORATION Top-stitching on panel seams, sparse embroidery, tassels, sash or drapery essential with evening dress.

UNDERGARMENTS Corsets continue long over the hips and short above the waist, lightly boned with little constriction at the waist. Petticoats simpler, in princess style trimmed with lace and ribbon. Shapeless camisole bra and girdle or hip-belt, suppressing rather than supporting the bust. Cami-knickers.

FOOTWEAR Boots with cloth top, fastened with laces or buttons, cover the calf completely, the top of the boots covered by the skirt. High, straight heel, 5–7cm (2–2¾in). Pointed shoes with high vamp. Leather brogues are popular for informal day or sportswear.

STOCKINGS Black cotton or woollen hose for winter, white silk for summer.

HATS Tricorne, toques, berets, also wide-brimmed hats with little trimming, fitting low on the head – cloth, soft felt, velour.

HAIR Coiffure continues to be drawn to the back of the head with bun or coil worn low on the crown. Hair is more tightly waved and 'bobbed' by the younger woman.

ACCESSORIES Gloves are worn long, in white silk or buckskin for evening, fastening with buttons. Gauntlet-style for day, knitted for winter. Leather handbags, clasp fastening.

MOVEMENT Relaxed and natural.

Left: A simple high-waisted frock with patch pockets and turned-over collar. The fur-lined coat is worn with a cloche hat.

Right: Drawing of loose-fitting top coat and barrel-line skirt (for the pattern see the pages 44–45).

DETAILS OF ILLUSTRATED PATTERNS

Loose-fitting top coat with wide lapels rolling from raised waistline, single-breasted centre-front button fastening and attached belt. Shaped panel seams at back and front incorporate deep pockets at side front, accentuating the hips. Two-piece, set-in sleeves fasten at slit cuff with single button. Coat hemline is stitched through to right side, finishing 10cm (4in) above the skirt hemline.

Barrel-line skirt reaching to lower calf in four panels, worn 19cm (7½in) from the ground.

The outfit is worn with soft-collared, loose-fitting shirt and tie (pattern not supplied).

FABRICS Coat in heavyweight gabardine; skirt in medium-weight twill wool.

COLOURS Soft browns, fawn.

HAT Straw, deep crown trimmed with grosgrain ribbon and shaped brim, worn straight on head.

NOTES ON CONSTRUCTION OF GARMENTS

Cut coat pattern along solid lines to separate side back and back pattern pieces. Separate side front and front in the same manner; the inserted pocket may be cut grown-on to the side front and stitched through to right side of fabric. Fine broken lines indicate position of belt. Ease back to front at shoulder seam. A 5cm (2in) hem is stitched through to right side.

The skirt has a form concealed placket opening in left side seam.

MEN

PREDOMINANT FASHION FEATURES

Lounge suit established as ordinary day wear, cut slightly shorter, with centre-back vent and seam. Single-breasted styles more usual with 2–4 buttons. Jackets are shaped into the waist with darts. Piped or bound (jetted) pockets replace flaps.

Waistcoats now made up in same fabric as the suit, with the back in lining fabric with adjustable half-belt and buckle. Trousers wider in the leg although still narrower at hem than knees, without turn-ups and retaining pleats into the waistband.

Light flannel suits for informal wear. British Warm and trenchcoats adapted for civilian use and cut on lines of officer's greatcoat: loose-fitting, double-breasted, with additional flap-yoke over the shoulders and belted. Raglan coats in rubber or waterproofed materials, fly fronts. Ulsters made in thicker, warmer fabrics, looser-fitting, with full or half belt.

FABRICS Suiting fabrics similar to previous fashion: flannel, alpaca, worsteds, wool and silk mixture fabrics. Melton cloth for British Warm.

COLOURS Black or dark grey suitings (for business lounge-suits). Camel or fawn for British Warm and overcoats. Lighter colours, grey and buff for light flannel suits.

SHIRTS Shirts similar to the styles of 1914, as with underwear.

FOOTWEAR Laced leather brogues in brown or black. Oxford-style lace-up shoes with more pointed toes, worn by younger gentlemen. Older gentlemen favour boots with suede or cloth tops, covering the ankle.

SOCKS Brightly coloured and sometimes striped.

HATS Less worn by younger men. Bowler, trilby, and Homburg most popular hat styles.

HAIR Centre-parting again popular, with hair combed back. Brilliantine hair ointment gives smooth, silky look.

ACCESSORIES Long ties with knot, known as four-in-hand. Gloves, gauntlet style with button fastening. Silver and gold tie pins, and cuff links. Walking sticks less fashionable. Wrist watches, worn before the war, now more common.

MOVEMENT More relaxed, although some retaining the upright military stance.

DETAILS OF ILLUSTRATED PATTERN

Knee-length raglan raincoat falls loosely from the shoulders with split sleeve and button and flap trim at cuff; high-fastening neckband, fly front and slit welt pockets, allowing the hands to reach inside trouser pockets.

Centre-back seam and vent allows for easy movement.

FABRIC Rubberized or waterproofed gabardine.

FOOTWEAR Low, laced brown calfskin boots, knee-length cloth leggings, buttoning over instep.

HAT Felt trilby with down-turned brim.

NOTES ON CONSTRUCTION OF GARMENT

Add vent to centre back of coat, 5cm (2in) wide and 51cm (20in) from hemline.

Add fly strap to left coat front to conceal buttons and buttonholes.

Slit welt pockets in lining fabric, to allow access to trouser pockets when worn.

Right: Drawing of a knee-length raglan raincoat (for the pattern see page 45).

TOP COAT

BACK

CB fold

TOP COAT

COLLAR

SKIRT

BACK

FRONT

cut 2

CB

POCKET

CB fold

TOP COAT

FRONT

cut 2

TOP COAT

BELT cut 2

RAINCOAT
SLEEVE BACK
cut 2

RAINCOAT
SLEEVE FRONT
cut 2

RAINCOAT
FRONT
cut 2

RAINCOAT
BACK
cut 2

RAINCOAT
UNDERSLEEVE
cut 2

NECKBAND
cut 2

TOP COAT
BACK SLEEVE
cut 2

TOP COAT
FRONT SLEEVE
cut 2

A

B

C

D

1919

WOMEN

PREDOMINANT FASHION FEATURES

The slim silhouette with straighter line for day wear and slightly longer skirts, frequently pleated, especially for sports, with flannel blazer or jacket.

One-piece frocks increasingly popular, with loosely accentuated waist. Hips are emphasized with gathers, drapery or sashes in all forms of fashion. Shorter sleeves for summer.

Evening dresses flimsy in character, retaining the barrel line, wide over the hips and drawn in above the ankle. *Décolletage* is frequently horizontal, with fine bodice straps, and a sash of contrast or matching fabric often drawn over the shoulder and falling to the floor at the back, creating the effect of a train. Diaphanous bodices open to the waist at the front and back, over a straight-cut underbodice, with high-waisted sash.

Outdoors, the barrel line is retained for coats, with large patch pockets emphasizing the hips.

FABRICS For evening crêpe de Chine, crêpe georgette, printed chiffon taffeta, satin charmeuse, voiles, foulards, velvet. Diaphanous, semi-transparent fabrics combined with satins, brocades, etc. Striped silks, ninon, zephyrs in checks, stripes and plain colours. Serge, tweeds, merino.

COLOURS Soft, subdued tones – salmon pinks, coffee, navy, putty, amethyst, sky blue, emerald, saxe, soft greys; silver and gold lamé. Brighter colours for evening – fuchsia, violet, lace pink.

DECORATION Evening dresses fringed for dancing – ostrich, swansdown and beaded edgings, velvet ribbons, silk tassels. Gold embroidery. Satin and chiffon sashes or drapery, tasselled and hanging to the front, sides or back, are essential to the evening dress.

UNDERGARMENTS Petticoats straight-hanging with flounce at lower edge. Knitted 'undies' in silk tricot, elastic-waisted. Satin underskirts. Dainty lawn chemise and knickers decorated with tucks and trimmed with broderie anglaise lace and narrow ribbon. Lightly boned or woven elastic corsets enclose entire torso, with suspenders and straps, little constriction at the waist. Shapeless camisole bra and girdle or hip belt, suppressing rather than supporting or emphasizing the bust.

SHOES Pointed toes, high heels with jewelled buckle trim or strap fastening. Black patent for day.

STOCKINGS Black usual for day wear, silk or artificial silk, matching the dress for evening.

HATS Wider at the sides, with turned-down brims, worn low on the head. Pleated tulle, ostrich feather (glycerined to ensure the correct droop), ribbons and veils. Also soft 'pudding-basin' styles.

HAIR Tightly waved, drawn forward on the forehead and cheeks in curls. For evening the hair is often drawn to the back of the head and held with combs.

ACCESSORIES Long, buttoned gloves for evening, light-coloured in silk or buckskin. Small handbags in tapestry, silk, brocade; metal and cord chains. Large ostrich-plume fans. Clasps, brooches, bracelets, rings and earrings all worn. Jewelled, diamanté or velvet forehead bands.

MAKE-UP Discreet rouging of the lips and cheeks becomes more acceptable and less associated with the stage and immorality.

MOVEMENT Relaxed and natural.

Left: Eveningwear becomes more frivolous in the wake of World War I austerity.

Right: Drawing of ankle-length evening dress (for the pattern see page 48).

Opposite: Men in 1919 evening dress admire the vogue for backless gowns.

DETAILS OF ILLUSTRATED PATTERN

Ankle-length evening dress with square-cut *décolletage* at front and back, and shaped hemline, accentuated by skirt drapery. The waist is cut fairly high, with jewelled clasp at right side seam, and side drape falling in folds to extended train. Hanging sleeves of soft contrast fabric trimmed with gold beading and tassels at shoulders and points.

FABRICS AND COLOURS Pink-and-gold brocade; rose-pink charmeuse contrast.

ACCESSORIES Large ostrich-feather fan; hair bandeau with single wired plume and centre jewel; long double pearl necklace.

NOTES ON CONSTRUCTION OF GARMENT

Leave opening at left side seam for hook-and-eye closure. Excess length is allowed at the waistline for draping of the fabric; catch in folds of fabric at side seam, and ensure a close fit. The bodice band is stretched to fit dress top and reduced in width in a similar manner to waistline, by stretching across the chest; finished width approximately 6.25cm (2½in).

The entire dress is mounted on a firm foundation and boned over the bodice, as illustrated by solid black lines. Shoulder straps are stayed with silk braid below gold-bead edge trimming.

Catch stitch folds of skirt drape at centre and side seams, as indicated by dots and arrows on pattern, and insert ends into right side seam. Additional drapery from the waist conceals stitching line and extends into train.

A narrow roll hem is recommended on bias-cut edges.

MEN

PREDOMINANT FASHION FEATURES

No major changes from previous year.

DETAILS OF ILLUSTRATED PATTERNS

Full evening dress consisting of dress coat and trousers with a white waistcoat. The coat is close-fitting with swallow-tails and high waist seam forming a continuous run to the front points. Two buttons are placed on the waist dart in front. The peaked lapel is finished to turn to the waist and is faced with silk to the edge. The skirt of the tail coat is long and smartly rounded away, and is not now cut with a strap. The entire length of the front is cut in the forepart, and the lapel is also cut in one with it. The lapel is of medium width with horizontal step, whilst the outer edge is shaped with very little curve. Two-piece set-in sleeves finish with slit cuff and two-button fastening. The tail coat is worn on all the more dressy occasions, but for the theatre or an informal dance the dinner jacket is worn. The latter is more usually worn with black waistcoat (vest), although for those who like just a little 'swank', a white or delicately coloured waistcoat is acceptable. All waistcoats are cut with long points in front and are well curved over the hips. The opening is generally U-shaped, but a V-style is also worn.

Dress trousers are usually finished with one or two rows of silk braid down the side. Two rows are more usual with dress jackets, and are placed approximately 6mm (¼in) apart. Trousers are slightly narrower than for general wear.

FABRICS AND COLOURS Fine black worsted suiting. White piqué for waistcoat and bow tie.

SHIRT Dress shirt with plain starched front and single stud fastening, white starched wing collar and cuffs.

FOOTWEAR Black silk socks; patent leather shoes with rounded toes and ribbon bow.

ACCESSORIES Matching shirt studs, waistcoat buttons and cuff links, white cotton or buckskin gloves and signet ring. Black bow tie with dinner jacket, white piqué with full evening dress.

NOTES ON CONSTRUCTION OF GARMENTS

Tail coat and trousers should fit closely to the figure – expert cutting and construction are essential to achieve correct proportion and balance. Make up waistcoat back in cheaper lining fabric with strap and buckle to ensure closer fit at waistline.

Right: Drawing of a man's dress suit (for the pattern see page 49).

DRESS
SIDE DRAPE AND TRAIN
cut 1

DRESS
FRONT
cut 1

DRESS
BACK
cut 1

A

A

fold

DRESS
BODICE BAND
cut 1 on fold

fold

DRESS
SKIRT DRAPE
cut 1 on fold

DRESS COAT
BACK
cut 2

CB

DRESS COAT
SIDE BACK
cut 2

DRESS COAT
FRONT
cut 2

DRESS COAT
SKIRT
cut 2

TROUSERS
——— BACK cut 2
······· FRONT cut 2

CB fold

DRESS COAT
COLLAR
cut 2 on fold

CB

WAISTCOAT
BACK

WAISTCOAT
FRONT
cut 2

DRESS
COAT
FRONT SLEEVE
cut 2

DRESS COAT
BACK SLEEVE
cut 2

The Twenties

Fashion in pre-war Britain had always infiltrated into society from the older generation. Now, for the very first time, fashion was dominated by the young. It was an age which idolized youth and freedom. 'The Gay', The Roaring', 'The Reckless', are but a few of the many adjectives applied to the 1920s, and as with any labelling of periods, they suggest the dominant flavour of the epoch. Both male and female fashions reflected the spirit of the age. The war had brought a new type of freedom and with it the abolishment of many pre-war social customs, particularly as regards formal morning and afternoon dress. It was at this time that the word 'casual' entered the fashion vocabulary.

Above: 1920s Flapper posing with a string of pearls.

Women's dress in 1918 had already set the standard to which it adhered throughout the 1920s. With each successive year women's clothing became increasingly mannish in character, with flat chest and narrow hips. Shoulders became broader, the fit looser, and hair was cut in masculine proportions. Hair was short throughout the 1920s. The bob was popular in the early part of the period, but was later followed by the shingle, a close, short cut with natural-looking waves. Finally, in 1927, came the Eton Crop, which made it even more difficult to distinguish between a woman and a schoolboy; make-up was her only feminine attribute. As *Vogue* remarked: 'if men and women have a similar outlook, it is natural that they should wear similar clothes'.

An often-cited reasoning behind the boyish, carefree cut was the new economic and social freedom enjoyed by women, and their fight for emancipation. Women seemed to be denying their femininity by appearing as two-dimensional as possible. Various measures followed the Act of 1918 which recognized women as morally responsible persons. Political emancipation was completed in 1928, when the Equal Franchise Act gave the vote to all women over twenty-one for municipal and parliamentary elections.

To say that the war brought votes for women is to make a very crude generalization, yet one which does contain essential truth. The suffragette movement may have come near to securing votes for women before 1914, yet the political advance of women was blocked by two major prejudices – the hostility of men and the reluctance, and indeed opposition, of many women. New developments during the war brought a new confidence to women and dissipated much of this apathy. Undoubtedly the replacement of militant suffragist activity by recruitment of women for the patriotic cause played its part as well, but more than this the war generated a tremendous mood favourable to change and innovation.

However, emancipation cannot be seen to give the full story of masculinity in dress, for it should be taken into account that immediately prior to the war, a time when suffragist agitation was at its height, fashion chose to restrict feminine movements to the minimum with the hobble skirt.

Another factor inextricably linked with the boyish ideal was the emphasis on youth. In March 1919 *Vogue* noted, 'never has the skirt been so youthful and irresponsible in character', and again in 1924, 'we shall be smart but not hard, there will only be one silhouette – the youthful one'.

Ankles, calves and knees became the new erogenous zones, with the bust suppressed in line with a younger figure. That women were baring more flesh is evident, the scantiness of their dress verified by the reduction in the quantity of fabric required for a complete outfit. This had declined from approximately 7.4–6.5m (19–7yd).

The drastic shortening of the skirt marked a startling innovation in fashion, and short skirts compelled all women to pay much more attention to, and spend more money on, shoes and stockings. Until this time very little had been seen of women's stockings, and black or some other dark shade was usual. All stockings now became flesh-coloured, or, at least, various tones of beige. This heightened the impression of nudity and caused further shock to moralists.

Although I have referred to the 1920s as though fashion was uniform throughout the decade, a subtle change of style was apparent during the year 1925–6, which Cunnington describes as an essential change from a 'schoolboy' to that of a 'schoolgirl'. The skirt ceased to be tubular, with fullness introduced in the form of pleats or godets. We can almost watch, as World War I receded, the process of growing up into maturity. The 'schoolgirl' era of the late 1920s, with a greater accent on femininity, led almost inevitably to the reappearance of the natural waistline at the end of the decade.

During this period fashion enjoyed a greater democracy, characteristic of the irreversible changes witnessed by post-war Britain in the structure of society. There were fewer class distinctions – an outcome of the middle-class expansion – and the standard of living rose, partly because lower prices and a tendency for smaller families brought about an increase in spending on luxury products. Greater uniformity in society was reflected in a greater uniformity in dress, for fashion in post-war Britain became less a symbol of nobility and wealth, and effectively spread down the social scale. The period witnessed the birth of 'fashion for all' – 'all' being very much of a generalization since, in effect, it only related to those who could afford it. The title really referred to the increased proportion of the population for whom fashion was now attainable. In many respects, the availability of fashion in post-war Britain served to make an even greater distinction between the very poor and the middle classes. To the former, fashion was as inaccessible as it had been before the war.

Increased spending power was an important phenomenon in the growing uniformity which fashion acquired in this period, since less obvious class distinctions were the inevitable result. In previous eras it had not only been the finer quality of the clothes of the aristocracy which had distinguished them; more importantly, they possessed an entirely different character, and their greater complexity put fashion well out of the reach of everyday folk. In the 1920s, clothes for women throughout the social structure were much simpler, and conformed to more or less the same essential character and line, providing the possibility of successful imitation.

The simplicity of 'high fashion' can be largely attributed to the influence of Gabrielle Chanel, whose distinctive style marked her out as the leading fashion designer. Her practical designs were easily adapted to the commercial market, as James Laver suggests: 'Chanel's originality lay in her introduction into high fashion of working-class modes.' She was largely responsible for the simple 'jumper' which suddenly became the day attire of almost every woman. This was the first garment to be used interchangeably by men and women. As universal as the jumper was the cloche hat, which was introduced in 1924 and continued in popularity throughout the decade. The cloche hat was particularly important, since its close fit finally compelled the majority of women to wear their hair short. In addition, it heightened the uniformity of fashion, since in the mid-1920s it came so low over the forehead as almost to cover the eyes. Make-up, too, tended to produce a standardized face.

Increased simplification of design not only brought fashion into wider availability commercially, but was also largely responsible for the increasing number of home dressmakers. Whereas previously dressmaking had been well beyond the capabilities of the average woman, women from all classes now began to make their own clothes. This development was given further impetus by the growth of the paper-pattern industry.

This is not to say that fashion in the 1920s was without its distinctions; these most definitely did exist, a fact clearly illustrated by the beautifully beaded and embroidered silk evening dresses of the wealthier set. Although machines had been developed for automatic beading, the cost of this technique was still relatively high, and the end product inaccessible to the majority of the population. Similarly, men's tailoring still relied on quality of cloth and cut, although it is significant that off-the-peg styles were more readily available.

The growing sophistication of man-made fibres during the inter-war years marked yet another leap forward in fashion for all. In the 1920s the rayon industry was in its infancy, and although artificial silk had been in use since the early days of World War I, the war had largely disrupted its development, and its influence in fashion at this time was negligible. The manufacture of artificial silk, which from 1927 came to be called by the less disparaging term 'rayon', expanded in various ways. New firms entered the industry, the most important of these in Britain being Courtaulds, ICI and British Celanese. New qualities and types of rayon were introduced; the best known was 'Celanese', which became very popular in the manufacture of women's underwear.

The rapid expansion of British textiles and fashion was aided by the 'Buy British' campaigns of the inter-war years, initiated by the government. Predominant among the methods used to recover from the war and deal with financial depression were the restrictions imposed on the freedom of world trade. Advertisers in all fields took advantage of the campaign to draw attention to the superiority of British products. Furthermore, duties on rayon imports in 1925 protected home producers against foreign imports and encouraged further growth of the industry. The British were thus able to close the gap between their products and those of foreign competitors which had grown during the war.

The availability of cheaper fabrics provided an essential impetus to the progress of ready-to-wear and the rise of the department store. Important changes were taking place in the patterns of trade and commercial activity which were to have far-reaching effects in the 1930s, and more importantly, in the period following World War II.

Many of the new developments also owed a great deal to the progress of advertising, which was in turn dependent on improved means of communication, in particular through the press and the cinema. During this period fundamental changes took place in the structure of newspaper companies, which resulted in concentration of ownership as opposed to numerous private concerns. In short, as with fashion, newspaper ownership was largely democratized, and daily attained vast and nationwide circulation. To attract women readers, each paper had its fashion page, at least fifty per cent of which was devoted to advertisements for clothes and beauty. The style of presentation was also changing; from 1924, the new 'photo-tone' process enabled photographs to be produced more cheaply in magazines and newspapers. For the first time women in beautiful clothes could be recorded in detail, and the importance of the model became obvious.

In the 1920s young people experienced a new freedom in dress synonymous with what seems to have been a complete change in attitude and outlook on life. This change was as much as a result of the changing social status of young women as of their political independence, which undoubtedly had its roots in the war years.

UN DOIGT DE PORTO

UN BRIN DE ROUGE

UN LÉGER SOMME

F. Fabiano

Above: Archetypal 1920s girl with bobbed hair.

In addition to the war experience, America also exerted a tremendous influence, and gave the lead in many social fashions. American tourists flooded into Britain in 1919, accelerating the infiltration of slang, smoking, jazz and cocktails. High heels, hitherto associated with the stage, Paris and immorality, came into general use, as did make-up. Beauty parlours were unknown in Britain in the early 1920s, although cream and powder were already used by 'fast young ladies who powdered their noses in public'. (R. Graves and A. Hodges, *The Long Weekend*). Before 1914, only ladies of doubtful reputation had painted their faces. It took the stress and excitement of war, the affluence among the lower classes and the greater spending power of middle-class girls to bring about the heavier use of cosmetics.

Increased interest in health and sport among the young set helped bring about the union of sports and day clothes. Sports personalities, like cinema stars, became important dictators of fashion, and there can be no doubt that they led the field in the revolution in sportswear which took place, a revolution that had important effects on fashion generally.

Golfing and tennis enjoyed a great popularity after the war, becoming a favourite leisure pursuit of the upper and middle classes. Sports costume tended to be an adapted form of day wear, and men's golf saw the revival of knickerbockers, which by 1925 had become looser and fuller 'plus fours', teamed with a Fair Isle sullover and patterned socks. The Fair Isle is characteristic of the more colourful, freer nature of men's clothes, coinciding with the development of knitwear. Knitted garments for men had been introduced in the early 1900s, but their importance in the 1920s was beyond compare. One of the first unisex garments, this gained equal popularity with females, who were keen to adopt many items from their partners' wardrobes, including hats, shirts, neckties and golf stockings. *Vogue* tells us in 1926 that the modern woman 'in the country wears almost the same clothes as her husband'. A short tweed skirt, however, remained more popular than trousers, which were most acceptable in the form of beach or lounging pyjamas.

Coupled with the advance in sportswear, men's fashions generally experienced a more casual and younger-looking trend. Tweeds and checks remained popular, promoted partly by the Prince of Wales, who set the trend to enliven menswear. From 1922, flannel trousers without braces included a waistband and adjustable side straps, worn with a blazer and fine straw panama hat in the summer. Sports shirts with an all-in-one collar, often coloured and in soft fabrics, superseded the traditional tunic styles.

The most distinctive trend came in the trouser width, which provided a sharp contrast to the tapered styles of pre-war fashion. Trousers widened as the decade drew on, with Oxford bags reaching a hem width of 60cm (24in) by 1926. During the latter years of the 1920s the extreme of the fashion was modified, although trousers remained generally wide and pleated into the waistband. Jacket lapels and ties followed suit to correspond with the increased trouser breadth, and jackets were worn shorter for all occasions. This trend extended to the tails of the dress coat, which still remained the correct formal attire for dinner dances, with the collar and lapels faced in silk. A starched shirt front completed the outfit, although the vogue for the dinner jacket with soft shirt and turn-down collar increased in popularity, the waistcoat in the late 1920s often replaced by a silk cummerbund.

A more casual outlook was evident by the greater frankness and relaxation of inhibitions on sexual topics. The morals and behaviour of the younger set seem to have undergone a thorough 'shaking up', related on the one hand to the new economic and social freedom, and on the other to the heightened intensity generated by the war and the colossal slaughter on the battlefields. The war marked a loosening of the standards of conventional morality. For many young women who had experienced freedom away from the sheltered home environment, a return to the old social customs would have been incongruous with the outlook on life and the opposite sex they had inevitably developed. Women were mixing freely with men without the chaperones of a previous era, and this, plus the wider availability of contraception, brought sexual liberty to women. This development was further aided by the work of Dr Marie Stopes, who set up a number of birth-control clinics in the East End of London.

An equally strong influence was exerted by the art world and was also indicative of a fresh approach and changing outlook. The *Exposition des Arts Decoratifs*, held in Paris in 1925, was far-reaching in its effect and set the modernistic and functional fashion. Taking its influence from cubism, the Bauhaus and the Ballet Russe, it introduced designs intended for mass-production in new materials and was not without its impact on design, architecture and furnishings, the rectangular futuristic designs characteristic of Art Deco replacing the luxuriance of Art Nouveau. Sleek geometric patterns and the modern desire for functionality clearly showed its impact.

Thus the 1920s witnessed more rapid fashion change, attributable to a number of fresh influences. As fashion began to spread downwards into all classes, large and commercial interests became involved. The pace of fashion accelerated, which may be seen as a manifestation of the generally increased rapidity of social and scientific developments. Flügel, writing in 1930, summed up this point:

'Motoring, aviation, cinematography, the gramophone, the wireless, have all come into general use in the course of two or three decades. Corresponding to this rapidity in change in our environment, we have become less conservative, more intolerant of the old and more enamoured of the new, a mental tendency which can best express itself in changing tastes as regards fashion. The fashions may indeed be looked upon as symbolic of our changing outlook on many other things' (J.C. Flügel, *The Psychology of Clothes*)

Above: Advertisement for crépe de Chine cami knickers.

1920

WOMEN

PREDOMINANT FASHION FEATURES

All styles follow the tubular line, with natural, loose waistline, with signs of a lower waistline towards the end of the year. Hips are emphasized with large patch pockets, sashes, bows, draped and pannier effects. Sleeves are long for winter, short in summer. Knitted jumpers, dresses, jackets and pleated skirts for casual wear. Blouses are loose-fitting, with wide, flat collars, worn like a jumper over the skirt.

Coat-frocks are popular. A typical coat-frock might be plain at the back, with matching or contrast embroidered front panel, and square neck opening. A narrow belt constricts the waist very little. Patch pockets on each hip. Collar, lapels and turn-back cuffs and belt of lighter, contrasting cloth. Outdoor coats are three-quarter length, fur-trimmed with large, floppy collars.

Evening wear is relatively close-fitting, retaining earlier fullness of the skirt for dancing. *Décolletage* horizontal, falling to the same distance front and back, uneven hemlines. Hems grow temporarily longer in 1921.

FABRICS Silks, wool, stockinette, gabardine, satin, velvet, chiffon, georgette, cashmere and facecloth for day. Silver and gold lamé, crêpe de Chine, printed chiffons and muslins and taffeta for evening. Transparent, diaphanous and firmer fabrics are combined. Undergarments are worn in crêpe de Chine, muslin and lawn.

COLOURS Duller and subdued: coffee, khaki, mustard, grey, navy and blue. Brighter colours for evening, and black-and-white.

DECORATION Fringing, tassels, bead embroidery, gold braiding and embroidery. Fur cuffs and collars for coats – monkey fur and coney. Bold borders on jumpers.

UNDERGARMENTS Princess petticoats in flimsy fabrics, elasticated at the waist, trimmed with lace and appliqué. Cami-knickers, combining camisole and knickers. Corset similar to 1919.

FOOTWEAR Buckled court styles predominant for day and evening. Oxford lace shoes for sports. Gaiters worn in winter.

STOCKINGS Black silk for day wear, coloured for evening.

HATS Wide-brimmed soft hats in cloth, wool or velour, decorated with feathers, flowers and ribbon, pulled well down on to the forehead. For evening, forehead bands and turbans.

HAIR Bobbed with a side-parting, or long hair combed into a bun at the nape of the neck, brought forward on to the face to imitate a bob.

ACCESSORIES Scarves, knotting low; long pearl necklaces. Ostrich-plume fans for evening. Headbands – brocade or velvet diamanté for evening. Wrist watches, leather and suede handbags.

MAKE-UP Similar to previous fashion.

MOVEMENT Similar to previous fashion.

DETAILS OF ILLUSTRATED PATTERN

Smart coat-frock with shaped collar cut grown-on to the side front and faced in paler fabric. The contrasting centre panel underlaps the side front, secured with a line of saddle stitching for ornamentation and to create the illusion of a separate coat and dress. Decorative stitching extends along hemline and is repeated at bodice, collar edges and on large, hip-level patch pockets. Rows of buttons accentuate embroidered front panel, divided by side-fastening belt at natural waistline, the latter indicated rather than emphasized. The back is cut whole with moderate flare. Two-piece, set-in sleeves end with attached cuff and two holes and buttons. The garment is loose-fitting throughout, allowing ample ease over the bustline and hips and creating the characteristic straight silhouette. Hemlines are raised slightly from previous fashions.

FABRIC Gabardine.

COLOURS Coffee and cream.

HAT Wide-brimmed soft felt hat with no trimming, worn straight on head.

ACCESSORIES Small clasp-fastening leather handbag with metal frame, buckle trim and narrow cord handle; cream, wrist-length buckskin leather gloves, gauntlet style.

NOTES ON CONSTRUCTION OF GARMENT

Ease back to front at shoulders. The collar is cut in one with coat fronts, with a single centre-back seam, and faced in a contrast colour.

Completed coat sides are attached to front dress panel using an overlaid seam, and saddle stitched 1.5cm (⅝in) from front edge. Broken lines on pattern indicate position of stitching.

Shaded section of front panel is cut in main fabric and decorated with embroidery, as illustrated on sketch.

Left: Fashionable court shoes from the 1920s.

Right: Drawing of smart coat-frock (for the pattern see page 56).

MEN

PREDOMINANT FASHION FEATURES

Single-breasted lounge suit, similar to previous fashion, 2–4 buttons or link fastening, shaped into the waist with darts. Trouser and waistcoat styles remain unchanged, knee width approximately 56 (22in), hem width 40cm (16in).

Overcoats continue in the previous style. Chesterfield, raglan and ulsters are worn well below the knee in length, single- or double-breasted according to style.

Morning coat only for most formal occasions, e.g. weddings, usually grey, and worn with striped shirt, white collar and cuffs, bow tie or Ascot silk scarf.

FABRICS Tweeds and checks in dark colours. Facecloth, gabardine, cashmere, worsteds. Oxford, taffeta and zephyr shirting fabrics. Undergarments in wool, Viyella and Aertex cellular fabric are worn.

COLOURS Various shades of grey popular.

SHIRTS AND UNDERGARMENTS Shirts white, striped, coloured with white double collars, stiff or soft. Stiff-fronted shirt always worn with formal lounge suit and evening wear. Vest and pants or combinations.

FOOTWEAR Oxford-style lace-up shoes, moderately pointed toes. Laced leather brogues in brown or black.

SOCKS Brightly coloured, sometimes striped.

HAIR Worn short-back-and-sides throughout the 1920s, centre or side-parting. Hair may be flattened with hair cream.

HATS Bowler (for city and business), trilby and Homburg most popular styles. Peaked tweed cap or trilby for sports and informal wear.

ACCESSORIES Patterned, spotted, striped and paisley bow ties and silk scarves. Umbrellas, wrist watches.

MOVEMENT Relaxed.

DETAILS OF ILLUSTRATED PATTERNS

Lounge suit demonstrates increasing trend of shapeliness, clearly defining the figure with a decided 'waisty' effect. The single-breasted, three-button jacket is cut shorter than formerly with pointed lapels, the roll is moderately low and the foreparts well rounded off at the bottom. There is a dart taken out of the forepart; an angled welt pocket on the breast and flap pockets on the hips are arranged slightly on the slant. Slit button cuffs and centre-back seam without vent are features of the lounge suit now worn.

Top button of the single-breasted waistcoat is just visible between the lapels of the jacket. For the back of the waistcoat, use the back waistcoat pattern from 1919 (see page 49).

The trousers are cut moderately wide in the legs and taper towards the bottom, with turn-ups. The back is cut higher to accommodate brace and buttons; buckle and strap to adjust waist measurement; side-seam pockets and button covered fly.

FABRICS AND COLOURS Fine, striped woollen suiting fabric in shades of grey.

SHIRT AND UNDERGARMENTS Soft-fronted striped shirt with starched white double collar and cuffs.

FOOTWEAR Black leather Oxford-style laced shoes and light-coloured spats. Spats less frequently worn among younger men.

HAT Felt trilby.

ACCESSORIES Plain four-in-hand tie, handkerchief in upper breast pocket for decoration only, gauntlet-style gloves, walking stick.

NOTES ON CONSTRUCTION OF GARMENTS

Adapt waistcoat back pattern from 1919; the back is usually cut in lining fabric and includes buckle and strap fastening at waistline to ensure a closer fit.

Left: A selection of single-breasted suits, worn with patch pockets, turn-ups and spats.

Right: Drawing of lounge suit (for the pattern see page 57).

COAT-FROCK
BACK
cut 2

COAT-FROCK
SIDE FRONT
cut 2

A

A   A

COAT-FROCK
FRONT PANEL
cut 1

CF

COAT-FROCK
FRONT SLEEVE
cut 2

COAT-FROCK
BACK SLEEVE
cut 2

COAT-FROCK
CUFF
cut 2

LOUNGE JACKET
BACK
cut 2

CB

LOUNGE JACKET
FRONT
cut 2

CB fold
LOUNGE JACKET
COLLAR cut 2 on fold

pleat   pleat

TROUSERS
BACK cut 2
FRONT cut 2

LOUNGE
JACKET
FRONT SLEEVE
cut 2

LOUNGE JACKET
FRONT SLEEVE
cut 2

WAISTCOAT
FRONT
cut 2

TROUSERS WAISTBAND cut 2 on fold

CB fold

1924

WOMEN

PREDOMINANT FASHION FEATURES

'We shall be smart but not hard, there will only be one silhouette – the youthful one' (*Vogue*, early autumn 1924).

Waistlines and hemlines lower after 1920, rising in 1923. From 1924 onwards the waistlines continue to lower while hemlines rise – 5cm (2in) below the knee.

The straight silhouette is established – the skirt widened with pleats and godets. Blouses begin to be worn like jumpers, pulled over the hips, obliterating the natural waistline. The contribution of knitted fabrics is significant: jumpers, jumper suits, cardigan jackets and cardigan coats.

Two-piece costumes popular; straight, loose-fitting, hip-length jackets, buttoning low, worn over straight skirts.

Coats three-quarter or seven-eighth length without belts, buttoning to one side.

For evening, dipping and transparent hems herald the shorter skirt, with drapery and sashes at hipline, or over the shoulder. Low backs, dresses mostly sleeveless or with flimsy 'winged' effect.

FABRICS Mostly plain fabrics, similar to previous fashion. Jersey and stockinette. For evening, diaphanous, floaty fabrics are worn; chiffon, crêpe georgette, crêpe de Chine, organza, voile, velvets, metallics, satins, beaded fabrics are popular.

COLOURS Beige and brown predominant, and fawn, grey, navy, black and white. Brighter colours for evening – cerise, pinks, mauves, red, blue, black, apricot, green and cherry.

DECORATION Coloured scarves, beading, fringing, embroidery and ribbon lattice work. Fur cuffs and collars for coats.

UNDERGARMENTS Boneless, elastic foundation garments known as 'flatteners' take the place of corsets. Princess petticoats in crêpe de Chine.

FOOTWEAR Russian boots for winter, wrinkled over the ankle, calf-length. Court shoes with buckle, silver or diamanté for evening, straps for day wear. Snake, crocodile, lizard skin, all popular. Lower-heeled brogues for sport with rubber or crêpe soles.

STOCKINGS Fully fashioned shaped and seamed stockings. White silk, tan, beige, flesh, fawn or grey. Woollen sports hose in check and plaid patterns.

HAT Cloche hat first worn, pulled well down over forehead. Brims turn down at the back, upwards at the front. Some rolled upwards all round.

HAIR Bob is abandoned in favour of the shingle, a closer style with natural-looking waves. Fringes popular.

ACCESSORIES Long pearls for day, silver fox-fur stoles and coloured scarves an essential fashion detail. Large shawls for evening wrap, chiffon scarves with evening dress draped from the shoulders or hips.

Handbags to match the outfit, beaded for evening. Jewellery important – long drop earrings, chokers, pearl necklaces, brooches and slave bangles.

MAKE-UP Rouge and lipstick, eyebrows plucked, eyebrow-pencil.

MOVEMENT Less upright poise, with the shoulders hunched and pelvis pushed forward, creating an inward curve to the torso.

DETAILS OF ILLUSTRATED PATTERNS

Tennis costume consisting of a white pleated skirt and blue blazer. The blazer is cut without shaping, and shorter than contemporary costume jackets, with large patch pockets at hips and shaped pocket on breast. Wide lapels with step collar roll low, fastening with two gilt buttons. Two-piece, set-in sleeves finish with straight turn-back cuff.

The skirt with all-round knife pleats is set on a silk hip-yoke drawn in with elastic at the top edge.

A stockinette hip-length jersey with low rounded neckline extends over the skirt hip yoke (pattern not supplied).

THE TENNIS GIRL.
Drawn by Elsa Courlander.

Far left: Suit with long jacket, made of gabardine and crêpe de Chine.

Left: Illustration of girl wearing a 1920s tennis outfit.

Right: Drawing of tennis costume (for the pattern see page 60).

FABRICS AND COLOURS Navy or royal blue flannel for jacket, white linen skirt. 'It is possible to make such a garment very attractive because of the possibility of the use of vivid-coloured flannels and sharp contrast in the form of braid or ribbon for the edge' (*Tailor and Cutter*, February 1924).

FOOTWEAR Low-heeled laced sports shoes of white buckskin with crêpe soles.

HAT Deep-crowned, pull-on type hat with turn-down brim, grosgrain ribbon and bow trim.

NOTES ON CONSTRUCTION OF GARMENTS

Ease back to front at shoulder seams of jacket. Position of contrast braiding is indicated by solid black lines on pattern. The jacket is loose-fitting throughout.

The skirt is cut perfectly straight with all-round 2.5cm (1in) knife pleats. A section of the skirt is given in the pattern section to illustrate spacing of the pleats. To construct the skirt, work directly on the cloth. Cut a piece of fabric depth 71cm (28in) plus 5cm (2in) hem allowance; width 285cm (112½in) (three times hips plus ease). It will be necessary to seam the fabric to create the full required width. Seams should be concealed at the inside fold of the pleats. Add seam allowance where required and to upper and outside edges.

The completed skirt is mounted on a silk hip yoke, elasticated to fit the waist at the top edge. To make up, cut a rectangle 12.75cm (5in) deep by 95cm (37½in) (hip measurement plus ease). Add seam allowances to side and lower edges and 2.5cm (1in) to upper edge to form a narrow casing for elastic. Ease the lower skirt to fit hip yoke; it may be necessary to overlap top edge of pleats slightly.

MEN

PREDOMINANT FASHION FEATURES

Lounge jackets shorter, with no back vent, and sometimes worn without waistcoats. Wider trousers with turn-ups now worn for most occasions, except the most formal. For business, dark lounge suits with striped trousers.

Oxford bags – wider trousers with turn-ups, up to 40cm (15¾in) and worn long (over the instep), teamed with a smart flannel jacket.

Flannel jackets and trousers, cut with a waistband, belt loops and adjustable side buckles. Tweed sports jackets or navy blazers with flannel trousers, grey or white in summer.

Overcoat as previous decade.

Knitted jumpers – Fair Isle or white with club colours replaces the waistcoat for sports.

Plus fours (looser and fuller than knickerbockers), with Fair Isle pullovers and patterned socks.

FABRICS Tweeds, herringbones, dark suiting fabrics for formal lounge suit. Gabardine for raincoats.

COLOURS As previous fashion.

SHIRTS AND UNDERGARMENTS Soft-fronted shirts with lounge or sports jackets, and coloured shirts with white double collar. Stiff shirt front with formal lounge suits, often striped. Essential to evening dress, always white. Pants shortened to trunks. Sleeveless singlets with no fastenings replace buttoned vests.

FOOTWEAR Shoes always worn in preference to boots by younger men. Brown or black leather, white buckskin with white flannels. Higher heels, patent-leather Oxford shoe worn with lounge suits. Crêpe and rubber soles for sports shoes.

SOCKS Brightly coloured, ribbed, patterned and striped socks. Mid-calf length with plus fours, supported by elastic suspenders, fastening below the knee.

HATS Trilby most popular style. Straw boaters or panama in summer. Tweed caps for sports and casual wear.

HAIR Short-back-and-sides, centre-parting with longer sideboards. Younger men clean-shaven.

ACCESSORIES As previous fashion.

DETAILS OF ILLUSTRATED PATTERNS

Stylish double-breasted reefer jacket with a six-button front. It is close-fitting and a front dart is taken out of the front. The revers are not too heavy, and the length of the turn is medium. Two slanted flaps at hip-level and left breast pocket. The back is cut whole without seam or vent. Two-piece sleeves finish with slit cuff and two buttons and buttonholes. The waistcoat is of white or very light-coloured material and has five buttons or holes. It is visible between jacket lapels. The bottom button is always left open (pattern not supplied).

White flannel trousers with permanent turn-ups, although remaining fairly narrow in the leg, are wider than previous styles. Trousers are cut with waistband and buckles and straps placed at the sides.

FABRICS AND COLOURS Navy blue serge or flannel jacket; white flannel trousers.

SHIRT Soft-fronted shirt with soft double collar, stiffened with celluloid tabs at collar points. It may be white or pale in colour.

FOOTWEAR White buckskin shoes with four-eyelet fastening, crêpe soles and more pointed toes.

HAT Straw boater.

ACCESSORIES Striped tie. Hatband and tie may be in school, club or regimental colours. Walking stick, cuff links, signet ring.

Right: Drawing of reefer jacket and flannel trousers (for the pattern see page 61).

CB

BLAZER
BACK
cut 2

BLAZER
FRONT
cut 2

BLAZER
FRONT SLEEVE
cut 2

BLAZER
BACK SLEEVE
cut 2

BLAZER
COLLAR
cut 2 on fold

CB fold

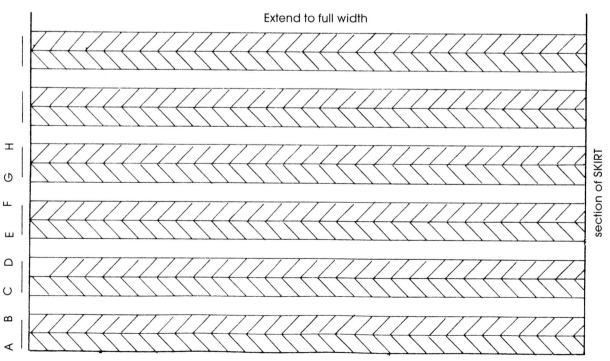

Extend to full width

A B C D E F G H

section of SKIRT

REEFER JACKET
BACK
cut 2

REEFER JACKET
FRONT
cut 2

REEFER JACKET
BACK SLEEVE
cut 2

REEFER JACKET
FRONT SLEEVE
cut 2

CB fold

REEFER JACKET   COLLAR   cut 2 on fold

TROUSERS
—— BACK   cut 2
······ FRONT   cut 2

pleat   pleat

TROUSERS   WAISTBAND   cut 2 on fold

CB fold

1925–1926

WOMEN

PREDOMINANT FASHION FEATURES

Extreme of present mode reached. Skirts are straight, the knee revealed for the first time in fashion history; worn with straight, long tops, often sleeveless. Many styles are adopted directly from men's tailoring – double-breasted waistcoats and jackets, link closure; shoulders are broader and the fit looser.

The years 1925–1926 also witness the first signs of change towards femininity in women's fashion. 'No longer are we all young boys... Yet we are not a day older; we are feminine before everything, slim as young birch trees, with a very real attempt to return to that old half-forgotten word – charm' (*Vogue*, November 1926).

Hem width is emphasized with godets and pleats, the fullness apparent only with movement.

The trend of informality in day dress continues. Sportswear trends influence fashion.

Two-piece suits and costumes remain popular. Blouses and dresses with boat-shape necklines, flat Peter Pan sailor collars, pouched at the hip. Coats are very loose fitting with wider shoulders and fur trimming.

Evidence of change in evening dresses, which begin to pouch at the 'waistline'; fuller in the skirt, often dipping at the back or sides. Low-back *décolletage*. One-sided designs dominate all fashions. Trompe l'oeil sweaters with scarves, bows and collars knitted into the design.

FABRICS   Crêpe de Chine, georgette, voiles, foulard, shantung, metallic laces, metallic cloths, beaded fabrics. Printed geometric and futuristic patterns. Tweeds and checks for daytime suits; knitted fabrics. Furs – Persian lamb, astrakhan.

COLOURS   Bold colours are worn: black, white, red, fuchsia, bright blue, orange, violet, jade. For evening all shades of purple, lavender, mauve. Cream, brown and beige remain popular.

DECORATION   Black lace, deep fringing, bead embroidery. Bold appliqué. Large, futuristic geometric and cubist patterns.

UNDERGARMENTS   Light, flimsy fabrics, ninon, crêpe de Chine. Elasticated corsets compressing the breasts and hips; these are pulled up at the front and down at the back to increase the flattening effect. Backless chemise for evening and strapless brassieres. Cami-bockers combine camisole and *Directoire* knickers.

SHOES   Toes not so pointed, heels higher and curved, two or three straps popular. Shoes frequently combine two colours and materials – leather, suede and skins: alligator, lizard, crocodile or snake.

STOCKINGS   Flesh tones, artificial silk and silk, silk and cotton.

HATS   Cloche hat universally worn, narrow-brimmed with close-fitting crown, pulled down well over the eyes like a helmet, and matching the outfit. Sparse trimming. Felts, velours and knitted styles all popular. Larger-brimmed hats for summer.

HAIR   Eton crop, extreme of short hair, closely cropped style cut above the ears and close into the nape of the neck. Sometimes waved for softer effects. Women frequent men's barbers.

ACCESSORIES   Gauntlet-style gloves – suede, calfskin, buckskin. Envelope handbags, containing make-up, cigarette cases, long cigarette holders. Ties, tie pins, cuff links. Scarves – silk, for day fastened at one side with brooch. Fringed scarves for evening. Long bead necklaces. Costume jewellery, slave bangles, bracelets, long drop earrings, shoulder brooch.

MAKE-UP   Orange rouge and lipstick, plucked eyebrows and pencilled brows create a mask-like face.

MOVEMENT   Pelvis pushed forwards and shoulders rounded, one hand frequently resting on the hips. No emphasis is therefore given to the bustline.

Left: A 1925 poster shows a fashionable young woman.

Right: Drawing of tubular evening dress with lowered waistline (for the pattern see page 64).

DETAILS OF ILLUSTRATED PATTERN

Knee-length tubular evening dress drawn in at lowered waistline with gathered band under bodice. The bodice is loose fitting, with scoop neckline bound with main dress fabric, and shoulder decoration harmonizing with 'waistline'. Heavy metallic lace insertion at centre front, back and sides reveals silk foundation, meeting the hemline of matching scalloped lace. Narrow bands of finer insertion trim the lower skirt section. Deep, cutaway armholes are bound in the same fashion as the neckline; the latter is cut low at the back.

FABRICS AND COLOURS Gold crêpe de Chine, matching fine silk for foundation.

FOOTWEAR Evening shoes of gold glacé kid with low vamp, pointed toes, curved heels and double T-straps.

ACCESSORIES Gold bandeau worn around the head and across the forehead; much jewellery including slave bangles, pearl-drop earrings, rings and choker necklace.

NOTES ON CONSTRUCTION OF GARMENT

Insert 6.25cm (2¼in) wide gold lace at front, back and sides of dress, and lower skirt. Position of lace is indicated by broken lines on pattern.

Gather at shoulders and lowered waistline, along broken lines, and stay with tape on wrong side.

Make up foundation and join to dress at neck and armhole edges with a narrow binding of self fabric, 6mm (¼in) finished width.

MEN

PREDOMINANT FASHION FEATURES

Menswear experiences more casual and younger-looking influence. Lounge jacket less defined at waistline. Lapels and shoulders widen to balance trouser width. Reefer jackets, blazers, sports jackets, flannel trousers – see previous fashion details. Oxford bags reach extreme in width, up to 62cm (24½in), lighter in colour than the jacket. Overcoats are shortened to just below the knee, velvet collars not so usual on chesterfields. Sleeveless, knitted pullovers, shorter than jumpers in length, in brightly coloured Fair Isle patterns, worn with Oxford bags or plus fours. Flannel jackets and soft felt hats for sports and casual wear.

FABRICS Tweeds and checks popular. Oxford shirting; light flannel or Viyella for sports shirt.

COLOURS Oxford bags – grey, brown, beige, light navy. Light colours for shirts – blue, grey and peach tones.

SHIRTS Coloured shirts with new soft collars and detachable supports.

SHOES Oxford style remains most popular. Shoes in two colours: white and tan or black and white. Not always considered to be in the best taste.

SOCKS Similar to previous fashion.

HAIR AND HATS Similar to previous fashion.

ACCESSORIES Wider ties in brighter colours – patterned or spotted. Collar pins, tie pins, cuff links.

DETAILS OF ILLUSTRATED PATTERNS

Full evening dress consisting of dress-coat, trousers and white waistcoat. The coat is close fitting, with tails ending above the knee and high waist seam, forming a continuous run to the front points. Three buttons are placed on the waist dart in front. The peaked lapel is finished to turn to the waist and is faced with silk to the edge. The entire front is cut in one piece and the lapel is cut in one with it. Two-piece sleeves finish with slit cuff and three-button fastening. The tail coat is worn for more dressy occasions, with the dinner jacket for informal evening wear. The latter is usually worn with black waistcoat and black tie.

The waistcoat, with deep U-shaped front and lapels, is cut with long points in the front and fastens with four buttons. A strap and buckle at the back enable a closer fit at waist-level.

Dress trousers are narrower than for day wear and without turn-ups. They are usually finished with one or two rows of silk braid down the side. The latter is more usual with dress jackets, and placed approximately 6mm (¼in) apart.

FABRICS AND COLOURS Black wool worsted; white piqué for waistcoat and bow tie.

UNDERGARMENTS Dress shirt with plain starched front and single-stud fastening, white starched wing collar and cuffs.

FOOTWEAR Black silk lisle socks; patent-leather Oxford laced shoes with rounded toes.

ACCESSORIES Matching shirt studs, waistcoat buttons and cuff links of onyx, pearl or mother-of-pearl on gold base; white cotton or buckskin gloves; signet ring; white bow tie.

NOTES ON CONSTRUCTION OF GARMENTS

The dress coat fits closely to the figure. Trousers may be finished with a row of braid at side seams.

Right: Drawing of full men's evening dress (for the pattern see page 65).

gather

gather

DRESS
FRONT
cut 2

CF

insertion lace

DRESS
BACK
cut 2

CB

insertion lace

insertion lace

DRESS
FOUNDATION BACK
cut 1 on fold

CB fold

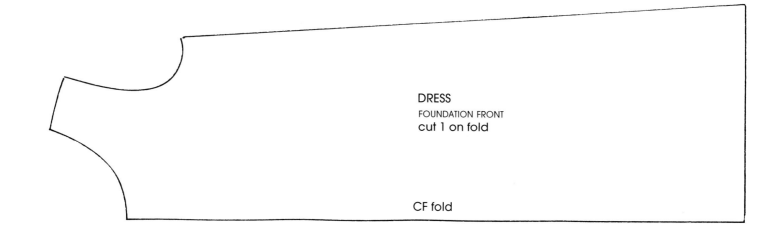

DRESS
FOUNDATION FRONT
cut 1 on fold

CF fold

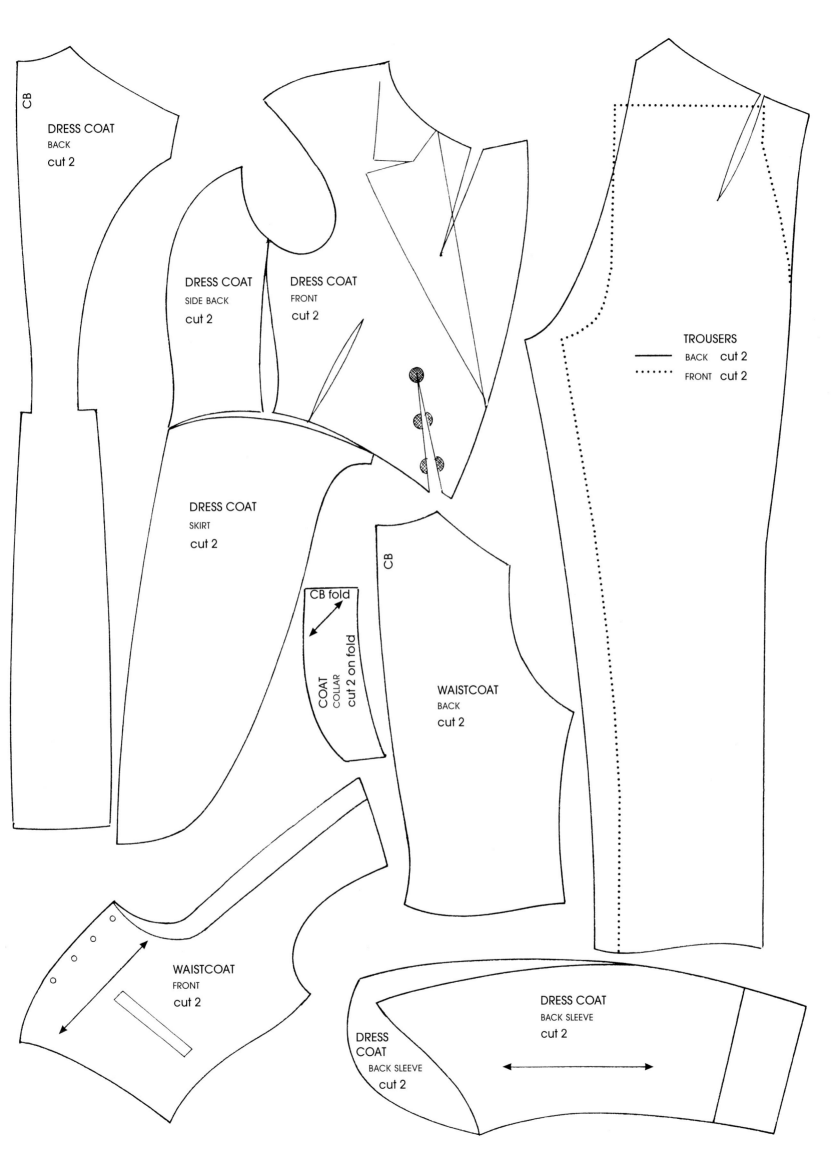

DRESS COAT
BACK
cut 2

CB

DRESS COAT
SIDE BACK
cut 2

DRESS COAT
FRONT
cut 2

DRESS COAT
SKIRT
cut 2

TROUSERS
BACK   cut 2
FRONT   cut 2

CB fold

COAT
COLLAR
cut 2 on fold

CB

WAISTCOAT
BACK
cut 2

WAISTCOAT
FRONT
cut 2

DRESS COAT
BACK SLEEVE
cut 2

DRESS
COAT
BACK SLEEVE
cut 2

WOMEN

PREDOMINANT FASHION FEATURES

Skirts knee-level, with pleats and godets. Length 38–40.5cm (15–16in) from the ground. Blouses with softer sleeves. Gathers, pleats, darts, tucks beginning to appear on all garments. Dresses are worn in a tunic style, tiered, drapery effects, especially in evening wear. One-sided asymmetrical effects, trompe l'oeil sweaters. Coats are three-quarter length, low revers, low buttoning with dropped waist, worn with short, pleated skirt. Long coats end just above the skirt hemline. Satin pyjama suits for cocktails. Popular golfing wear consists of jumpers, tweed skirt culottes or plus fours. Leather sports coats.

FABRICS Artificial silk, now known as 'rayon', manufactured by Courtaulds. Knitted fabrics, striped stockinette, fine silks. Tweeds and checks. Velvet and metallic fabrics, georgette, crêpe de Chine, lace.

COLOURS Black and white, bold and pastel shades all popular.

DECORATION Silver fox fur, ruffles, jabots. Bold geometric designs.

UNDERGARMENTS White less popular than peaches and pinks for undergarments. Separate brassieres constrict rather than support the breasts. Cami-knickers, cami-bockers.

FOOTWEAR Suede, buckskin, crocodile, snakeskin, lizard; pointed toes, higher heels.

STOCKINGS Checked or striped woollen stockings for golf. 'Flesh-coloured' (beige) artificial silk or silk stockings.

HATS Cloche hat is cut higher at the back, with the brim turned up on one side, linking with the often asymmetrical nature of the dress.

HAIR Extremely short hair less popular. The shingle, a short cut with natural-looking waves, softer than previous fashion. False hair pieces add length to the back of the hair, if needed.

ACCESSORIES Shoes and handbags match. Umbrellas with day costume. Costume jewellery.

MAKE-UP Plucked eyebrows, kohl to blacken eyes, rouge and lipstick. Suntanned skin fashionable.

MOVEMENT As previous fashion.

DETAILS OF ILLUSTRATED PATTERNS

Hip-length lounge jacket of plain material, cut with panelled front and single-breasted fastening. Wide, pointed lapels roll from lowered waistline, with upper collar faced in velvet. Shaped patch pockets, with velvet trim and button tab, harmonize with collar. There is corresponding decoration at pointed cuffs of two-piece set-in sleeves.

The skirt is cut quite straight with single inverted pleat at centre front to allow greater freedom of movement.

A long-line, single-breasted waistcoat fastening from V-shaped neckline with a single row of closely spaced buttons, and a masculine collar and tie, complete the outfit (pattern not supplied).

FABRICS AND COLOURS Fine woollen suiting fabric in tan, blue or grey shades.

FOOTWEAR Snakeskin shoes with pointed toes, double T-bar straps and high curved heels.

HAT Close-fitting cloche hat pulled down well on the head. Narrow brim turned up at the back, and braid trim.

Far left: Advertisement for cigarettes shows a woman wearing a cloche hat.

Left: A woman dressed for travel in a knee-length coat with patch pockets.

Right: Drawing of a lounge jacket and skirt (for the pattern see page 68).

ACCESSORIES Pearl-drop earrings; patent leather belt worn at lowered waistline; wrist-length, gauntlet-style kid gloves to match the outfit.

NOTES ON CONSTRUCTION OF GARMENTS

A 6mm (¼in) seam allowance is included in the pattern.

Jacket back is cut in one piece. Ease back to front at shoulder seams. Separate jacket front and side-front pattern along panel line A to B. Add seam allowance to cut edges.

The pleated skirt is cut perfectly straight. If a seam or seams have to be introduced they are concealed at inner folds of pleats or at centre back. To cut the skirt work directly on the cloth. Cut a piece of fabric: depth = skirt length, eg 57cm (22½in), plus hem and seam allowance; width = 95cm (37½in) (hips and ease), plus a 32cm (12½in) pleat allowance. Total width = 127cm (50in), to which seam allowances must be added. The construction of the pleat at centre front is shown on the section of the skirt pattern illustrated.

The completed skirt is then mounted on to a silk bodice, which supports the skirt without bulk.

MEN

PREDOMINANT FASHION FEATURES

Styles are similar to previous fashion. Lounge jacket often cut straight at the hem. Single-breasted styles with three buttons, only the middle one fastened. Lapels and shoulder width increase. Permanently pressed turn-ups on trousers.

Oxford bags – less exaggerated trouser width. All trousers remain wider in the leg, pleated into the waistband.

Reefer jackets, blazers, sports jackets and flannel trousers are similar to 1924.

Evening-wear tail coats for formal wear. Collar and lapels faced in silk. Dinner jacket for less formal occasions. Black waistcoats, matching the suit, occasionally replace white, with the dinner jacket only. Trousers follow day styles, never with turn-ups. Sleeveless, knitted pullovers, shorter than jumpers in length, in brightly coloured Fair Isle patterns, worn with Oxford bags or plus fours. Flannel jackets and soft felt hats for sports and casual wear.

FABRICS Tweeds and checks popular. Oxford shirting; light flannel or Viyella for sports shirt.

COLOURS Oxford bags – grey, brown, beige, light navy. Light colours for shirts – blue, grey, peach tones.

SHIRTS Coloured shirts with new soft collars and detachable supports. Dress shirt with starched front of marcella or piqué, with plain, double cuffs or pleated front, worn with wing collar and white bow tie. Pleated shirts not usually worn with dinner jackets.

SHOES Oxford style remains most popular. Correspondent shoes in two colours, white and tan or black and white.

SOCKS Brightly coloured, ribbed, patterned and striped socks.

HATS Trilby most popular style; straw boater or panama in summer. Tweed caps for sports and casual wear.

HAIR Short-back-and-sides, centre-parting with longer side-boards.

ACCESSORIES Wider ties in brighter colours – patterned or spotted. Gauntlet-style leather, suede or buckskin gloves, may be string-backed. Collar pins, tie pins, cuff links, wrist watches; umbrella with formal lounge suit.

MOVEMENT Carefree, casual attitude of the 'bright young things', with their interest in sports and dancing, is reflected in their behaviour and movement.

DETAILS OF ILLUSTRATED PATTERNS

Single-breasted blazer with wide, pointed lapels and three-button fastening. It is close-fitting, with two front darts, and rounded lower edges. Two large patch pockets at hip-level and shaped breast pocket, which may be embroidered with the crest or badge of club or regiment. Two-piece, set-in sleeves finish with slit and single gilt button, harmonizing with front jacket fastening. The back is cut with centre-back seam and no vent.

White flannel Oxford bags are wide in the leg with turn-ups. They are cut with front pleats and belted waistband. Braces are not required.

A striped shirt, with white detachable soft collar, and striped club tie, complete the outfit.

FABRICS AND COLOURS Navy flannel for jacket, white flannel trousers.

HATS It is permissible for young men to go hatless.

NOTES ON CONSTRUCTION OF GARMENTS

The blazer may be bound with silk braid in club or regimental colours on outside edges, cuffs and pockets.

Oxford bags are loose fitting in the leg, constructed with a waistband and belt loops. Waistband pattern includes front extension.

Right: Drawing of a blazer and Oxford bags (for the pattern see page 69).

JACKET
BACK
cut 1 on fold

CB fold

A

JACKET
SIDE FRONT
cut 2

FRONT
cut 2

B

JACKET
FRONT SLEEVE
cut 2

JACKET
BACK SLEEVE
cut 2

CB

JACKET
COLLAR
cut 4

BODICE
TOP BACK
cut 1 on fold

CB fold

BODICE
TOP FRONT
cut 1 on fold

CF fold

SECTION OF **SKIRT**

fold line

fold line

CF fold

BLAZER
BACK
cut 2

CB

BLAZER
COLLAR

BLAZER
FRONT
cut 2

pleat   pleat

OXFORD BAGS
——— BACK cut 2
········ FRONT cut 2

BLAZER
BACK SLEEVE
cut 2

BLAZER
FRONT SLEEVE
cut 2

OXFORD BAGS   WAISTBAND   cut 2 on fold   CB

1929

WOMEN

PREDOMINANT FASHION FEATURES

Designers endeavour to lengthen the skirt by means of transparent or false hems and trains. Day wear follows suit, with dipping or pointed hems and a general lengthening of skirt, but the trend is more extreme in evening fashions.

Tweed coats and skirts worn with jumper. Blouses are tucked into the skirts at the waist. Dresses and skirts flare low, moulding closer to the figure around the hips.

Evening wear is often sleeveless with back *décolletage* more pronounced, dipping with the hem and reaching halfway down the back. All dresses fit closely over the hips, flaring to the hemline. Higher 'waist', with drapery effects from the shoulders and hips, sometimes trailing the ground.

FABRICS Lighter-weight woollen fabrics, firm silks and satins, tweeds, cashmere, shantung, wool crêpes. For evening wear satin, chiffon, voile, moiré, georgette, tulle and metallic brocades are worn. Patterned and plain fabrics combined.

COLOURS During the day beige, brown, navy, black and white are worn. For summer and evening wear, brighter colours are popular such as blue, yellow, rose pink, pale green, black and white.

DECORATION Scarves, jabot collars and frills. Geometric patterns. Chiffon flowers worn on one shoulder or one side of 'waist'.

UNDERGARMENTS Foundation garments cease to achieve the straight-line effect. 'Corselettes' mould rather than constrict the figure, and include two breast pockets. Camisole almost obsolete as separate garment.

FOOTWEAR Frequently employing two colours and materials, e.g. white and tan, suede and snakeskin. Cuban and Louis heels.

STOCKINGS Coloured stockings and 'flesh' tones in silk or artificial silk.

HATS Brim of cloche hat becomes larger and softer, tilted back at the front to reveal more of the face.

HAIR Worn longer, with rolls of curls at the nape of the neck. For women growing their hair, a small slide is worn to keep straggling ends in place.

ACCESSORIES Gauntlet-style gloves in dyed leather. Envelope handbags often co-ordinate with shoes. Large evening wraps, chiffon squares; plaid or striped scarves for day wear, wrapped tightly around the throat with tails hanging behind. Jabot collars. Strings of pearls shorter than previous fashion. Costume jewellery.

MAKE-UP Vaseline and kohl on eyelids. Black mascara, rouge and darker lipsticks.

MOVEMENT Similar to previous fashion, although shoulders now less hunched.

DETAILS OF ILLUSTRATED PATTERNS

Bias-cut evening dress with draped cowl from lowered neckline, bloused bodice and dropped waist. The shaped skirt falls from fitted hip yoke with draped inserts at side fronts and back. Set-in bishop sleeves fasten at deep pointed cuffs with rouleau loops and covered contrast buttons. Contrast bands at shoulder and hip yokes harmonize with matching binding at dress edges, emphasizing design features. The dress remains loose-fitting over the natural waistline. Displaying characteristics of the 1920s, the style is indicative of a more feminine trend in ladies' fashions, and lengthening skirt hem.

FABRICS AND COLOURS Pale peach crêpe de Chine, brown satin contrast binding.

FOOTWEAR Evening shoes of gold kid with single strap fastening and high curved heels.

ACCESSORIES Clasp-fastening, beaded clutch handbag, supported by a metal frame.

NOTES ON CONSTRUCTION OF GARMENTS

Bias cut requires more careful handling of the fabric. Additional length is allowed in the dress bodice for blousing at lowered waistline.

Skirt drape is stitched in at side front and back seams between A and B. There are no side seams in the skirt.

1.5cm (⅝in) bias-cut strips are applied at shoulder and hip yoke edges; cuff, hemline and drape edges are finished with 1cm (⅜in) binding. Cut all strips on true bias of fabric (measurements indicate finished widths). Position of binding is indicated by heavier black areas on pattern.

Sleeve cuffs are finished with rouleau loops and covered buttons, also in contrast fabric. Underneath, wear knee-length, princess petticoat and closely fitted, elasticated corset – the bust remains unaccentuated.

Left: Illustrated advertisement shows a stylised flapper girl walking a toy dog.

Right: Drawing of bias-cut evening dress (for the pattern see page 72).

MEN

PREDOMINANT FASHION FEATURES

Day wear styles remain similar to previous fashions, with trend for wider, more pointed lapels and increased shoulder width. Double- or single-breasted. Lounge suit waistcoat fronts more usually match the rest of the suit. Trousers with permanently pressed turn-ups.

Overcoats: 'Breadth of shoulder and a short, broad lapel is the most predominating feature of this season's styles' (*Tailor and Cutter*, September 1929). Chesterfield for more formal wear, double or single-breasted, the latter usually with fly front. This style ceases to feature a velvet collar. Ulster – looser-fitting style, belted, with patch pockets. Raglan – usually single-breasted, belted, with patch pockets. Raincoats of proofed tweed or gabardine.

FABRICS Flannel suiting, tweeds and checks, worsteds, cashmere. Raincoats of proofed tweed or gabardine.

COLOURS Black and white for evening. Shades of grey for day wear. Dark grey or black for formal lounge suits. Putty or camel for less formal overcoats.

UNDERGARMENTS Soft-fronted shirt with turn-down collar worn with double-breasted dinner jacket. Stiff shirt front remains correct with formal lounge suit and other evening styles. Singlet and trunks or combinations in knitted wool, aertex or artificial silk.

FOOTWEAR Oxford-type laced shoe, plain black calf or brogued, black for town, brown for sports or country. Correspondent leather shoes in two colours.

SOCKS Coloured or striped ribbed socks, reaching to mid-calf and secured with garters.

HATS Trilby remains most popular style, available in soft felts, straw and tweeds. Bowler hat for business.

HAIR Centre-parting with hair slightly raised at the hairline and brushed back, short-back-and-sides.

ACCESSORIES Gloves fasten at the wrist in chamois, kid, buckskin or cloth in pale colours, grey or white. Rolled umbrellas, wrist watches.

DETAILS OF ILLUSTRATED PATTERNS

Dinner jacket and dress trousers worn with black waistcoat. The waist is not close-fitting but shape is suggested by giving breadth and squareness at shoulders and ease at the chest; the waist is defined without the abrupt shaping of earlier styles.

Pointed lapels are bold in proportion, faced with silk and rolling to a one-button fastening. Outside breast pocket and jetted hip-pockets preserve the slim, smoother appearance of the skirt, the length just covering the seat of the trousers. The back is cut with moderate drape and centre-back seam and vent. Two-piece, set-in sleeves finish with slit cuffs and single button to harmonize with front.

A black waistcoat or vest is more usual with dinner jackets, although white or delicately coloured versions may be worn. Low U-shaped opening with lapels, fastens with four buttons.

Trousers are generally slimmer than for day wear, without pleats or turn-ups.

FABRICS AND COLOURS Jacket and trousers in black wool worsted; black silk for waistcoat and tie.

SHIRT White dress shirt with starched front and single-stud fastening, separate starched wing collar and cuffs.

FOOTWEAR Black patent-leather Oxfords; black lisle socks.

ACCESSORIES Shirt studs, waistcoat buttons and cuff links to match in onyx, jade, smoked mother-of-pearl, pearl. White handkerchief worn in breast pocket, for decoration only.

NOTES ON CONSTRUCTION OF GARMENTS

Expert cutting and tailoring skills are required to achieve the correct balance and proportion. The back shoulder seam requires easing on 1.3cm (½in); the back scye (armhole) held in and the front scye worked up to form a breast shape.

Trousers may be finished with two rows of braid at side seams; if two, they are placed approximately 6mm (¼in) apart. The latter is more usual when worn with a dress coat; one row with a dinner jacket.

Left: Formal, sporty and casual fashions for men.

Right: Drawing of dinner suit (for the pattern see page 73).

DRESS
BACK
cut 1 on fold

CB fold

SHOULDER YOKE
cut 2

C
C
D
D

DRESS
FRONT
cut 1 on fold

CF fold

DRESS
SLEEVE
cut 2

SKIRT
YOKE
cut 1 on fold

CB
CF fold

DRESS
CUFF
cut 2

DRESS
SKIRT BACK
cut 1 on fold

CB fold

A

DRESS
SKIRT SIDE
cut 2

A
A
B
B

DRESS
SKIRT FRONT
cut 1 on fold

CF fold

A
B

DRESS
SKIRT DRAPE
cut 4

A
B

The Thirties

By the opening of the decade the waist had resumed its normal position, and throughout the 1930s emphasis was on the shoulders and hips. Hair was worn longer and with more waves, all contributing to a more feminine, mature emphasis on dress, in contrast to the boyish, youthful line of the 1920s.

By the mid-1930s the all-in-one corset and brassiere was the most popular advertised garment, and the word 'uplift' entered the fashion vocabulary. Before the advent of World War II the bosom was well re-established, along with the hips and the pinched-in waist. Vionnet introduced the bias cut in 1930, and dresses grew more clinging and complex in cut, perhaps as a reaction to previous simplicity and the growth of the ready-to-wear industry. The new cut necessitated careful handling of the fabric and there was thus a more observable distinction between those who could afford the work of expensive couturiers and those who had to buy imitations in the cheaper shops.

The standardization of male costume in the 20th century continued, as did the trend of informality and ease in men's dress witnessed during the previous decade. By 1939 dark-coloured shirts appeared in navy, wine, red or brown with light-toned coat and trousers for informal wear, and striped fabrics became an acceptable alternative to the white business shirt. The popularity of summer resorts in the Mediterranean, Florida and the Bahamas and the vogue for sunbathing inspired the introduction of summer evening jackets and light-coloured suits. Lower and middle classes, too, enjoyed more leisure; in the early 1920s only about one-and-a-half million people had paid holidays, whereas by 1939 the figure was over eleven million. To capitalize on the holiday boom, the first all-in holiday camps on the American model appeared; Billy Butlin opened his first camp in Skegness in 1937.

A rising standard of living, paid holidays and public transport put holidays and day-trips within the reach of a wider section of the population than ever before. With the increased popularity of seaside resorts the bathing costume inevitably assumed greater importance.

The 'bare-back' craze, with emphasis on the rear of the female dress, can be partly attributed to the backless swimsuit and sunbathing craze. Evening and summer wear throughout the period often gave the impression, from the back, of the wearer being 'stripped to the waist', and decoration and embellishments were often reserved for the back view. It is for this reason that the decade has acquired the name 'the Dorsal Period'.

The ready-to-wear market, in its infancy during the 1920s, was now being more firmly established as fashion became available to a larger proportion of the population. The salaried middle class, civil servants and clerks, were able to enjoy new luxuries. As prices fell they found they could buy houses, small cars, household gadgets and furniture as never before. A small car – an Austin 7 or a Ford 8 – cost £105 by 1932, a third of a year's salary. With the rise of the mass market Britain increasingly became a consumer society, and with the introduction of hire purchase a man without capital could for the first time equip himself on credit, although this was much frowned upon at the time. In the field of entertainment the cinema provided a cheap means of escapism; half the population went to the pictures at least once a week. The period between the wars was one of technical revolution, with change and improvement accelerated at a pace far beyond that achieved in similar time spans in previous centuries. It is significant that in a time of mass unemployment the one industry that steadily increased its labour force was the service industry, providing comforts and entertainment to those able to afford them.

Kestos lavish on grateful femininity, lingerie garments of charm and delicacy which delight to the full their capricious hearts and fancies. The Backless Brassière is their latest creation—it is a clever adaptation of the Kestos Brassière which allows its wearer to adopt décolleté fashions with a dignity that is seemly with present-day manners. Sold everywhere.

Catalogue on request.

KESTOS LTD.
Maddox House, Regent St., London, W.1.
(Wholesale only)

KESTOS
BACKLESS
BRASSIÈRE

Above: Advertisement from 1935 for the Kestos backless brassiere.

The development of man-made fibres also accelerated at this time, and further discoveries in the production of artificial silk, in its early stages in the 1920s, overcame many of the initial problems. Rayon, as it became known from 1927, was greatly improved in quality, one advance being the discovery of how to dull the metallic gleam of the early product, making possible the production of fine, flesh-coloured yarns suitable for knitting into women's stockings. The sum total of all these changes was a gigantic increase in the output of rayon; moreover, as competition grew fiercer and as costs of production were cut, prices fell sharply – much more than those of silk, cotton or wool. Cheap woven or knitted fabrics and hosiery in rayon or rayon mixtures tapped new levels of demand in all classes.

Research into new fibres continued in Britain and abroad, and in 1938, in the USA and the UK (jointly by ICI and Courtaulds) the first fully synthetic fibre was produced; this was the polyamide Nylon 66. Innovations to improve the properties of natural fibres were also introduced: 'zingale' (uncrushable) and 'sanforized' (pre-shrunk) finishes for cotton fabrics. Stiffening methods such as 'Trubenizing' were used for men's shirt collars, which required no further starching. Separate collars also ceased to be the norm, and ready-to-wear shirts were made with collars attached.

Improvements in mass-production techniques had in themselves simultaneously raised standards and lowered costs. Combined with the wider availability and variety of cheap fabrics, the growth of factory-produced clothes forged ahead particularly rapidly. Because of the growing sophistication of clothes in the early 1930s, as we have seen, home dressmaking became less viable for the amateur, and the factories were able to take over a large share of the market with passable imitations of *haute couture*. Many of the clothes produced for the retail trade were very shoddily made; the financial depression seems to have provided an excuse for a general lowering of standards. Despite the enormous improvements that had been made in the production of rayon since its inception, it is not naturally a durable fibre, and mass-production techniques generally tended to lower standards in garment construction. These two factors, both of which reduce the life of garments, served to accelerate the pace of fashion. Thus this period witnessed a basic change in attitude towards clothes, from those which had been made to last a lifetime to the new mass-produced, short-lived garment. Other inventions, such as simplification of dress fastenings, facilitated both wear and mass-production. Elastic replaced laces in underwear, and the press stud the hook and eye. Press studs often lay concealed beneath a row of decorative but useless buttons. The metal zip fastener, at first limited in use to heavier and stronger materials, proved indispensable in sports and leisure wear, and buttons were replaced by zip fly fronts on men's trousers. Refinements, including attaching the zip to a band of stronger material, extended its use in connection with lighter fabrics employed in evening wear.

Advertising, too, continued to stimulate the fashion industry. Mass-circulation of the women's press did not really take place until *Woman* was launched by Odham's in 1937. This was the first magazine to be printed by the colour-gravure process, and offered readers and advertisers plenty of high-quality pictures much cheaper than the upper-class 'glossies'. It had a readership of half a million by the end of the year. Such developments in communication placed increasing demands on the retailer to produce new and exciting trends to attract customers. Competition between rival firms increased with the growth of advertising, which was not without its advantages for the consumer. Reduced prices and improved standards were one method of capturing the market.

Above: Woman modelling a silver fox fur coat.

The monopoly of Paris designers and couturiers on fashion was not only threatened by ready-to-wear and the rise of the department store, for now fresh influences came into play. The cinema was unparalleled in the influence it exerted on fashion. With the massive expansion of the cinema after the advent of the 'talkies' in 1927, it became a leading force in promoting new modes and methods of attraction. By 1939 the cinema was easily the most important and persuasive form of mass entertainment. It was vitally important for a number of reasons, but mostly because its influence was unambiguous and direct. There was an obvious link between fashion and the screen – the vogue for wide shoulders, slim hips and a flat chest was unmistakably popularized by the silhouette of Greta Garbo, one of the most influential stars of the period. This trend also affected the male silhouette, and by the end of the decade men's jackets were well padded and featured broader shoulders and chests. Lapels, too, became wider and more pronounced, and the vogue for turn-ups continued on the wide trouser leg.

The romance and glamour of the cinema was readily exploited by the women's journals at all levels. *Vogue* continued to emphasize Paris, the theatre, and society as the main trend-setters, and gave little recognition to the cinema until the early 1930s. Yet the growing sophistication of the film and the widespread building of new super-cinemas at this time made it a respectable form of entertainment for the middle and upper middle classes at least. By 1934 *Vogue* talked of 'clothes to wear to the cinema', and fashion models were now photographed in cinematographic style. The feminine reaction in dress was no doubt heightened by the romance of Hollywood. The term 'sex appeal' entered the fashion vocabulary, and inevitably led to emphasis on the more obvious womanly attributes. The influence of the cinema was much more marked on 'glamour' dress than on practical day costume. However, more important than the dress itself was the total impact or 'look' to which every important film star made some individual contribution. The actual costume thus became representative, its aim being to create an impression of the glamour of the film world. The majority of women achieved this idea by imitating the make-up and hairstyles of their favourite film star. Naturally, this gave an overwhelming stimulus to the cosmetic and beauty industry. It is a vivid commentary on the changes that had taken place that a woman's journal advertised in 1919 a lipstick which was 'imperceptible when properly applied', while another in 1935 claimed that 'the alluring note of scarlet will stay on your lips for hours'.

Popular imitation of the stars is a fundamental consideration in understanding the fashions of the 1930s. Their essentially escapist character is perhaps symbolic of the uneasiness of the decade, for it is important to remember that despite the steady rise in living standards, the period was characterized by depression and unemployment. The decade began with financial crisis in 1931, and unemployment remained at a high level throughout the 1930s, reaching a peak of 3,750,000 in September 1932. Although the slump did not dramatically affect fashion, an ever-present, underlying insecurity was felt by everyone, employed or unemployed. This, plus the concern from the mid-1930s onwards about the possibility of a second world war, undoubtedly affected attitudes.

Concurrent with escapism was the amusing note which entered many fashions as the 1930s continued. Hats became smaller and madder, often tilted to a degree which now seems purely ridiculous; they were a popular topic of many cartoons. Frills and decorations were often exaggerated. In 1933 the fashion emphasis fell still more heavily on the shoulders; evening gowns and summer frocks had frills arranged in tiers which

Above: Fashionable woman with her dog, wearing leather Oxfords with her suit.

jutted out over the sleevehead. Shops were full of bows, ruffles and frills, all meant to accentuate the shoulder width. Women were able to appear more feminine without sacrificing any of their new-won liberties in dress or life.

The influence of the sports world also continued to be felt throughout the 1930s, seen mostly in the more casual approach adopted by both men and women in dress. Tennis clothes had, however, followed the influence of the day dress with the reversion to a longer skirt, and by 1931 had already returned to halfway down the calf. Men's plus fours, too, became longer. Despite the evident reluctance to return to the short skirt in sport, it was inconceivable that women should return to the disadvantages of dress endured earlier in the century. Another solution was thus found which led to the wearing of shorts. This began in 1931 with the 'short sports dress', consisting of a trousered skirt reaching well below the knee, with inverted pleats. Shorts grew in popularity, and in 1935 a new kind of pleated shorts was introduced, with a double advantage: 'while the trousers allow plenty of freedom of action, you cannot tell it from a flared skirt when you stand at ease'. As the 1930s drew to a close, sports clothes became increasingly functional, and complete physical freedom was established. The stylization of sports clothes, their development and tendency to become uniform, robbed them of any chance of influencing fashion. Sports clothes were now dominated by separate rules which stressed practicality and freedom of movement, regardless of the modes of contemporary fashion trends.

The same trend is apparent in day wear during this decade, which in many ways also came to be influenced by separate rules. In the mid-1930s particularly, when industry was reviving after the depression, the number of women in paid employment was expanding. During the entire span of the war, the number of women employed in commerce and its associated occupations doubled. It is in such statistics that we encounter a central phenomenon in the sociology of women's employment in the 20th century – the rise of the business girl. The development of large-scale industry and bureaucracy would undoubtedly have brought this development in time, but it was the war, by simultaneously creating an abundance of government committees and departments, and a shortage of men, which brought an instantaneous and permanent step forward in the economic and social power of women. During the 1920s both day and evening wear, although different in many respects, followed essentially the same lines, both keeping to the straight silhouette and short skirt. However, in 1928, when designers endeavoured to lengthen the skirt by means of transparent or false hems and trains, the movement was on the whole confined to evening wear. To a limited extent day wear did follow suit, with dipping or pointed hems and a general lengthening of the skirt, but it remained essentially practical. This gap continued to widen as the 1930s progressed, until there were almost two separate fashions. Comparing the elaborate fantasy evening wear with the jumpers, skirts and dresses of the business girl, it is difficult to realize that they were contemporary. Day wear was, in effect, becoming an occupational costume, designed primarily for that purpose. Evening dress no longer shared the same demands or influences.

The 1930s, then, a decade of technical innovation and change, developed a characteristic approach to fashion. The period significantly marked the end of the pre-mass-production era, and the beginning of ready-to-wear clothes with the consequent wider availability of fashion. Perhaps there was a certain quietening down after the 'roaring twenties' in fashion and social life; certainly much of the outrage died away. Many phenomena persisted however: high heels and the use of make-up; and *décolletage* in evening wear, continuing to expose a large portion of the female body. The 1930s, then, were not a period of startling innovation, but more a period of consolidation of many of the movements which had begun in previous years.

Female fashions, in particular, reached extravagant heights during the latter part of the decade, but this reaction was curtailed by the probability of war in 1939. World War II broke out on 3 September 1939, bringing with it yet more changes to the fashion world.

Above: Two evening dresses from 1932, by Norman Hartnell (left) and Victor Stiebel (right).

WOMEN

PREDOMINANT FASHION FEATURES

'There is more than emphasis placed on natural feminine lines, there is exaggeration' (*Vogue*, October 1931).

The waist has resumed its normal position, and emphasis falls on the shoulders and hips. Dresses grow more clinging and complex in cut, constructed largely on the bias of the fabric to achieve the necessary smooth lines and flowing hems.

The day costume evolves along practical lines, cut with long, shaped panels, fitting at the hips, flaring low and continuing to dip at the sides. Skirts finish 30–35cm (12–14in) and dresses approximately 30.5cm (12in) from the ground. Shorter blouses are often worn over the skirt.

For evening, sheath-like, slinky dresses swathe the figure, tightly moulding the hips and flaring from the knees to the ankle or full-length. Low back to the evening dress – sometimes as low as the waist.

Some collarless coats, some with shorter, broader lapels. All with broad shoulders, belted to nip in the waist. Patch pockets.

FABRICS Luxurious, heavier, clinging fabrics – satin, crêpe (rayon, silk), chiffon, shantung for evening. Fabrics are softer for day wear. Wool, rayon or silk jersey or crêpe, satin; tweeds and firm woollens for suits. Undergarments are worn in tricot, washing satin, crêpe de Chine, Celanese.

COLOURS Evening – black and white, pinks, blues, cyclamen, mauve. Day – black and white, navy, beige.

DECORATION Intricate seaming, often cut diagonally across the figure. Small prints, diagonal lines and stripes. Scalloped edges. Drapery at neckline and on bodice.

UNDERGARMENTS Princess slips with attached brassiere, shaped closely at the waist. With the close-fitting evening gown and heavier fabrics the slip is sometimes discarded. Corsets mould the figure to achieve the desired slimness of hips and waist. Cami-knickers and cami-bockers.

SHOES Low-cut, court style with higher, straighter heels. Frequently in two colours and materials; pointed toes.

STOCKINGS Darker shades following vogue for suntanned skin.

HAT Shallow crowns with upturned brim worn tilted forward over one eye.

HAIR Worn longer with more waves, side-parting.

ACCESSORIES Gloves tighter fitting in darker shades, matching the handbag. Scarves fill in low V-necklines.

MAKE-UP More natural-looking than mask-like face of the 1920s.

DETAILS OF ILLUSTRATED PATTERN

Wedding dress cut in similar style to contemporary evening wear. Diagonal-cut bias panels ensure the bodice drapes the figure closely. The bodice continues through defined waistline, giving essential slimness of hip. The full-length skirt is also cut on the bias, flaring from hip yoke to full hemline. The centre-back panel is cut entirely in one – extended to form a sweeping train. Moderate V-neckline faced in satin, and wrist-length slim-fitting sleeves. A simple headdress of orange blossom and small pearls secures the full-length veil; the proportion of the head must always remain small.

Far left: Woman in a white dress with a low-cut back and velvet sash.

Left: 1931 illustration of a bride arriving at church on her father's arm.

Right: Drawing of wedding attire in 1930s evening dress style (for the pattern see page 80).

FABRICS AND COLOUR White crêpe de Chine with white satin contrast fabric at neckline; white tulle for veil.

FOOTWEAR White satin slippers, frequently made in the same fabric as the dress.

ACCESSORIES Mid-length white suede gloves, worn wrinkled over wrists; large bouquet.

NOTES ON CONSTRUCTION OF GARMENT

Bias cut requires careful handling of the fabric – the dress should mould the upper figure and hips, with easing allowed at the waistline. Lower part of dress back is illustrated by broken lines on pattern. The pattern pieces should be joined at 1 and 2 before cutting; back and extended train are cut in one panel.

Separate back neckband from dress back by cutting pattern piece along dotted line. Adjust the pattern pieces as necessary to achieve required slimness of hips and fullness of skirt in proportion to the figure.

The veil is gathered on the narrow headdress and secured to the head with combs. It may be cut from one length of wide tulle and rounded at corners. Allow sufficient length to cover the train at the back and form a short face veil. For undergarments, use full-length, princess-style petticoat and close-fitting, ready-made corset. The bustline must not be emphasized.

MEN

PREDOMINANT FASHION FEATURES

'The emphasis in tailoring is on the chest, and the main object is to imply breadth and fullness in that region' (*Tailor and Cutter*). The waistline is above the natural hollow; buttons and pockets are higher. Lapels have diminished in length and increased in width. The double-breasted reefer jacket is a very popular style, with two rows of buttons and wider front. Jetted pockets remain the vogue because they help to suggest narrow flanks.

Trousers are of medium width, cut rather long in the leg, with turn-ups. Pleats and a top welt or waistband persist. For business and formal wear black jacket with striped trousers continues, and a dark lounge suit is frequently worn. Two-piece suits often worn, with the waistcoat replaced by a pullover or sleeveless slipover. Flannel trousers and sports jacket are worn for sports, or tweed lounge suit. Overcoats feature squareness and breadth of shoulder.

FABRICS Fine woollen suiting, serge, worsted, in dark colours, grey or navy for business attire. Striped flannel, herringbones and checks. Large checks or patterned tweeds for sports jackets and suits or overcoats.

COLOURS Browns and blues as suitings, grey and fawn for summer. Also subdued colours with brighter overcheck or woven flecks.

DECORATION Hand-stitched edge of collar and lapels of informal suits is a new feature during 1930s. Racoon-fur collars for winter overcoats.

SHIRTS AND UNDERGARMENTS Similar to previous fashion.

SOCKS Plain or ribbed, silk or lisle, black or dark blue. Half-hose to tone with suits, white and cream half-hose for sports.

SHOES Lower in heel than previous decade. Spats continue to be used with low shoes or Oxfords. Summer and sports shoes of white buckskin. Generally, shoes tend to be heavy to balance the wide trouser leg, as in the 1920s.

HAIR Short hair remains fashionable for men, although fuller and with more waves than the former flattened style.

HATS Trilby for day wear. Bowler hat for more formal and business attire.

ACCESSORIES As previous fashion.

DETAILS OF ILLUSTRATED PATTERNS

Formal wedding outfit consisting of morning coat, waistcoat (pattern not supplied) and trousers. The coat fits closely over the hips, with cutaway fronts, and length of skirt reaching to around the bend of the knee. Pointed lapels roll low from single-link fastening at high waistline. Other variations of the morning coat include one or two bone or silk-covered buttons and right-angle step collar. A front dart which defines the waist and gives breadth and ease over the chest; squareness of shoulders also imparts size to the chest. An outside breast pocket can be incorporated if desired. Two-piece set-in sleeves finish with slit cuff and four-button fastening. The jacket back is cut with centre-back seam, vent and side pleats in the skirt, ending with two covered buttons at waist seam. The trousers are cut on the same lines as day wear, and always without turn-ups. Team with a light-coloured double-breasted waistcoat, cut low in front, and just visible both above and below the buttoning of the coat. The Ascot cravat is more usual, since it balances the large expanse of shirt, although a narrow knot or bow tie may also be worn.

Note: Younger men often wear a black lounge jacket waistcoat and striped trousers.

FABRICS AND COLOURS Black or grey woollen worsted suiting; black-and-white striped cashmere for trousers.

SHIRT White linen shirt with starched wing collar and cuffs.

FOOTWEAR Plain laced shoes in black patent leather worn with white spats.

HAT Silk top hat.

ACCESSORIES White kid gloves, walking stick, white flower in left lapel, white handkerchief for decoration, tie pin, cuff links.

NOTES ON CONSTRUCTION OF GARMENTS

Tailoring skills are required to achieve the correct balance and proportion. Additional ease is allowed in the back shoulder seam and over front armhole to provide fullness over the chest.

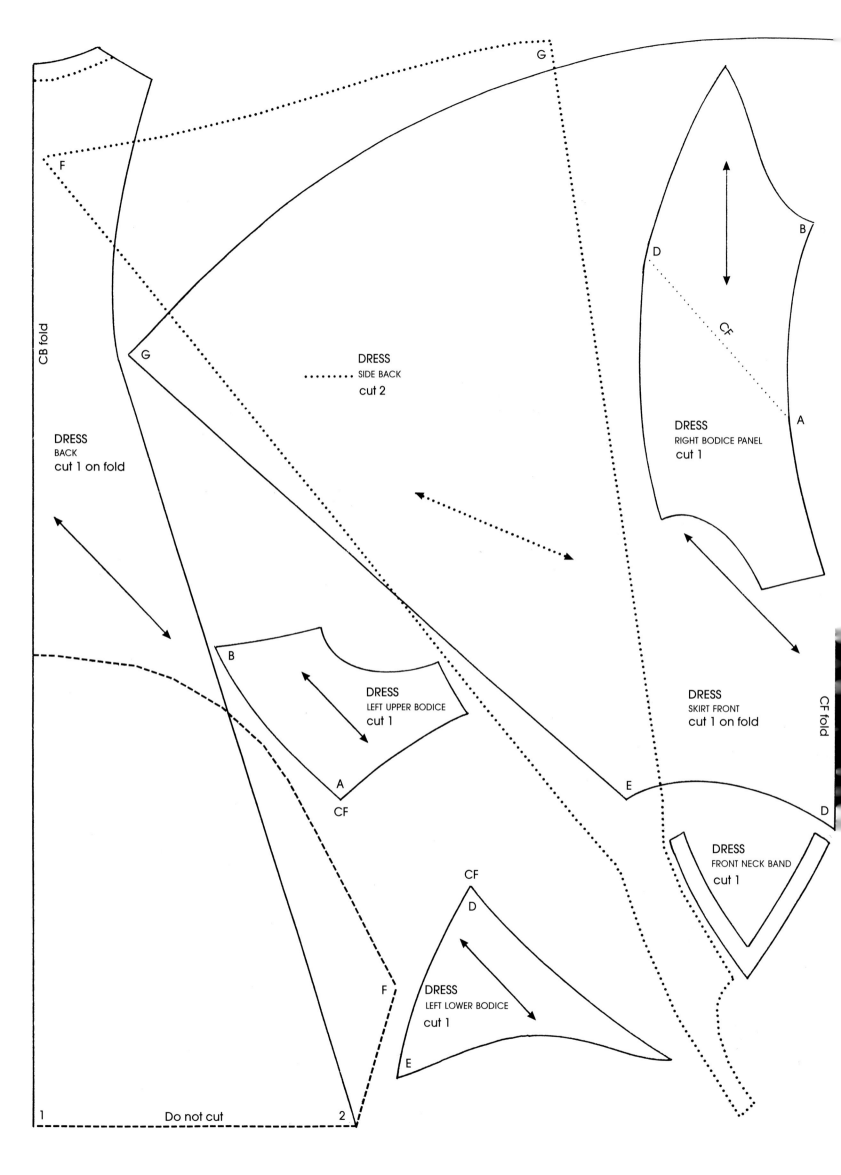

CB fold

F

G

DRESS
SIDE BACK
cut 2

DRESS
BACK
cut 1 on fold

G

DRESS
RIGHT BODICE PANEL
cut 1

D

B

CF

A

B

DRESS
LEFT UPPER BODICE
cut 1

A

CF

DRESS
SKIRT FRONT
cut 1 on fold

E

D

CF fold

DRESS
FRONT NECK BAND
cut 1

CF

D

DRESS
LEFT LOWER BODICE
cut 1

F

E

1

Do not cut

2

CB

MORNING COAT
BACK
cut 2

SIDE BACK
cut 2

MORNING COAT
FRONT
cut 2

MORNING COAT
SKIRT
cut 2

MORNING COAT
FRONT SLEEVE
cut 2

MORNING COAT
BACK SLEEVE
cut 2

TROUSERS

——— BACK cut 2

······ FRONT cut 2

MORNING COAT
COLLAR
cut 2 on fold

CB fold

1934

WOMEN

PREDOMINANT FASHION FEATURES

Fashion emphasis falls more heavily on the shoulders. Long coats are longer than the dresses they are worn with, 117cm (46in) from nape of neck. Coats belonging to costumes are rather short, all heavily padded. Lapels are broad and pointed, tailored along masculine lines, waists fit closely and appear very small in comparison to the broad shoulders. Capes are a popular feature, especially with single-breasted styles.

Three-quarter-length swagger and jigger coats create a triangle over a slim skirt, cut with additional fullness at back.

Skirts for morning and afternoon take rather a straight, tight line, with fullness below the knee. Short inverted pleats, box and knife pleats, are placed at the sides and back to give freedom of movement. Diagonal seams are frequently used. Short overblouse often worn belted over the skirt.

Evening gowns and summer frocks have frills, arranged in tiers, which jut out over the shoulders. Bows, ruffles and frills all accentuate the shoulder width. Decoration and low necklines confined mostly to the back of the dress. Fullness is low, close-fitting over the hips and flaring from the knee, with long trains.

Summer dresses in softer fabrics follow the contour of the figure. Cowl necklines and sleeves popular. Dresses finish approximately 30.5cm (12in) from the ground. There is a short vogue for Tudor-look fashion with slashed and padded sleeves. Sports clothes become briefer.

FABRICS Fine dress woollens, jersey, crêpe. Luxurious evening fabrics – velvet, reversible satin, taffeta, moiré, crêpe de Chine, crinkle rayons. Heavily flecked angora and Scotch tweeds for coats, suits and sportswear; diagonal and honeycomb weaves, checks, tartans, plaids and stripes.

COLOURS Black and white, browns, dark chocolate, navy, grey. Other favoured colours are Persian red, raspberry red, royal and midnight blue, terracotta, mulberry. Plain and figured fabrics are frequently combined; a plain dress may have a figured coat, or the dress may be figured while the coat is plain.

DECORATION Diagonally striped fabrics; large bows in bold checks or stripes with tailored suits; brighter trimmings and scarves in orange, turquoise, pink, emerald, purples. Furs such as silver and blue fox, grey astrakhan, seal and skunk are popular and used wherever possible, especially for collars and cuffs. Large, square wooden buttons or brass buttons. Top-stitching detail on plain fabrics.

UNDERGARMENTS Brassieres begin to separate and support. Lightweight bras of bias fabric cut low for evening wear. Backless evening slips and princess petticoats, moulding the figure closely. Lastex yarn effects revolution in undergarments, providing two-way stretch, support without stiffening. Step-in hip belts and 'roll-ons', entirely composed of lastex yarn. Singlettes – brassiere, vest, girdle and pantie combined.

FOOTWEAR Dyed leathers to co-ordinate with the costume.

STOCKINGS Medium or subdued tints, 'skin tones'.

HATS To match the outfit, tricornes and berets, worn well tilted over one eye or at the back of the head. Tudor fashions – velvet Tudor halos, Juliet caps.

HAIR Side-parting with flat crown and curls at the side and back of the head, swept back from the face.

ACCESSORIES Long gauntlet-style gloves. Bags coordinate with shoes, gloves and stockings – brown and grey leathers, pochettes and clutch handbags. Large box-calf belts; luxurious fur capes.

MAKE-UP Imitation of favourite cinema stars. Eyebrows plucked into thin, arched line and reshaped with eyebrow-pencil. Make-up dark, following craze for suntans. Red lipstick.

DETAILS OF ILLUSTRATED PATTERN

Double-breasted collarless coat, with shoulder cape cut in one with back panel. The cape is edged with a separate band of self-fabric and top-stitching detail. The coat is slim-fitting over natural waistline, accentuated by quarter-belt at the front and two-button fastening. It is calf-length, fitting slimly over the hips and with only moderate flare in the skirt. Plain, two-piece, set-in sleeves are narrow throughout. The coat is worn longer than the skirt or dress.

Left: Tailored outfit in black wool with astrakhan trimming.

Right: Drawing of double-breasted collarless coat (for the pattern see page 84).

FABRICS Fine woollen facecloth or twill weave.

COLOURS Brown, beige or cream.

SHOES Leather court shoes with high, slim heel, dyed to match the outfit.

HAT Felt hat with narrow brim and grosgrain ribbon trim on shallow crown, worn tilted.

ACCESSORIES Gauntlet-style gloves to match outfit, worn over coat sleeve; cream suede, leather and patent clutch bag with clasp fastening and metal frame; a silk scarf fills in the low neckline.

NOTES ON CONSTRUCTION OF GARMENT

Coat back panel is underlined with firm linen or cotton fabric and joined to main fabric from A to B. The underlining is therefore left free below top caped section. Join back to side back from A to B; break the stitching at point B and continue to stitch side back to underlining only as far as C. The lower band of the cape may then be attached, and is caught into front neckline dart only after shoulders, side seams and sleeves are complete. Position of coat back underlining is indicated by broken lines on pattern.

Separate band from cape pattern along dotted lines before cutting in fabric. Seam allowance will be required on both edges for joining, and at lower edges of band. Seam allowance must also be added to outer edges of front belt pattern.

A 1cm (⅜in) seam allowance is given on all remaining edges. Hem allowances are not included.

Top-stitch cape and front belt as illustrated.

MEN

PREDOMINANT FASHION FEATURES

Jackets continue popular trend with fullness over the chest, square-cut shoulders and closer-fitting over the hips. Lapels slightly rolled, wide and pointed.

Thick overcoats in fleecy woollen fabrics – 'teddy bear' coats. Raincoats and mackintoshes, loose-fitting, trench styles with belts popular.

Evening – dinner jackets and dress coats cut with wide, pointed lapels with wide-chested effects. Link-fastening and jetted pockets popular. Backless waistcoats of white piqué, joined at the back of the collar and with a strap and buttons or buckle at waist-level. Black waistcoats with dinner jackets.

FABRICS Similar to previous fashion.

COLOURS Similar to previous fashion. Midnight blue an acceptable alternative to black for evening wear.

UNDERGARMENTS Many shirts with attached collars, celluloid stiffeners inserted between a double piece of fabric in the undercollar. Short-sleeved sports shirt with polo collar, the sleeves reaching to just above the elbow. Plain fronts for dress shirts and decline in use of fancy fabrics. Shorts and trunks with lastex waistbands.

FOOTWEAR Similar to previous fashion.

SOCKS Similar to previous fashion.

HATS Similar to previous fashion; crowns generally higher and brims broader.

HAIR Similar to previous fashion.

ACCESSORIES Gloves essential item of male dress; short gauntlet style. Ties are in spotted, striped, or small-figured silks. Tie-clips used when no waistcoat is worn.

DETAILS OF ILLUSTRATED PATTERNS

Lounge suit consisting of jacket, waistcoat and trousers. Single-breasted lounge jacket with two-button fastening is cut with square shoulders and wide back stretch. There are two darts on each front, an angled welt pocket on the chest and flap pockets at hip-level. The roll is cut moderately low with wide, notched collar and foreparts rounded at lower edges. Two-piece set-in sleeves with slit button cuffs, and centre-back seam with no vent.

Trousers are generously cut with pleats into waistband at fronts, and side seam pockets. Permanent turn-ups at lower edge are 4.5cm (1¾in) in depth.

The single-breasted waistcoat (pattern not supplied) is just visible between jacket lapels, fastening with five buttons.

FABRICS AND COLOURS Fine, striped worsted suiting of grey or blue.

SHIRT Plain white shirt with attached collar.

FOOTWEAR Laced Oxford-style shoes.

HAT Bowler hat with curled brim.

ACCESSORIES Grey leather gloves, bold striped tie with pointed ends, handkerchief in breast pocket for decoration only.

NOTES ON CONSTRUCTION OF GARMENTS

Ease back to front at shoulder seams of jacket. Padding is required to achieve fashionable squared shoulders and wide-chested effect.

Right: Drawing of lounge suit (for the pattern see page 85).

CB

JACKET
BACK
cut 2

vent

JACKET
FRONT
cut 2

JACKET
FRONT SLEEVE
cut 2

JACKET
BACK SLEEVE
cut 2

TROUSERS   WAISTBAND   cut 4

CB

CB fold

JACKET
COLLAR
cut 2 on fold

pleat   pleat

TROUSER
—— BACK cut 2
······ FRONT cut 2

1935

WOMEN

PREDOMINANT FASHION FEATURES

Similar to fashions of previous years, with less severe emphasis on the shoulders. The sleeves, belts and necklines are important and softness at the neckline is achieved with scarves and cowl necks. Ruffles, collars, jabots, frills, exaggerated bows on blouses, and loose, full bishop sleeves are all features.

In contrast, the daytime look is severely military with square epauletted shoulders, frogging and regimental-style buttons. 'Women have set themselves the rather difficult task of producing the military silhouette during the day, and an alluringly feminine silhouette for evening wear' (*Daily Express*, October 1932).

Short bolero jackets are worn over wool dresses. Panel skirts are slim fitting from waist to hips with hip basques, pleats, intricate seaming and low flaring. Coats are loose three-quarter-length with large collars, bold revers and dropped shoulder lines. Swagger coats are worn with a bias cut and swing back, creating a triangle over close-fitting skirts. Capes for day and evening are worn in every length, as are caped coats and evening dresses.

For evening greater emphasis is given to the bust, with pleated fullness and shirring between and under the breasts; unbelted dresses are cut up in a triangle with the bodice gathered to it. The necklines are less low-cut than the previous year. Interest, fullness and low neckline continue at the back.

FABRICS Textured fabrics are worn, such as crêpe (silk, wool, rayon), crinkle silks and rayons, soft woollen dress fabrics, small checks, diagonal stripes, tweeds, checks, fancy worsteds and Bedford cords. For evening velvets, satin, chiffon, artificial silk, ninon and lamé are worn.

COLOURS Black and white are predominant, with navy and white for town and business. During the day red, orange, yellow, green, purple, plum are worn and for evening, black, white, gold, silver, dark blue. Pastel shades are also worn for day and evening – soft and subtle smoky greys, pinks.

DECORATION There is a predominant use of contrasts – matt and satin textures, plain suits with striped, checked or spotted bows, prints with reversed backgrounds. Embroidery, scallop edgings and top-stitching detail is used. Fur is used on collars and sleeves.

UNDERGARMENTS Seamless, roll-on hip belts in lastex, zip fastenings. Lastex yarn and lace brassieres and corsets with new 'uplift' brassiere and insets of lastex for diaphragm control are worn. Open-mesh elastic is used for sports and summer. Backless bras and corselettes are cut on true bias.

FOOTWEAR AND STOCKINGS As 1936.

HATS Hats are getting smaller and smaller – 'little nothings perched at precarious angles on your head'. They match the outfit and are sometimes made in the same fabric as the coat. 'Veils will be more important than hats' (*Vogue*, December 1935). Large-brimmed hats with tiny, shallow crowns in straw or taffeta are worn for summer, trimmed with fabric bows, bindings and tulle.

HAIR Mass of curls worn high on the head for evening, all hair swept back from the face and curled.

ACCESSORIES As 1936.

MAKE-UP Similar to previous fashion with blue eyeshadow, black mascara and red lipstick. Eyelash dye and false eyelashes are used. Make-up is more pronounced for evening.

DETAILS OF ILLUSTRATED PATTERNS

Norfolk-style jacket, panelled at front and back. Wide revers are cut moderately high with wide notched collar and lapels, faced in contrasting check fabric, and single-breasted four-button fastening. Four patch pockets are trimmed with check material and the buttons match the collar and revers. The natural waistline is emphasized by wide insertion of check fabric, forming a mock belt. Narrow two-piece sleeves are set into broad shoulder line.

A divided sports skirt completes the costume. It carries a single knife pleat at each side front, also a small strapping with three imitation holes and buttons. The skirt is cut with hip yoke and separate waistband.

The outfit is worn with a masculine collar and striped tie.

FABRICS Fine tweed or worsted.

COLOURS Tan, brown or blue with toning overcheck for contrast.

SHOES Low-heeled, brown or black leather brogue lace-ups.

HAT Small felt hat with a shallow, flattened crown and narrow, curled brim, turned up at sides. Narrow grosgrain ribbon trim.

ACCESSORIES Gauntlet-style, wrist-length suede gloves to match the outfit.

NOTES ON CONSTRUCTION OF GARMENTS

For the jacket, cut the belt, pocket decoration and collar and lapel facings in check fabric. The position of pockets is indicated on pattern.

Cut jacket front and side front pattern pieces along belt lines. The belt is cut as a separate section and constructed with jacket front. The same applies at jacket back with panel seam stitched through belt. Padding is required over the shoulders to give a squared appearance. Allow for all seams except the scye.

For the skirt, the waistband is split for the side seam and placket each side.

Right: Drawing of golfing outfit (for the pattern see page 88).

MEN

PREDOMINANT FASHION FEATURES

Similar to previous fashion. Overcoats are shorter in length, just covering the knee. Shorter pullovers and knitted slipovers are worn for sport. Knitted cardigans are worn in plain colours with overworked check in self shades.

FABRICS   Fancy tweeds, whipcords and worsted suitings, sports tweeds, flannels and serges are worn.

COLOURS   Similar to previous fashion. Midnight blue is an acceptable alternative to black for evening tail coats and dinner jackets.

SHIRTS   Shirts are coloured grounds with coloured stripes. The semi-stiff collars are white or match the shirt. Striped shirts predominate.

FOOTWEAR   As previous fashion.

SOCKS   Short socks are worn for summer sports, flannel greys, oatmeals, and white being prominent with darker suiting shades for everyday wear. Lastex yarn in the top holds the sock firmly in position, below the calf of the leg. Suspenders or garters are unnecessary.

HATS   As 1936.

HAIR   As previous fashion.

ACCESSORIES   Silk ties are worn in two-colour stripe effect, such as brown and white, or black and grey. Handkerchiefs are worn with borders of a similar stripe arrangement. Other accessories are as previous fashion.

DETAILS OF ILLUSTRATED PATTERNS

Golfing costume consisting of single-breasted, lounge jacket, sports vest and long striped plus fours. The jacket is cut on contemporary lines, with fullness over the chest, square-cut shoulders and closely fitting over the hips. Pockets with flaps are worn at hip level and a breast pocket shows a handkerchief. Step collar is worn with three buttons on front, but with only the middle one fastened, throwing additional ease over the chest by making the waistline appear smaller. The jacket back is cut with centre-back seam and vent. Two-piece, set-in sleeves finish with slit cuff and three-button fastening.

Long plus fours are made wide at the knee, pleated into wide bands at lower edges and fastened with buckle and strap. Two darts are put in the front waist on each side and pockets are inserted in side seams.

The outfit is worn with a sleeveless vest-pullover of tweed with linen trim, replacing the traditional waistcoat. The garment buttons on left side seam with fly and four buttons; waistband buttons through with two holes.

FABRICS   Flannel or serge for jacket, striped flannel for plus fours.

COLOURS   Muted shades of grey, brown or tan.

FOOTWEAR   Brown leather shoes with fringed over-tongue to cover laces. The ribbed golf hose tones with the suit.

ACCESSORIES   Tie with cream background and overcheck to match the suit; suede or leather gloves; the handkerchief in the breast pocket is for decoration only.

NOTES ON CONSTRUCTION OF GARMENTS

Padding is required over the shoulders of jacket to indicate broad chest and wide shoulders.

Pleat the plus fours into knee straps. Fly front opening may fasten with zip or buttons. Pockets may be inserted at side seams.

Add overlap of 2cm (¾in) to the left side of vest-pullover for button opening. V-neckline and armholes are bound with bias linen tape, with a waistband also of linen fabric. The vest-pullover should fit the figure closely and is especially trim at the waist.

Left: Fashionable players prepare to begin their round of golf.

Right: Drawing of golfing costume with lounge jacket and striped plus fours (for the pattern see page 89).

1936

WOMEN

PREDOMINANT FASHION FEATURES

The fashion lines of the previous year continue, with prevalent use of contrasts in fabric and colours. Jackets and coats are lined with shirt or dress fabrics, with padded shoulders – less accentuated shoulder width than first half of the decade – arge collars and rounded lapels.

Tunic-styles predominate. Peplum jackets flare from the waist to finger-tip length over bias-cut skirts. Tunic coats or loose swagger or jigger coats flare from the shoulders.

Blouses are high-necked with short, puffed sleeves. Matching knitted jumpers, short-waisted cardigans and skirts are worn.

Sports and informal wear include dull tweeds, boxy or swagger coats over slim skirts, divided sports skirts or flannel trousers. For tennis, shorts or sports dresses are worn well above the knee and have evolved from the shirts and shorts outfit.

Evening fashions change in emphasis to show a more romantic, feminine appeal. Some have Empire line, bustle effects with large bows and drapery. Backs remains low. Fullness swings to the back of the dress, remaining straight at the front and slim on hips. Short boleros cover evening gowns.

Dinner suits are worn as long slim skirts, flaring from the knees with jacket and closely fitting blouses, in luxurious fabrics such as velvets and satins.

FABRICS Tweeds, alpaca, fine dress woollens, crêpe and taffeta all feature. Flannel and tweeds are worn for sports and informal wear. There is a wide range of crease-resistant fabrics. 'Lystav' – a new linen-look, rayon fabric – is used as is 'Tootal Linen' – a pure dress linen.
Satin, velvet, crêpe and taffeta are worn for evening.

COLOURS Black and white, navy and white, royal blue and turquoise are worn, with pastel shades worn for evening.

DECORATION Contrast effects are created using reverse grounds of prints and contrast textures. Black-and-white novelty prints such as newsprint, handwriting, pins, pigs and matches are used. Drapery is used on shoulders or hips and sunburst pleats of chiffon are favoured. Shirring and cording is used under the bust for emphasis. Flowers are worn on bosom or belt or as hair and hat decorations. 'Real or artificial – it doesn't matter – but somewhere, somehow, you must have a flower' (*Vogue*, 1936). Novelty buttons include birds, flowers, bows and geometric shapes.

UNDERGARMENTS Tailored, bias-cut slips fit smoothly over the hips, swinging at the hemline towards the back. Brightly coloured taffeta petticoats are worn with bias-cut hip belts, seamless roll-ons or with zip fastening. Uplift brassieres are worn as are panties and girdles in one for under trousers.
Underwear is worn in fashionable peach, candy and shell-pink, edged with ecru or coffee lace.

FOOTWEAR Open-toed sandals are worn in leather for day, or gold and silver kid, satins and brocades for evening. Shoes are frequently made in two materials and colours to co-ordinate with contrasts in dress – white and navy, white and brown, white buckskin and black patent are popular. Higher heels are worn, up to 6.35cm (2½in). Lower-heeled shoes for sport are around 3cm (1⅛in). Overshoes are worn over the ordinary shoe for protection in wet weather.

STOCKINGS Darker shades are worn for day wear. Ladder-proof stockings are constructed with lastex. Ribbed lisle stockings or knee-high stockings with lastex supports are worn for sports.

SOCKS As previous fashion. Ankle-length socks are worn for tennis, supported with lastex yarn.

HATS Slightly shallower crowns and narrow brims, Bretons, pill-box and panama styles, turbans and toques are worn. Fabric, flower and veil trimmings are all popular.

HAIR Upward curls frame the face flat on sides and back.

ACCESSORIES Suede gloves match the outfit and are worn gauntlet-style, long or short. Short gloves are worn for evening in satin, organdie, taffeta. Belts are wide at the front, sloping to narrow width at the back: 'so wide that they come up and support the bust'. Other accessories include pochettes (large clutch bags), Spanish shawls, velvet and fur evening wraps and capes. There is a revival of small muffs. Jewellery includes earclips, wrist bangles and strings of pearls worn high at neck. Brooches are worn on wide revers.

MAKE-UP Matching rouge, lipstick and nail enamel are worn in 'bright red', 'gay red', 'poppy', 'geranium', 'rich raspberry'and 'terracotta'. Run-proof mascara.

DETAILS OF ILLUSTRATED PATTERNS

Swagger coat and skirt featuring a slightly dropped shoulder line with a front and back yoke into a narrow panel. Pin-tucks are arranged to give a wider appearance to the upper section. The cross-fastening tabs – which are cut on at the neck – are high, but low enough to wear a decorative scarf in a large bow if desired. The coat is cut on straight lines and can be made either in three-quarter or seven-eighth length. The sleeves are two-piece, slit through the centre and finished with two buttons and tabs at wrist. Two roomy outside patch pockets with a cut-on strap and button are placed fairly high on the foreparts. The skirt is cut with a front yoke and panel with an inverted pleat in the centre and a knife pleat either side. The centre pleat is 28cm (11in) long, and the knife

Right: Drawing of swagger coat and skirt (for the pattern see page 92).

pleats 20.25cm (8in) long, providing ample ease for movement. The skirt is cut on modest lines, and only widened by pleats below the knees.

FABRICS Medium-weight flannel, tweed, alpaca.
COLOUR Beige.
FOOTWEAR Two-tone court shoes of white buckskin and brown leather.
HAT Flat-brimmed felt hat with a rounded crown and cream and brown striped ribbon trim, worn tilted over one eye.
ACCESSORIES Brown leather clutch bag with strap buckle fastening. Silk cream-and-brown-striped scarf worn in large bow at neckline. The suede gauntlet-style gloves match the outfit.

NOTES ON CONSTRUCTION OF GARMENTS

Make pin-tucks along broken lines indicated on front coat pattern. Padding is required at the shoulders, extending to outer yoke line. A 1cm (³⁄₈in) seam allowance is included in the pattern, except at front edges.

MEN

PREDOMINANT FASHION FEATURES

The style of the early 1930s, with wide-pointed lapels and broad shoulders, continues. The trousers remain moderately wide in the leg with turn-ups. Sports jackets might be worn with an open-neck shirt or pullover, longer plus fours or flannel trousers. Waist-length golf jackets of suede or proofed gabardine are worn with knitted welts at waist and wrists. Fastenings are to one side with zips or buttons. Overcoats follow a loose, square-cut trend, with patch pockets.

FABRICS AND COLOURS Similar to previous fashion. Striped flannels and worsted suitings are predominant. Tweeds and checks are worn for sports in brighter colours than before, such as greens and tan.
SHIRTS AND UNDERGARMENTS Coat-style shirts (button-through) are easily available ready-made. Sports shirt with attached polo collar are worn – the sleeves reach to elbow-length while the body part is more fitted than the day shirt. Singlets are sleeveless with jersey or low round necks. Trunks and shorts have lastex waistbands.
FOOTWEAR Oxford laced shoe is the most popular style, brogued for sports with a fringed tongue protecting the laces. Monk shoes are worn with side buckle fastening.
SOCKS Golf hose in ribbed styles are worn in plain fawns, browns and greys, toning with the suit. Lastex tops support the socks below the knee. Golf hose to match pullover.
HATS Trilby is worn with a with snap brim, which can be turned up or down according to taste. Porkpie hats are worn, which are flatter than the trilby with rounded dent in crown. Loose-fitting tweed peaked caps are worn for sports and country.
ACCESSORIES Similar to previous fashion. Gloves are coarser leather and knitted for sports and country but with smoother leather and kid for summer. Light-coloured gloves are worn with formal evening dress. Brief- and attaché cases accompany business suits.

DETAILS OF ILLUSTRATED PATTERN

Single-breasted, knee-length raglan overcoat is worn fastened high at the neckline; roomy patch pockets with flaps are worn at hip-level and split sleeves have stitched double cuffs. The style retains fullness across the chest and broad shoulders characteristic of the period. The top button may be worn unfastened with the collar turned up. The coat is easy-fitting throughout, with a centre-back seam and vent.

Team with bold checked trousers cut wide in the leg, pleated into waistband at fronts, with turn-ups at lower edge.

FABRICS Proofed gabardine or Melton cloth.
COLOURS Dark tan or beige.
HAT Felt trilby.

NOTES ON CONSTRUCTION OF GARMENT

Split, raglan sleeves are top-stitched 1cm (³⁄₈in) from centre seam line. Padding is required at shoulders. Use trouser pattern from 1934.

Left: A day at the beach, with the men wearing sports jackets and the girls in daring shorts.

Right: Drawing of raglan overcoat with checked trousers (for the pattern see page 93).

OVERCOAT
FRONT
cut 2

OVERCOAT
UNDER SLEEVE
cut 2

OVERCOAT
BACK
cut 2

CB

vent

OVERCOAT
TOP SLEEVE BACK
cut 2

OVERCOAT
TOP SLEEVE FRONT
cut 2

OVERCOAT
COLLAR
cut 2
on fold

CB fold

COLLAR STAND

CB fold

1938

WOMEN

PREDOMINANT FASHION FEATURES

The broad-shouldered look continues, although the effect is softer and less square. Romanticism continues to be apparent in evening wear with full-flowing or circular skirts and frills and flounces. The skirts are full-length and touching the ground, but rarely seen with trains. Crinoline dresses of diaphanous and transparent materials are worn over stiffened slip.

Low and scooped *décolletage* at the front and back remain important features of the evening dress, with draped interest at shoulders, often worn with a short box jacket or small, tightly fitted bolero.

The day skirt is shorter and fuller with draped, gathered and tucked bodice and fuller sleeves, tightening towards the wrist.

POPULAR FABRICS For evening, organza, voile, coloured tulle, crêpe and taffeta (printed or plain), slipper satin, chiffon, crêpe de Chine are worn. For day, crease-resistant and textured cotton and linen fabrics, crêpe, Celanese (rayon), jersey are worn.

COLOURS Bright colours are worn for evening wear. White is a popular background for boldly coloured or black prints. Large floral designs are worn for summer and evening dresses.

DECORATION For evening bold flowers, applied or printed, ribbons, sequins and gold embroidery are used. Garlands of flowers or coloured feathers are worn around waist, on the bodice or to accentuate neckline. For day, tucks and pleats decorate the bodice and emphasize the bust. Feathers are used at the waist and for lace trimming. Ribbons are worn everywhere, trimming dresses, hats, gloves, shoes and bags. 'Ribbon is young and gay and decorative and belongs to this era of feminine clothes' (*Vogue*, December).

UNDERGARMENTS Uplift brassieres become known as bras and feminine curves are enhanced although the hips remain slim. A wasp waist is essential, held in by a lightweight, boned corset. Brightly coloured stiff taffeta petticoats are worn with full skirts.

SHOES Elegant slim heel and rounded toes are worn. Leather is often perforated and combined with mesh fabrics, suede or two-tone. The first cork or wooden wedge soles are worn for day and evening along with the 'hooded heel' – a seamless heel covering all in one with the back of the shoe. Open-toed sandals are worn with 6.35cm (2½in) heels.

HATS Generally smaller than previous fashions, although they often achieve more height, become more elaborate and are worn tilted. They are also becoming an essential feature in evening wear. Berets decline in popularity.

HAIR Worn 'off the ears' – well off forehead and temples to show nape of the neck – swept on to the top or back of the head in curls or waves, braided or in a figure-of-eight chignon. Hair is fastened with tortoiseshell hairpins or held by combs.

ACCESSORIES Costume jewellery as previous fashion. Jewelled wrist bracelets are worn with bare arms for evening. Bags are small with clip fastening or are satchel style with long handles, while evening bags are embroidered or sequined. Dorothy bags are also worn. Other accessories include ostrich feather or fur stoles and bright handkerchiefs or scarves, worn with plain coloured day suits and brighter belts.

MAKE-UP There is a continued use of false eyelashes. Blue, green or blonde mascara is sometimes used instead of black. Lips are full and deep red with sucked-in cheeks and eyebrows are plucked and arched.

DETAILS OF ILLUSTRATED PATTERN

A floor-length evening dress with a full skirt gathered into bodice at front, with applied ribbon rosettes. The fitted bodice is tightly ruched at the front and supported with fabric stay and boning, emphasizing the bust and a narrow waist. Wide tucked shoulder straps serve to accentuate the shoulder width. The dress is worn with a separate, matching cummerbund, tucked in the same manner as shoulder straps. There is a light zip fastener and hook-and-eye closure at side seam.

FABRICS Taffeta or heavyweight satin, with a tulle overskirt.

COLOURS Powder blue with deep blue ribbon decoration and accessories.

Left: Woman wearing an elegant evening dress of spotted organdie.

Right: Drawing of floor-length evening dress (for the pattern see page 96).

Shoes Satin or gold kid open-toed, sling-back evening shoe with slim, high heel.

Hair Hair is swept up with curls towards the back of the head, with just one wave in front.

Headdress A cluster of three ostrich feathers in shades to tone with dress, mounted on a composition tortoiseshell comb and finished with fancy-edged circular veil.

Accessories Small pearl earclips are worn. Other accessories include a gold-plated jewelled vanity case holding cigarettes, lighter and make-up. Long, white or pale-coloured kid gloves are decorated with ribbon bows.

NOTES ON CONSTRUCTION OF GARMENT

For the undergarments use a ready-made, tightly fitting, backless corset. Layers of silk and organdie, or tulle petticoats are cut on similar lines to the dress skirt to support the bouffant style. Cut two layers of tulle for the overskirt and one layer of firm silk fabric for foundation.

Bodice sections are boned to the waist at the front, back and side seams. The bodice is underlined with firmer silk fabric. To join the bodice to the skirt, cut a piece of tape to waist measurement and gather the skirt and front bodice to fit.

For the cummerbund cut a piece of fabric 66 x 28cm (26 x 11in) and pleat as for shoulder strap. The belt is attached to the dress at the side seam opening and meets edge to edge. Add a seam allowance to all belt edges. Leave an opening at the left side seam of dress for fastening.

MEN

PREDOMINANT FASHION FEATURES

Follows the menswear trend throughout 1930s, although a less exaggerated cut is noted in men's suits, which are straighter, with well-padded square shoulders and wider lapels. The trousers are narrower in the leg, with a zip-front fly fastening replacing buttons.

Waistcoats are discarded for informal wear with lounge suits. Trousers are frequently of a different shade to jackets.

Fabrics and colours Wool worsted or flannel, or light-coloured linen for summer suits.

Shirts and undergarments As previous fashions. Rayon shirts are worn, as are jockey shorts, which are briefer than trunks.

Shoes The popularity of Oxford-style shoe continues, fully laced or with two eyelets for less formal wear. Two-tone, white and tan or white and black are worn for informal occasions, or 'monk' shoes with side buckle fastening. Chukka or desert boots with two-tie fastening is introduced for sports and casual wear, and sandals, sometimes with crêpe sole, are worn for summer.

Socks As previous fashions.

Hats As previous fashions, although crowns are generally higher and brims broader to balance squarer shoulders.

Hair Often worn without a parting, brushed back and slightly raised at the sides. Small, clipped moustaches are worn.

Accessories Tie pins, clips and collar bars (to hold points of collar beneath the tie) continue in use.

DETAILS OF ILLUSTRATED PATTERNS

Informal evening dress consisting of a dinner jacket, waistcoat and dress trousers. The single-breasted jacket fastens with single link button, throwing ease over the chest and making the waistline appear smaller. The fashionable broad-chested and wide-shouldered effects are indicated. Wide pointed lapels, faced in silk satin, have buttonhole at left. Welt pockets retain slimness over the hips. A slanted welt pocket can be added on the breast to display a handkerchief with double points. Two-piece, set-in sleeves finish with a slit cuff and single-button fastening. Double-breasted dinner jackets are also popular, but regarded as slightly less formal.

Dress trousers are cut on similar lines to day wear trends, pleated into the waistbands at fronts, with ample ease over the seat and wide in the leg, but without turn-ups. A single row of silk braid may be present at outer leg seams.

The waistcoat is single-breasted, fastening with five buttons. Welt pockets can be added at waist-level and on the left breast if desired. A silk cummerbund may replace the waistcoat.

Fabric Wool worsted.

Colours Deep midnight blue is an acceptable alternative to black, although black remains popular. The waistcoat is of white piqué or marcella, or black silk.

Shirts Stiff-fronted shirt and wing collar are considered correct, although soft-fronted styles with a turn-down collar are frequently worn for less formal wear.

Shoes Patent leather Oxford-style, fully laced.

Socks Plain blue or black silk.

Hair As previous fashion.

Accessories A black silk tie is correctly worn with a dinner jacket. The gloves are a light-coloured kid. A white linen handkerchief is worn in the top jacket pocket and a second, for use, tucked in the sleeve. The boutonniere is a dark red carnation, either fresh or artificial; white is worn with tails. Gold cuff links and a signet ring are also worn.

Right: Drawing of informal evening dress (for the pattern see page 97).

CF fold

gather

DRESS
SKIRT BACK AND FRONT
cut 2 on fold

C   B

DRESS
SHOULDER STRAP
cut 2

E   D

E
D

DRESS
BODICE BACK
cut 1 on fold

CB
fold

C   C
B   B
A   A

DRESS
BODICE UPPER FRONT
cut 1

CF

B   B
A   gather along dotted lines   A

DRESS
BODICE
LOWER FRONT
cut 1

CF

DINNER JACKET
BACK
cut 2

DINNER JACKET
COLLAR
cut 2 on fold

CB

DINNER JACKET
FRONT
cut 2

TROUSERS
——— BACK cut 2
········· FRONT cut 2

pleat   pleat

CB

WAISTCOAT
BACK
cut 2

DINNER JACKET
BACK SLEEVE
cut 2

DINNER JACKET
FRONT SLEEVE
cut 2

WAISTCOAT
FRONT
cut 2

WOMEN

PREDOMINANT FASHION FEATURES

Before the outbreak of war fashion looked set towards wasp waists and fragility. 'Now with the brilliance of an acrobatic somersault, it turns a new fashion face towards a new future' (*Vogue*, November). Two contrasting fashion trends are thus observable.

The military look of the early and mid-1930s is revived: severe suits, epaulettes, wide shoulders and revers. Skirts are shortened dramatically. Coats are fuller with loose sleeves and backs, not nipped in at the waist.

Trousers are flannels and slacks in grey, stripes and checks. 'Your wardrobe is not complete without a pair or two of the superbly tailored slacks of 1939' (*Vogue*, November). These were sharply creased, with turn-ups and fitted waistbands and worn with sweaters and cardigans.

War has its impact – 'If we dress at night we dress down' (*Vogue*, November). 'Afternoon dresses will often function as dinner dresses now.'

The main trends observable in the fashions of 1939 are wide shoulders, small waists and shorter skirts, which continue as the main trend of the war years.

FABRICS As previous fashion. Tweeds, twills, worsted, pin-stripes, checks, herringbones and 'zingal', a new uncrushable fabric, are used. Slacks are made with flannel, serge, heavy linens, tweeds, corduroy and velvet. Jersey suits use firmer silks.

COLOURS Navy and white are fashion favourites along with beige and brown, camel and fawn. Raspberry, prune, cocoa and sage are also seen.

DECORATION Bold top-stitching is used alongside navy and white polka dot, stripe and check prints. The use of contrast continues as before.

UNDERGARMENTS Similar to the previous year with shaped princess petticoats. Brightly coloured taffeta underslips are worn with fuller skirts. Pantie-girdles are used for wearing under slacks. The foundation of the mode is uplift and small waist. 'The nipped-in waist, dresses demand it – corsets contrive it' (*Vogue*, January).

FOOTWEAR The accent is on heels – wedge, high, Dutch boy, solid, square-heeled shoes and platform soles. 'In this war we walk tirelessly in our chunky shoes' (*Vogue*, November).

HATS Hoods and snoods and knitted caps are worn.

HAIR Usually worn longer and curled, drawn back from the face and above the ears.

ACCESSORIES 'Elizabeth Arden's fitted handbag-cum-gasmask case' is worn, as are large boxy handbags. Brightly coloured contrast belts and scarves are worn.

MAKE-UP 'Burnt sugar' rouge and lipstick are worn with khaki shades. 'Stop red' is ideal with navy blue uniforms, as well as dark town clothes. Helena Rubenstein 'regimental red' lipstick and nail groom is also worn.

DETAILS OF ILLUSTRATED PATTERN

A day dress with a yoke effect cut in one with front and back panels extending over squared shoulders. The shoulder width is further emphasized by a gathered sleevehead and band of contrast fabric. Saddle stitching on the front bodice continues around the raised scallop neckline and is repeated on the front skirt panel. The natural waistline is well defined by a contrast fabric belt and the panelled skirt fits slimly over the hips, flaring softly towards the hemline, with single knife pleats at the side fronts for ease of movement. The long sleeves fit tightly from elbow to wrist.

Far left: Illustration showing a woman wearing a pair of wide-leg trousers with a blouse and high heels.

Left: Tweed suit by Lelong.

Right: Drawing of day dress with yoke effect (for the pattern see page 100).

Fabric Wool or rayon crêpe.

Colours Sage green with medium-brown contrast.

Footwear Pre-war brown leather court shoes with high, slim heels and rounded points.

Hat Brown felt hat with shaped brim and dented crown perched forward on head. The hat features a grosgrain ribbon trim.

NOTES ON CONSTRUCTION OF GARMENT

Leave the centre front open above small triangle. Cut the dress bodice band and belt in contrast fabric. Padding is required over the shoulders to give the essential squareness and broad-shouldered effect. Leave an opening in the left side seam for a zip fastener. The dress should fit closely over the waist and hips. Secure tops of pleats with a hand-worked arrowhead.

MEN

PREDOMINANT FASHION FEATURES

The three-buttoned lounge jacket with pointed revers usually fastens only at the centre, throwing ease at the chest and making the waist look smaller. Waistcoats are not always worn with summer suits. Sports jackets are worn with a yoke at back and front, knife pleats to waist, patch pockets with pleats and a belt reaching the front of pleats. The jackets are worn with pullover and flannel trousers.

For evening a double-breasted dinner jacket is worn with with wide, pointed lapels and a soft double collar and shirt. Narrow turn-back cuffs and lapels are faced in silk. Single-breasted dinner jackets are regarded as slightly more formal – a wing collar and stiff shirt are considered correct. The dress coat is worn for most formal occasions – short in the waist, with long tails, broad lapels and a moulded chest.

Overcoats are double-breasted ulsters worn for travelling, motoring or informal wear. Lapels may be buttoned across the chest and the collar fastened to the throat with a ticket pocket on the left sleeve. They are often lined with checked woollen material, with silk for sleeves and around shoulders. Large patch pockets and split sleeves are other features. Single- and double-breasted chesterfields are also worn.

Fabrics Similar to the previous fashion – pin-stripes, checks and plaids are all popular.

Colours Similar to the previous fashion.

Decoration Top-stitching detail is worn on overcoats and sportswear.

Shirts and undergarments Striped shirts are worn for business. Rayon is used increasingly for men's undergarments. Dark-coloured shirts in navy, wine, red or brown are worn with a light-toned coat and trousers for informal wear.

Shoes Similar to the previous fashion.

Socks Similar to the previous fashion.

Hats Similar to the previous fashion.

Hair Similar to the previous fashion.

Accessories Similar to the previous fashion. Coloured handkerchiefs, striped or plaid in rich colours, are used only for informal wear. White linen or batiste is correct for the evening. Spotted, striped or small-figured silk ties are also worn.

DETAILS OF ILLUSTRATED PATTERNS

A double-breasted reefer jacket, with wide, pointed lapels rolling from waistline, gives fullness over the chest and emphasizes the broad, square shoulders.

The fronts, with four buttons and squared lower edges, have straight flap pockets at hip-level and a slanted welt pocket on left breast. The back is cut wide across the shoulder blades with a shaped centre-back seam and moderate flare at the skirt. Two-piece set-in sleeves finish with a slit cuff and two buttons and buttonholes. The jacket is cut squarer than previous styles, with less definition at the waistline.

Trousers are cut generously over the seat with pleats into the front waistband. The legs are wide with a sharp centre crease, and permanent turn-ups are a common feature.

Fabrics and colours Blue woollen suiting fabric with a bold overcheck.

Shirt Pale-coloured shirt with an attached, turn-down soft collar.

Footwear Black leather Oxford shoes, fully laced.

Hat Felt trilby.

Accessories Spotted tie with pointed ends, grey leather gloves, handkerchief (worn in breast pocket for decoration only) and a tightly furled umbrella.

NOTES ON CONSTRUCTION OF GARMENTS

This style of jacket is designed for tall, slim and shapely men as it is apt to pull at the front if not properly fitted and adjusted.

Additional ease is required at the sleevehead, which must be carefully manipulated to achieve a smooth finish at the armhole.

The dotted lines show extension for left waistband.

Right: Drawing of reefer jacket with trousers (for the pattern see page 101).

DRESS
BODICE BACK
cut 1 on fold

CB fold

A •

A

• B

DRESS
BODICE
SIDE BACK
cut 2

• C

C

DRESS
BODICE
SIDE FRONT
cut 2

• D

DRESS
BODICE
FRONT
cut 1
on fold

CF fold

• D

S •

DRESS
BODICE BAND
cut 2

• B

S

gather

DRESS
SLEEVE
cut 2

CB fold

DRESS
SKIRT BACK
cut 1
on fold

DRESS
SKIRT SIDE BACK
cut 2

DRESS
SKIRT SIDE FRONT
cut 2

pleat

DRESS BELT

DRESS
SKIRT FRONT
cut 1
on fold

CF fold

REEFER JACKET
FRONT
cut 2

CB fold

COLLAR
FREEFER JACKET
cut 2 on fold

TROUSERS
BACK cut 2
FRONT cut 2

pleat

pleat

JACKET
FRONT SLEEVE
cut 2

JACKET
BACK SLEEVE
cut 2

REEFER JACKET
BACK
cut 2

CB

CB fold

TROUSERS WAISTBAND

The Forties

'A bare month before war broke out... we were all set to lace in our waists to suit the new waspish lines... Yet though the fashion tide was running at its strongest, at the first impact of war the designers and the public swung round instantly, instinctively and went full-steam ahead for fashions with a new feeling – fashions that fitted both the practical needs and atmosphere of war' (*Vogue*, January 1940).

It is evident that in the late 1930s a new style in women's fashions was emerging which looked set to revive the more feminine silhouette and tight-waisting of an earlier era. 'Fashion was as fantastic, as mad as world affairs' – a conspicuous comment on the uncertainty felt throughout Europe. With the outbreak of war fashion became attuned to that purpose, and women's dress evolved a definite military flavour, with large patch pockets, braiding and epaulettes; 'military braiding' also featured in hairstyles, with the hair plaited and knotted at the back of the head. A shorter skirt, up to 48cm (19in) from the ground, and an exaggerated shoulder line, initiated in the late 1930s by the Italian designer Schiaparelli, formed the most distinctive style features of the war period. The fashion, once set, continued without conspicuous change until late in the decade, the severe military cut softening gradually with the progress of the war.

The cut of men's clothes also remained virtually at a standstill, with suits following the line set in 1939. With the majority of the male population in uniform, the main focus, for the present, was on female fashion.

A considerable proportion of younger females also adopted a uniform and, as in World War I, women were to play a fundamental role in the war effort. From 1938 women could enlist in the Auxiliary Territorial Service (ATS), which formed part of the Territorial Army. Then in 1941 the War Office announced the National Service Act, involving the unprecedented conscription of women into the armed services. This initially 'called up' all unmarried women and childless widows between the ages of 20 and 25, the age limit later being extended from 19 to 30 years. In the Defence Regulations of the same year the ATS were given equal status with men, initiating another vital step in the direction of emancipation. For the first time, too, women were involved in active service, and were used in operational duties from mid-1942. Soon the majority of women, apart from mothers of children under the age of 14, had enlisted, with each employed woman required to work a stipulated number of hours per week. In 1943 came the 'grannies' call-up' requiring women between 46 and 50 to register for war work.

Once again the manner in which women tackled new jobs brought about changes in attitude to the working woman.

For the lady in civilian dress, shortages in cloth and labour, and the directing of the clothing industry towards the war effort, necessitated government intervention and began a period which Cunnington describes as 'dictated fashion'. In 1941, when the war-time clothing situation became critical, the Board of Trade introduced the Utility scheme, which regulated the quality and

Below: Garbardine shorts and white shirt by Jaeger.

Once of manufactured cloth. The leaders of London's couture banded themselves together to cooperate with the government on a practical clothing policy. They formed the Incorporated Society of London Fashion Designers, under chairman Edward Molyneux.

Upon the introduction of the Civilian Clothing Order in 1942, which reinforced the Utility scheme, the Society produced for the Board of Trade utility designs which proved to the world that shortage of labour and material need not mean restriction of elegance and taste. Utility designs followed the prevailing taste of square shoulders and straight lines, but adhered to set regulations as to the amount of cloth, incorporated trimming and standards of workmanship. In September 1942 *Vogue* noted, 'Your Autumn suit will be devoid of trimming, tailored on austerity lines,' and Cunnington remarked in an article in 1941, 'Your wardrobe, instead of being a three-volume novel will now be a short story in which each line will count.'

Men's Utility suits likewise followed a slimming and simplification, using a lower-grade quality wool, usually mixed with other fibres and available in three major colours – brown, grey and navy. As with women's clothes, all additional features such as fastenings were reduced to a minimum. The single-breasted jacket had no drape or shoulder pads, trousers were devoid of turn-ups, back pockets and pleats, and the waistcoat disappeared completely.

Vogue and *Harper's Bazaar* ran a series of articles on making every coupon count, and offered ideas for renovating and updating an existing wardrobe. Clothes rationing was to continue well after the war ended; the Utility scheme was maintained until 1952 and clothing coupons to 1949.

Clothes rationing represented but one of the many shortages of the period. As shipping was disrupted food-stuffs began to be in short supply. With food rationing introduced in 1940 'lemons and oranges became as exotic and rare as caviare', and women learnt to introduce dried eggs, evaporated milk and tinned meats and fish into trusted recipes. The nation was encouraged to 'dig for victory', to turn lawns and any available open space into vegetable gardens, while parsley, herbs and small vegetables decorated window boxes. In every way people tried to avoid waste; all edible scraps were collected and used for pig and poultry food, and transport was restricted to war supplies and the constant movement of troops and evacuees.

Rescheduling of production lines for the national effort caused the scarcity of a number of fashion accessories such as cosmetics and stockings. After the ban on silk stockings in 1941 women went bare-legged throughout the summer months, from necessity. Coloured creams were often applied to give a meagre form of coverage, but proved unsuccessful, often causing indelible stains on precious clothing. Some swimming pools banned bathers 'bronzed by art' and the Board of Trade published 'Rules for Rayons' to ensure longer life for an essentially weak fibre. For factory work women adopted slacks, while short-sleeved shirts saved fabric, and hats were generally replaced by headscarves.

Shortages, too, encouraged the use of unconventional materials such as raffia and straw for hats and bags. Leather, as a munition of war, was in short supply for civilian shoes and other goods, and clumpy wooden soles and cork wedge heels came into use. With cotton, rubber and steel on the priority list, underwear factories were converted to produce kites, balloons, sails and flags. Alongside this, though, production of underwear for the women's forces still continued. Make-up was cherished – a last desperately defended luxury – and hair, remarkably, defied the World War I trend of a short bob, and hung in bleached curls to the shoulders.

Restrictions did not end with the war, and a period of 'silence' was observed in the fashion world. The British fashion industry actually emerged from the war in a stronger position than it had enjoyed during the 1930s. The designers of Utility wear concentrated their efforts in establishing the prestige of British fashion abroad. Collections were designed for export to South Africa, South America and Canada, and to the women at home appeared like forbidden fruit among the pages of the glossy magazines. In the field of mass-production, the lack of outside competition, the experience gained in the mass-production of uniforms

Above: Typical 1940s hair style, with the front and sides rolled and the length at the back falling into lustrous curls.

and government regulations which stipulated quality and sizing standards as well as quantity of cloth, led to improved methods and provided the essential impetus of stability and prosperity necessary to organize the clothing industry. Better wages and set profit margins enabled women to enjoy far higher standards in mass-production techniques than in the pre-war years.

New technology, too, had been developed for the war effort, with the production of nylon as a strong and lightweight fabric refined and concentrated in the manufacture of parachutes and other war accessories. Resins developed to stabilize mosquito nets in the Pacific held the promise of permanently starched, water-repellent, crease- and stain-resistant finished fabrics. Resins could be further used in binding seams without stitches in the way that army tents had been constructed, and further developments were promised in the development of vinyl plastics for lightweight raincoats, and costume jewellery in electro-polished steel. The role of television, too, as a major force in the promotion of fashion was established, although it was more importantly an asset of the 1950s. In January 1947 *Vogue* was the first magazine asked to televise a Basic Wardrobe in the BBC's programme 'Editor's Choice'.

Two years after victory there was still no end to drabness in fashion and food, and it was in such a climate that Dior presented his 'New Look' in 1947. This represented the ultimate in femininity, with a neat waistline, accentuated by a rounded hip-line, natural sloping shoulders and long, swirling skirts. Dereta was the first British ready-to-wear firm to capture the Paris look, and had sold its first designs in a West End store within the first day. Not all were so ready to welcome the New Look. The Board of Trade criticized its extravagant use of fabric, for with Britain still under the restrictions of the Utility scheme, production was restricted and delayed, and the New Look could only develop along non-Utility lines. However, despite opposition, the New Look was to dominate the fashion scene until the end of the 1940s. Dior presented an alternative, equally elegant, straight and slender silhouette with the brief jacket worn over a long, straight skirt. Such designs used 'reasonable' quantities of fabric. As skirt hems lengthened to 30–35cm (12–14in) from the ground, *décolletage* in evening and cocktail dresses became very wide and deep, revealing a large expanse of bosom seldom seen since the 18th century. Underwear took on a new importance with the introduction of the strapless wired bra and the return of the corset as an essential foundation of the mode, producing a small, tight, boned waist, trim above and rounding below. The petticoat also added to the line; stiffened and flounced and worn in two

Above: Underwear with a nipped in waist and padded hips give the right silhouette to late 1940s 'New Look' fashions.

Opposite: Belted coat and umbrella.

or three layers, the swirling skirt stood away from the figure. Hip pads provided roundness of hip for the slimmer woman.

A 'New Look' in men's clothing was to lag behind women's fashions, but post-war styles did lose the exaggerated shoulder line. More relaxed clothing became common for day wear in preference to the ill-fitting Utility suits. Sports clothes included the short battle dress bought from army surplus, often worn with the new 'Daks' – trousers made with pleats at the front and a waistband which required no belt. The duffle coat, also sold as government surplus at the end of the war, attained a new popularity for males and females, sometimes dyed blue. It was not until 1949 that a large range of clothing became coupon-free.

With the end of the 1940s some form of recovery was apparent and Britain looked to reestablishing itself. The new Labour government, elected by a landslide victory immediately after the war, had made important inroads in the field of social welfare. The National Health Service established free health care for all, and nationalization of the Coal Board and British Rail looked set to provide a country for the people. The outlook was one of hope – a 'New Look' for fashion and a new look for the country.

WOMEN

PREDOMINANT FASHION FEATURES

'Feminine and ever more feminine is the way fashion is moving. Most is made of every curve and every hard line is softened… Squared-up looks are out; curved lines are here' (*Vogue*, December 1947). Dior's 'New Look' makes fashion headlines, but it can only develop along non-Utility lines. The natural shoulders are narrower and less padded and are rounded with kimono or raglan sleeves. Neat waistlines are accentuated by rounded hiplines. Hiplines are made apparent by actual padding or pleats or patch pockets. Skirts are perfectly straight or really wide. The width is gained by circular cuts, gores, pleats and gathers. The hemlines are longer – around 35cm (14in) from the ground and 12.75cm (5in) below the knee. The day version of the New Look is a suit – a tiny, brief jacket with a short, flared peplum over a long, straight or full skirt.

Coats are either tiny-waisted or full and loose, with contrast linings of fur, plaid or satin.

Ankle-length cocktail or full-length evening dresses fasten demurely high at the neck or are cut very wide and very low and are often strapless.

Fabrics Tweeds, soft fine dress woollens, wool and rayon jersey and velvets are used. For evening, failles, satin and tulle is used. Small checks are worn in contrast to bolder patterns and closer-woven, higher-quality fabrics are used.

Colours Blended colours – grey-greens, grey-blues, aubergine, cactus, sage, olive and bay – are worn, along with geranium red. For evening, browns and greys or soft, subdued greens are favoured.

Left: Flared skirt typical of the 'New Look' fashionable in the late 1940s.

Right: Drawing of a close-fitting day dress (for the pattern see page 109).

Decoration Knotted girdles, bows and cascading draperies concentrate interest at hip-level. There is new interest at the neckline with frills and ruffles.

Undergarments Dior's New Look necessitates a return to the corset as the foundation of the mode, fashioned in lighter fabric. 'Waspies' are worn for a nipped-in waist and are made from 15.25–20.25cm (6–8in) deep, rigid material, boned and laced at the back, worn on top of the roll-on. These are a luxury item. Circular stitched bra cups are worn for emphasis, while evening wear brings about the strapless wired bra. The petticoat takes on a new importance; two or three are worn, flounced and gathered in taffeta or tulle, and stiffened with horsehair braid or feather boning. Lace, denied during the war, begins to return in non-Utility. Synthetic fabrics, such as nylon, are used increasingly for undergarments. Parachute nylon and silk are now sold for this purpose.

Shoes Less clumpy than previous years, with higher, slim heels, up to 10.25cm (4in) in 1948.

Stockings Rayon Utility is worn or sheer nylon stockings.

Hats Hats are worn 'off the brow'. With the New Look, small half-hats are generally smaller and neater. Summer straw hats with wide brims and shallower crowns are also worn. 'As skirts swirl wider, as coats get bulkier, so must the hat get neater, smaller to balance your outline' (*Harper's Bazaar*, October 1947).

Hair Cut short again into an urchin cut, following the line of the head.

Accessories Long evening gloves are worn with sleeveless dresses.

Make-up Bright red lipstick, bluish and tawny shades, and rouge are worn. Eyebrows are plucked into natural arched line with black mascara and blue-green eye-shadow.

DETAILS OF ILLUSTRATED PATTERN

A close-fitting day dress with interest centred at hip-level. A wide bias girdle wraps around to tie in large bow at the right hip. By contrast, the bodice is simple with a high neckline and small Peter Pan collar, with long, tight-fitting sleeves, and a softened, rounded shoulderline. The dress is characteristic of the gentler, more feminine vein that is replacing the mainly functional fashions of the past years.

Fabrics Wool or rayon jersey.
Colours Deep cherry red or amethyst.
Footwear Court shoes with high, slim heel, fine platform sole and ribbon bow decoration.

HAT Soft fabric hat with raised crown and drapery to match the outfit.

ACCESSORIES Gauntlet-style suede gloves are worn over the dress sleeve. Small pearl earclips are also worn.

NOTES ON CONSTRUCTION OF GARMENT

The sleeves should fit closely over the arm; adjust to fit as necessary. The wrist opening is finished with single covered button and loop. If a woven fabric is used, the dress and sleeve should be cut on the bias. Insert a 23cm (9in) zip at the left side seam. Extend the girdle pattern to 3m (3¼yd). Cut on the bias. The centre of the girdle is caught into the back of the left side seam, along line A to B, thereby concealing the opening when tied. Leave an opening of 10.25cm (4in) at the centre-back neckline for a second zip fastening.

MEN

PREDOMINANT FASHION FEATURES

Utility regulations still apply. There are no significant changes in men's dress in the late 1940s.

Two-piece lounge suits without waistcoats continue to be worn. Lounge-suits are now worn for all occasions except the most formal. Black lounge suits with a white carnation and handkerchief in breast pocket are acceptable wear for weddings, whereas a morning coat was always required previously.

Summer suits are made less skimpy and are closely fitting over the chest, with a less squared shoulder line and lower waist than the war years. They are made unlined by ready-to-wear firms in lightweight fabrics.

Trouser legs are wider again, pleated into the waistband and longer over the instep. Flannel trousers are favoured, requiring no belt. Lounge and sports jackets, influenced by American service styles, are adapted for the British market with wide shoulders and double-breasted styles.

From army surplus, a short battle dress is worn for casual wear with a loose, blouson-style jacket.

The duffle coat is an unlined loose-fitting coat with a yoked back, raglan sleeves, large patch pockets, attached hood and toggle fastening. It is worn by men and women.

FABRICS Man-made, synthetic and mixture fabrics enable lighter-weight suiting fabrics. Flannel, gabardine, corduroy, cavalry twill and tweeds are all worn.

COLOURS Deep navy and midnight blue are worn in preference to black for dinner jackets and dress coats. Shirts are worn in pastel shades with bold stripes.

SHIRTS AND UNDERGARMENTS Shirts with longer points on collars are American influenced. Soft shirt collars are worn with dinner jackets. Sports shirts are worn with attached collars in flannel, cotton and rayon, sometimes worn open-necked. American-style beach shirts in spun rayon are worn in plain colours with white collar. Underpants are made in cellular cotton fabric with no front yoke and straight fly front.

SHOES Chukka boots of brown or black leather are based on army officers' boots. Elasticated side gussets eliminate fastenings. Crêpe-soled shoes with rounded toes are worn.

SOCKS Worn long again after the war, up to knee-length, with elasticated tops and are often striped. Wool and nylon mixtures are used.

HATS Less popular after the war, though trilby and snap-brim hats, porkpies, bowler hats (for business) are all worn.

HAIR Remaining short-back-and-sides for business. The American influence popularizes the crew-cut, where hair is cut short all over.

ACCESSORIES Gloves with string backs and leather palms are worn for driving, featuring a strap fastening with gap at the back of the hand.

DETAILS OF ILLUSTRATED PATTERNS

A three-button single-breasted summer jacket with notched lapels and rounded fronts. There are three patch pockets finished with stitching trim below upper edges. The jacket is cut on easy-fitting lines at the waist with additional width at the chest and shoulders. The back is cut in one piece.

The trousers have darts and pleats at the waist and are finished with permanent turn-ups. They are of generous width throughout.

FABRICS AND COLOURS Very fine worsted suiting fabric with a smooth finish, or lightweight woollen mixture fabric, in several shades of grey, blue, brown or tan. The jacket may be worn with trousers of the same material or in combination with other shades as a sports coat, for street wear, business or social activities. Lightweight mixture fabrics are also suitable.

UNDERGARMENTS Pastel-coloured shirt with soft attached collar, worn with a spotted tie.

FOOTWEAR Black leather laced shoes with rounded toes.

NOTES ON CONSTRUCTION OF GARMENTS

The edges, collar and welts are single-stitched 6mm (¼in) from the edge. The dotted lines on the trouser waistband indicate the extension for the left side.

Right: Drawing of summer jacket with trousers (for the pattern see page 109).

The Fifties

The 1950s often seem to have passed unnoticed, an interim age between the turbulent 1940s and swinging 1960s. By comparison, the 1950s lack excitement and colour, but significant movements were developing which transformed Britain from the age of austerity to prosperity. Stability was essential to Britain's reconstruction programme, and fashion responded to this influence. Restrictions were still imposed, even after five years of peace: the Utility scheme continued until 1952, and petrol rationing continued well into the decade. In 1954 food rationing ended after 14½ years, and coal rationing and price control only in 1958.

It was in such a climate that the government presented the 'Festival of Britain' in 1951, 'a year of fun, fantasy and colour, a year in which we can while soberly surveying our great past and our promising future, for once, let ourselves go'. Situated on the South Bank of the River Thames, the Festival set out to celebrate Britain's achievements in the introduction of the welfare state, new nationalized industries, our progress in the arts and sciences and design, free from Utility regulations. *Vogue* ran a feature on the 'Rise of Ready-to-Wear' to coincide – 'the most fastidious and fashion-conscious woman can dress in ready-to-wear clothes'. All seemed to signify that Britain was emerging from austerity into a new era.

The next event to brighten the lives of the British people was the coronation of Queen Elizabeth II in 1953, televised for the first time and seen by millions all over the country. The sale of television sets at this time rocketed, and television became firmly established; in 1959 the BBC had over 26 million viewers. Black-and-white sets usually had 23–26cm (9–10in) screens at this time, housed in a wooden cabinet. Independent broadcasting from 1955 brought a wider range of viewing choices.

Despite Britain's floundering economy and recurrent financial crises throughout the 1950s, for most people economic difficulties were less apparent than rising prosperity. The Festival of Britain was followed by the return of the Conservative government, which abandoned wage restraint, lifted much rationing and actively encouraged a consumer boom. Almost full employment and higher wages brought increased spending power and, as the government abolished systems of control, this stimulated business and industry, with consequential growth of manufactured goods. These were the years when the car, the television, the refrigerator, entered the average British household. With strict control on the number of cars manufactured for the home market, the expansion of the motor-car industry was delayed. Nevertheless, car sales more than doubled and by 1959 it was estimated that one in every three families in Great Britain owned a car, compared with one

Above: Town suit in charcoal grey flannel, with diagonal fastening and basque curves over the hips.

in seven in 1950. 1959 was also the year of the Mini-car; relatively inexpensive at £497, it was an immediate success. The progress and expansion of the car industry was to provide the basis of prosperity in the 1960s.

Nearly four million women, including a growing number of married women, were going out to work. This brought a second income into the home and contributed to rising living standards. Women provided a cheap labour source and were actively encouraged by the government to play their part in the country's recovery. However, advertising was still directed very firmly towards the housewife, and reinforced women's role in the home. It was in trying to fulfil these two roles that conflict arose in the following decades. Support for the family in various ways eased some of the financial pressure; the establishment of the welfare state provided benefits and relieved financial strain. The post-war 'housing drive' increased the rate at which families could be re-housed, causing much overcrowding. On cleared bomb-sites temporary dwellings, known as 'prefabs' (short for prefabricated), were set up to provide immediate accommodation. However, they continued in use well beyond the 1950s and some are still in existence today. A more permanent planning measure was the 'new town' which was designed to relieve congestion in the cities by the setting up of housing estates and large shopping developments, with supermarkets and department stores in the country. The 1950s also witnessed the first high-rise flats, extensively constructed throughout the 1960s, and problem-creators of the 1970s. The face of the environment was changing rapidly, the Clean Air Act of 1952 introducing the compulsory use of smokeless fuels such as coke, and thus ending smogs. The increase in sales of the domestic motor car brought a new form of pollution, and town planning now included essential roundabouts, traffic lights and car parks.

Fashion expanded alongside other British industry, as ready-to-wear, with improved standards and advanced technology, forged ahead. In very much the same way as war had provided the essential impetus to the expansion of commercialized fashion in the inter-war years, World War II, and in particular the Utility scheme, which had regulated quality of workmanship and cloth, helped to overcome many of the problems created by mass-production, and the industry emerged in a strong position. Conversely, in restricting clothes production for the home market, the Utility scheme delayed the availability of fashionable ready-to-wear. It was abolished in 1952, and was superseded by the more flexible 'D' scheme, in which garments below a certain price limit remained exempt from purchase tax, and above that level tax was graduated according to cost. The scheme was discontinued in 1955 and replaced by five per cent purchase tax on all clothes other than children's. Output of yarn and cloth increased, and ready-to-wear firms were thus able to develop their own materials and original styles of garments. Marks and Spencer was one of the most important firms of the period, rapidly establishing new stores and following a policy of value and quality. As Goronwy Rees, in his book on Marks and Spencer, states: 'Their prices after the war were not cheap. But given the quality which

their merchandise embodied, it offered better value for money than anything else on the market.' Their share of national clothing sales more than doubled between 1950 and 1968, and was to increase to ten per cent of the total national consumer spending on clothing. In their centenary year, 1984, Marks and Spencer with its two hundred and sixty stores in the United Kingdom took one pound in every seven which was spent on clothes. Their large and powerful organization also played an important part in the textile revolution, initiating their own research from which many took a lead. The production of nylon, promoted after the war, effected its own revolution in underwear, and was followed by a succession of other new fibres: ICI introduced 'Terylene' in 1952; DuPont was next on the scene with 'Dacron' and 'Orion' in 1953; and in 1957 'Courtelle', the first British acrylic fibre, was produced commercially by Courtaulds. Most incredible was the speed at which the textiles, once discovered, were applied to industry. New fibres increased the range and variety of materials available to the textile industry enormously. Raw materials which were no longer artificial forms of existing fibres, but fibres in their own right, possessed properties quite distinct from those of natural fibres. Thermoplastic qualities enabled fibres to be bulked, and fabrics embossed and permanently pleated were light in weight, drip-dry and easy to iron. The fabrics themselves, then, influenced fashion, creating new styles and simultaneously lowering costs. Lightweight, easy-care clothes were appropriate to the needs of modern life.

By the early 1950s, with the import restrictions lifted and the overwhelming success of the New Look in 1947, Paris had re-established itself as the predominant fashion leader. Success in ready-to-wear was achieved by establishing close links with French couture, and designs were readily copied and adapted for the mass market. Until 1956 two silhouettes prevailed, with skirts either full

the famous comfort-in-action trousers

TAILORED BY SIMPSON

or pencil-slim. For the most part the full bouffant skirts were retained for evening dresses, which could be floor- or cocktail-length. The ubiquitous strapless bodices of evening wear, heavily boned for support, relied on constructed foundations; numerous petticoats and weighted hems supported the skirt, where full.

The tailored suit was the basis of every woman's wardrobe, and usually consisted of a tight-fitting jacket, jutting out over a slim skirt. A scarf filled in the neckline, as the close fit often made a blouse superfluous, and tapes at the waistline heightened the fit at this point. Hemlines had risen slightly since the New Look, falling to the mid-calf and remained more or less stable until the late 1950s, when skirts became significantly shorter. Fashion, and more importantly hemlines, made front page news, although this was usually only a matter of 2–5cm (1–2in) variations introduced by individual designers. Christian Dior, Balenciaga and Chanel, who reopened in 1954, were the major designers of note. Dior introduced a succession of new fashions, based on letters, until his untimely death in 1957. Each gave a specific emphasis to the silhouette: the low-waisted, slim 'Ligne H' in autumn 1954 was closely followed by 'Ligne A', widening towards the hem, and 'Ligne Y' which expanded above the tapered skirt with dolman or full sleeves. His own version of Givenchy's sack dress, a waistless shift narrowing towards the hem, was his *coup de grâce*, but his fashion house continued to create new modes, with the young designer Yves St Laurent introducing the 'trapeze line' in 1958. The skirt was remarkably short, barely covering the knee, and flared from the shoulderline, creating a silhouette not dissimilar to the 'A line'. By 1959 the waist had returned.

Accessories were all-important; gloves and hats were always worn and could be large and flat or small and closely following the line of the head. Hair remained short with waves or bubble cut until the later years of the decade, when longer hair was brushed upwards, creating full-blown beehive effects. Shoes, round-toed and relatively clumpy in 1950 became shapelier and, as hemlines rose, heels became higher. From the mid-1950s toes became increasingly pointed and heels stiletto. Clothes were generally well-designed, elegant and feminine.

Much of the character of the constructed fashions of the 1950s, with their boned bodices, built-in petticoats and weighted hems, looked back to an earlier page of history. Menswear, too, took a nostalgic influence from upper-class Edwardian fashion. The Neo-Edwardians wore long, tight-fitting, single-breasted jackets with velvet-faced lapels and cuffs, fancy waistcoats and narrow, fitted trousers. A bowler hat and winklepicker shoes, pointed well beyond the natural toeline, completed the look. The style was created by Savile Row and was adapted in a simpler form to the wider market.

Above: Fashion design by Victor Stiebel for a full-skirted gown typical of the period.

Men's clothes generally were slimmer fitting, losing much of their previous bulkiness and squareness of cut. Trousers were more shapely, with fitted waistbands, adjustable elastic inserts and zip fly fronts (now universal); turn-ups were phased out in the early 1950s. Trousers were also lighter in character, resulting partly from a more relaxed attitude towards dress, and increased use of man-made fibres meant they could be permanently creased. Shirts were often made of mixed fibres, incorporating a percentage of cotton for comfort, in bold colours and patterns, cut straight at the lower edge. These were sometimes worn outside the trousers and open at the neck, with either long or short sleeves.

Overcoats likewise became shorter and closer fitting, with single-breasted opening, and by the late 1950s were knee-length. Motoring had ceased to be the dusty sport of its early days and no longer required protective clothing. The duffle coat, brought out by ready-to-wear after the war in heavy wool, also became popular. In the 1950s the dress suit ceased to be worn for all formal occasions and the dinner jacket or dark lounge suit was favoured.

Young fashions began to take on fresh influences, distinct from those directing mature dress. Adolescence, to this date unacknowledged, was recognized as the important interim stage between child and adult. The needs of this younger set could not be met within the existing range of entertainments and fashions, and the 'teenage market' expanded at a phenomenal rate. Traditional family values declined and the idea of the 'generation gap' emerged, since parents often could not understand, nor participate in, the lives of their offspring. The young almost seemed to be hostile to their parents, and in dress, music and attitudes opposed the values of their parents' generation. The affluent society gave a new spending power to the young, and they found a world and culture of their own, different from, and often at odds with, those of their parents. American rock-and-roll idols, including Elvis Presley and Bill Hayley, and young film stars, like James Dean, a rebellious crazy mixed-up kid, became leaders, worshipped and imitated. The Teddy boys, or 'Teds', from 1953, were the first teenage sub-culture, and contributed to feelings of teenage anti-social behaviour. Their dress, not unlike that of the Neo-Edwardians, was inspired by the Edwardian age, with long jackets with narrow velvet lapels and cuffs worn over fancy waistcoats, white shirts with bootlace ties, crêpe-soled brothel-creeper shoes and winklepickers, and long hair slicked into quiffs and 'sideburns' with Brylcreem. Wimpys, youth clubs and coffee bars, with juke boxes sounding out the latest records, became new meeting grounds. Teenagers were to lead fashion in the 1960s, but the seeds of the movement were sown in the previous decade.

THE QUEEN. DECEMBER 5. 1951

[just that]

Above: Advertisement for Wolsey nylons.

In November 1952 *Vogue* photographed the blueprint teenager, with ponytail and coke, and from 1953 dedicated a section of their magazine to young fashion. *Harper's Bazaar*, too, began The Young Outlook' in January 1958. Teenage girls wore full circular dirndl skirts with numerous petticoats of paper nylon, ideally suited to rock-and-roll dancing, worn with scoop-neck blouses or tight polo-necks and 'flatties' – flat-soled shoes. For casual wear tight trousers, tapering to just above the ankle, and chunky sweaters were adopted throughout the 1950s. The bust assumed a new importance, and large, pointed breasts became the new feminine ideal. Pre-formed, conically stitched and often padded bras pushed the bust upwards and outwards, the 'sweater-girl bra', from 1953, exaggerating the bustline in the desired manner. Strapless bras were cleverly constructed for plunging necklines and low-back styles, and 'Lycra' was introduced for underwear, making possible strength and control without stiffening.

In many ways casual fashions were derived partly from the teenage market, with full-skirted shirtwaisters and tight-fitting trousers or slacks and jumpers. The look also owed a great deal to Italian designers, including Pucci and Simonetta, who led the field in casual wear with bright colours – cerise, orange, scarlet and emerald green – and loosely fitting, but nevertheless 'chic', comfortable clothes. Italy also effected a revolution in knitwear, which became smoother and less bulky in the late 1950s. Development of machinery and textiles enabled fine, knitted tubular structures, and twelve denier nylon stockings, without seams, could be produced. Fine, knitted sports shirts for men, with turned-down attached collars, short sleeves and tunic-style opening, became popular for general casual wear. Accessories, too, became dominated by this overriding influence: pointed shoes for both sexes and classic stiletto shoes and soft leather handbags for women. Italian fashions in menswear differed from the Edwardian look with extended shoulders and significantly shorter, straight, boxy jackets and narrow trousers. Despite the square silhouette clothes were well-fitted and shapely. Hair was short and tidy, cut in even length all over, in contrast to the more conventional short-back-and-sides.

By the end of the decade life in Britain had changed in many ways. The British people felt optimistic, with outward signs of success in the rebuilding programme and emergence of the affluent society. The average family was beginning to enjoy the luxuries that had previously been accessible only to the middle and upper classes. The fashion industry, likewise, expanded rapidly, the success of styles in ready-to-wear becoming instrumental in establishing fashion. Fashion was never to be the same again after the 1950s.

WOMEN

PREDOMINANT FASHION FEATURES

During the 1950s women's clothes are generally elegant, well-designed and easily available from ready-to-wear. Two silhouettes prevail throughout the decade: narrow, form-fitting bodices and pencil-slim skirts or full, flaring from the waist to wide hem. 'Skirts are sometimes longer, but nowhere shorter' (*Harper's Bazaar*, 1951) – skirt lengths are at least to mid-calf.

The Dior 'princess line' features shaped panels that fit the figure, with the waistline outlined rather than specified. It is worn with a blouson jacket gathered into a wide belt at the hips.

A tailor-made suit is the essential item of any wardrobe. All have narrow skirts, with three types of jacket – very neat and close-fitting, with a defined waist and peplums; long, belted tunic jackets or loose, casual fingertip jackets.

Coats feature three main outlines. They are fitted and often belted, with full skirts that may be three-quarter, seven-eighths or full-length, just covering the skirt; tubular shape; or tremendously big greatcoats, sloping from dropped shoulders into enormous fullness and made in shaggy wools. The pockets are generally large and deep.

General characteristics of 1950s clothes include shawls or stand-away collars, half-belts above or below the natural waistline, swing backs, angled shoulders and three-quarter-length sleeves. Casual wear includes sweaters with 'V or 'U' necklines, worn with tapered trousers or full dirndl skirts. For evening, narrow or full skirts are worn. Stem dresses flare low from just above the knees. Plunging necklines appear, along with strapless or one-shoulder effects. Evening wear is ground- or cocktail-length, around 15–20cm (6–8in) from the ankle, just longer than the day dress. Evening clothes with skirt and petticoats are sometimes joined, with boned bodices and weighted hems.

FABRICS Day suits are made with smooth woollens (no nubbly weaves) and tweeds are firmer and smoother, occasionally with metallic threads. Flannels and gabardines are used for sharp, tailored suits. Velvets and velveteens are also worn. Surface interest is created with silks. Long-haired, deep-piled fabrics, such as mohair, plush, 'teddy bear' fabrics, is used for coats. For evening, lace, slipper satin, plain and façonné, faille, silk and jersey is worn.

COLOURS Black combined with white. Neutral shades are used for woollens. Not many strong colours are worn. For evening, ice pink, lemon, olive, black and white are worn.

DECORATION Fur is widely used as trimming on linings, borders, collars, cuffs, hems, muffs, hats, fur and necklets on dresses. Much white fur, also Persian lamb, mink, beaver and leopard is also worn. Fine pleating is a feature, alongside embroidery, beading and sequins on evening dresses.

UNDERGARMENTS 'The hourglass look is out; a new silhouette has come in, narrow and controlled all the way down. The narrow shape must be built on a new sort of foundation, smoothing your hips and behind into a long, slinky line' (*Harper's Bazaar*, January). Boned and wired bras feature adjustable straps, which can be removed for one shoulder or strapless dresses, and are wired to separate between the breasts for deep, plunging neckline. Nylon fabrics revolutionize underwear, making possible lightness and stretch. Layers of net and paper nylon petticoats are worn to emphasize the full silhouette.

SHOES Fairly clumpy in the early 1950s.

STOCKINGS Fine, seamed nylon stockings worn in natural shades.

HATS Hats are always worn. A large brim with flat crown (mostly for summer) or a small biretta type, are perched above the front hairline and worn straight on the head. Chinese coolie hats are also worn.

HAIR Worn slightly longer and often swept to one side. Hair can be curly or flat and sleek.

ACCESSORIES Accessories take on a new importance. Scarves fill in necklines of tightly fitting, tailored suits as blouses are not always worn. Long evening gloves are worn, pushed down to the wrist for day. Evening accessories include embroidered and lace stoles. Jewellery includes black beads, graduated pearls worn high at neckline, pearl earclips, diamanté earrings and bracelets.

MAKE-UP 'Doe eyes' with eyeliner are drawn in with an upward turn at outer corner. Emphasis is on the eyes, which are heightened with plenty of eye shadow and mascara. Lips are shaped into a 'Cupid bow' line and are vivid red. Faces are fresh looking, the skin glowing through a filmy foundation or tinted powder.

Left: Fashion design illustration for a pink linen and silk surah summer dress.

Right: Drawing of top coat (for the pattern see page 116).

DETAILS OF ILLUSTRATED PATTERN

A lady's top coat, which might be described as semi-double-breasted, as it has a narrow front panel, with a pair of fastening buttons at the waist, set very close together laterally. The upper buttons are ornamental and set well back. The back of the coat is panelled, the centre panel being relatively narrow at the waist and hips. The waist is sharply defined by means of shaped panels and side dart. The skirt flares over the hips to calf-length.

The roll-collar revers are made to swell out prominently over the bust and to roll softly down to the waistline. The slanting pockets with curved flaps are made in velvet to match the collar facing. The two-piece sleeves fasten with a slit and two buttons at the cuff, and are cut fairly narrow.

FABRICS Flannel, fine worsted twill.

COLOUR French grey, with black velvet trim.

FOOTWEAR Black leather court shoes with an all-over punched design, leather bow trim, rounded toes and elegantly high, straight heels.

HAT Small, veiled felt hat with a velvet ribbon trim and large bow at the back.

ACCESSORIES A black-and-white check scarf fills in the neckline. Short grey buckskin gloves are worn and a tightly furled umbrella with knotted cane handle is carried. Pearl earclips are also worn.

NOTES ON CONSTRUCTION OF GARMENT

Attach tapes inside the coat at the waistline to ensure a close fit. Padding may be required over the hips to give the essential roundness. Cut the velvet facing for the fronts and collar in one piece. A 1cm (³⁄₈in) seam allowance is provided in the pattern, except at the fronts. No hem allowance is included.

MEN

PREDOMINANT FASHION FEATURES

The lounge suit is worn for all occasions in lighter colours for informal or summer wear. Heavier woollens are worn for weekend and country, and dark grey or black for business or formal wear.

Lounge jackets are generally longer, more fitted and with a lower waist than previous years. The skirt is flared with side or central back vents and three to four buttons. Single-breasted styles are popular, as are two-piece suits.

Trousers are narrow in the leg, but not peg-top. They are fitted over the hips and thighs and turn-ups may be present.

Chesterfield and raglan-style overcoats are still worn and are loose-hanging with step collars. Flap or patch pockets are usual. For duffle coats see 1947–1948.

Lumber jackets or anoraks in leather or cloth are based on army battle dress and are worn for informal wear.

FABRICS Man-made synthetic and mixture fabrics make possible lighter-weight suiting fabrics. Worsted suitings, gabardine, flannel, tweeds, herringbones, cheviots and checks are also popularly worn.

COLOURS Black and darker greys are worn for business. Lighter greys, blues, fawn and tan are used for summer wear.

SHIRTS AND UNDERGARMENTS Coloured and boldly patterned shirts are worn, as are dark shirts with light-coloured ties and suits.

SHOES Pull-on boots with elasticated gussets are worn, just covering the ankles. Rounded toes and Oxford-style laced shoes are also favoured, with sandals for summer.

SOCKS Short socks with patterned sides are fashionable – their elasticated tops are reinforced with nylon.

HATS Bowler hats are worn with Neo-Edwardian fashions and for business. Porkpies and trilby hats are also worn.

HAIR Short-back-and-sides.

ACCESSORIES Driving gloves in unlined leather, or leather palms, with string or fabric tops are fashionable. Dark ties are worn with light suits, or spotted or striped ties. Cuff links are used for shirts without buttons at cuffs. Long, tightly furled umbrellas are business accessories.

DETAILS OF ILLUSTRATED PATTERN

A knee-length, loose-hanging chesterfield overcoat with a single-breasted, three-button fastening and a step collar. Flap pockets at hip-level are set horizontally with an optional slanted welt pocket on the left breast. Split set-in sleeves finish with shaped turn-back cuffs. The top-stitching detail emphasizes the front edges and is repeated on the sleeve seams, cuffs and pocket edges.

FABRICS Wool gabardine or Melton cloth for winter wear.

COLOURS Camel or grey.

FOOTWEAR Laced, Oxford-style shoes in brown or black.

HAT Snap-brim hat.

ACCESSORIES Gauntlet-style gloves.

NOTES ON CONSTRUCTION OF GARMENT

Top-stitch front, collar, cuffs and flap pocket 1cm (³⁄₈in) from the outer edges and at the centre sleeve seam. Ease back to front at shoulder seams. Adapt the trouser pattern from 1948 (see page 109).

Right: Drawing of chesterfield overcoat (for the pattern see page 117).

COAT
BACK
cut 2

CB

COAT
SIDE BACK
cut 2

COAT
COLLAR
cut 2

CB

COAT
SIDE FRONT
cut 2

COAT
FRONT
cut 2

COAT
FRONT SLEEVE
cut 2

COAT
BACK SLEEVE
cut 2

OVERCOAT
BACK
cut 2

OVERCOAT
TOP SLEEVE BACK
cut 2

OVERCOAT
TOP SLEEVE FRONT
cut 2

OVERCOAT
FRONT
cut 2

OVERCOAT
BACK SLEEVE
cut 2

OVERCOAT
SLEEVE CUFF
cut 2

COLLAR
cut 2

1953

WOMEN

PREDOMINANT FASHION FEATURES

Similar to the previous fashion, with the bust assuming greater importance. Suits are padded over the bust. Loose, stand-away necks and dropped armholes are also a feature.

Dior's 'tulip line' features added padding over the bust and a skirt shortened to 40.5cm (16in) from the ground. The sack or sheath dress is completely straight from the neck down and worn without belt, while a chemise dress is straight and simple, similar to sheath.

For casual wear 'the sweater has grown in importance and size. Buy it two sizes larger for a casual look' (*Vogue*, June 1953). Teenage fashions feature chunky sweaters, scoop-neck blouses or tight polo necks with full, circular skirts or drain-pipe pants. For evening, strapless, full-skirted ball gowns are worn.

FABRICS Tweeds with neat, definite patterns, such herringbones, dogtooth checks and Donegal tweeds are used, along with mottled, streaky, two-tone weaves. 'Manufacturers are smoothing the surfaces of their tweed cloths' (*Tailor and Cutter and Women's Wear*, January 1953). Wool mixed with rayon and nylon and ribbed jersey fabrics are used. Cotton prints – black and white, small designs and polka dots – are also used. DuPont introduces Dacron and Orion. For evening, lace, satin, organza, chiffon, tulle and paper taffeta are often worn.

COLOURS The coronation year means that heraldic reds, blues, white and regal glints of gold and purple are popular. Bright colours are worn with black and white. Tweeds – in sandy beige, mustard, brown-yellows – are worn with black.

DECORATION Black-and-white prints, small designs and polka dots are worn. Other decoration includes jewels, sequins and beading inspired by the coronation.

UNDERGARMENTS Lycra is introduced for underwear, giving firmer control without stiffening and rolling up. The sweater-girl bra – two stiffened cones, circular-stitched, with tight shoulder straps for uplift – is worn to enlarge size of the breasts and push upwards and outwards. Padded bust forms of foam rubber are used to give fuller, pointed bust. Cheap paper nylon petticoats and stiffened nylon net are worn with circular or full skirts.

SHOES Round toes, sling-back or court shoes with cutaway sides are worn. Flatties or pumps are teamed with casual and teenage fashions.

STOCKINGS Two-way-stretch nylon, seamless stockings.

HATS Small and neat, similar to previous fashion.

HAIR Worn sleek and waved or curly, and swept up at the sides, revealing the ears.

ACCESSORIES Scarves are used to fill in sweater and jacket necklines. Long day gloves are worn in light colours, well above wrist. Evening gloves reach above the elbow with strapless styles. Jewellery is worn in the hair for evening, and chokers and earrings are also favoured. Graduated pearl necklaces are worn for day. Other accessories include umbrellas and neat handbags with short straps.

MAKE-UP Liquid rouge is worn on the temples and under the brows, with tinted foundation and powder. Brown or blue-green eye-shadow is worn, with eyeliner drawn in upward turn at outer corner. Mascara, pencilled eyebrows, red and pink lipstick and nylon false eyelashes are also in fashion.

DETAILS OF ILLUSTRATED PATTERN

A summer dress with a low, bias-cut, stand-away neckline. The bodice is close-fitting with high-fitting kimono sleeves and a side panel cut in one

Left: Bolero and dress of lightweight wool georgette.

Right: Drawing of summer dress (for the pattern see page 120).

with the undersection of the short sleeves. The straight skirt fits closely over the hips with front tucks into waist seam.

FABRICS AND COLOURS A white-spotted silk shantung or cotton poplin with red or blue background.

FOOTWEAR Silk brocade, barred, toeless court shoes with rounded toes. Seamless stockings are also worn.

HAT White fine straw hat with a shallow crown and wide brim. Navy or red ribbon trim is used with a silk-bound brim.

ACCESSORIES A white patent-leather belt emphasizes the narrow waistline. Long cotton gloves are worn wrinkled over the arm. A navy leather pochette and white clip earrings complete the look.

NOTES ON CONSTRUCTION OF GARMENT

Ease the bias-cut collar to the neckline, overlapping at centre front. Attach belt loops at the waistline. Leave an opening in centre back above the small triangle for a zip fastener. Two small pleats on skirt front are caught in at waistline seam.

MEN

PREDOMINANT FASHION FEATURES

Menswear slims down this year, with more sloping shoulders, less pointed lapels and narrow trousers. Single-breasted styles predominate and double-breasted styles have the same general characteristics. Dark lounge suits are usually worn for business and formal wear.

Trousers are tapered and more shapely, with a waistband and permanently pressed creases. Turn-ups die out. Casual tweed sports jackets are worn with flannel or corduroy trousers.

The trend of informality in menswear continues with open-neck shirts, slacks, unlined casual jackets for summer and cardigan jackets.

Shirts are no longer considered as an undergarment – jacket-style shirts are worn outside the trousers, with long or short sleeves. The plain white shirt is re-established with business lounge suits.

For evening, tail coats are cut square, narrower and longer. Lapels are also narrowed. The tail coat is worn less than the dinner jacket.

Teenage fashions include leather jackets, T-shirts, blue jeans and leather belts.

FABRICS Similar to previous fashion. Man-made and cotton mixture fabrics are used for shirts.

COLOURS A bolder variety of colour and pattern is used for men's shirts, such as paisley and spot prints.

UNDERGARMENTS, SHOES, SOCKS, HATS, HAIR, ACCESSORIES Similar to the previous fashion.

DETAILS OF ILLUSTRATED PATTERNS

This double-breasted jacket is characteristic of the slimmer line in menswear. The shoulders are less broad and square, giving a more natural line, and the lapels are narrower with less fullness evident across the chest. Straight welt pockets eliminate bulk, and the left breast pocket is set at a slight slant. The jacket is long and fitting fairly closely over the hips. Narrow two-piece set-in sleeves finish with a slit cuff and three-button fastening, harmonizing with the jacket front. The foreparts are cut square at the lower edges.

The trousers are cut narrower in the leg, with turn-ups and pleats into the waistband, and are more fitted over the seat.

A plain white or light-coloured shirt with a turn-down attached collar completes the outfit.

FABRIC Fine herringbone tweed.

COLOURS Black-and-white and grey-and-white mixture.

FOOTWEAR Half-brogues of black box-calf with welted leather toes and heels and rounded toes. Grey or black ribbed socks are also worn.

HAT Snap-brim felt hat in grey or black.

ACCESSORIES Handkerchief in breast pocket. Leather gloves and cuff links are also worn.

NOTES ON CONSTRUCTION OF GARMENTS

For the trousers, use the waistband pattern from 1947–1948.

Left: Formal pin-striped suit with a double-breasted jacket and a trilby hat.

Right: Drawing of slimmer line suit (for the pattern see page 121).

JACKET
FRONT
cut 2

CB fold

JACKET
COLLAR
cut 2 on fold

TROUSERS

——— BACK cut 2

•••••• FRONT cut 2

pleat

JACKET
FRONT SLEEVE
cut 2

JACKET
BACK SLEEVE
cut 2

JACKET
BACK
cut 2

CB

1955

WOMEN

PREDOMINANT FASHION FEATURES

Main silhouettes continue in the style of previous years and are narrow or full, the 'waist' fluctuating between Empire line and hip. Half-belts are popular on suits, coats and dresses and are positioned high or low. Semi-fitted suits with shorter jackets are worn. Padding is used over the bust. Built-in petticoats are worn with full skirts.

Dior's letter shape designs are highly influential – in 1954, Ligne H featured pulled-out-telescope silhouettes, tunic suits with low-waisted long jackets (sometimes reaching to the knee) over longer, slim skirts. In 1955, Ligne Y featured dolman sleeves with longer, tapered skirts. Ligne A designs widened from small head and shoulders to full pleated and stiffened hems. Chanel's collarless jackets and skirts were also worn.

For coats the seven-eighths length is popular and trench-style raincoats are worn. 'Suits everywhere tend to be jackets and dresses' (*Harper's Bazaar*, September 1955). Close-fitting jersey or crêpe dresses are worn with belt interest just above the hips.

There is an Italian influence on casual clothes, and bright blouses with tapered corduroy pants are worn, as are knitted tops. Evening wear is similar to the previous fashion.

FABRICS   Black or grey and white tweeds, smoother hopsacks and basketweave are popular fabrics. Jerseys, crêpe, cotton and rayon prints are also worn, with brocade, satin, velvet, lace, silk, faille, tulle and chiffon used for evening.

COLOURS   Black is the predominant colour for day and evening. For day suits, soft browns, slate and graphite, mauve, bronze and vanilla are worn. For evening, colours include red, pink, green, yellow, white and ivory.

DECORATION   Bold prints are worn, with small floral prints for summer. Bow trimmings, jewels, sequins, bead embroidery on evening gowns, Persian lamb trimmings and fur collars are also worn.

UNDERGARMENTS   Similar to previous fashion.

SHOES   Less clumpy than previous years with more shapely narrow heels. Low-cut court shoes with pointed toes are worn. Slipsters – slip-ons without heels, usually in suede or satin – are worn for casual evening and day wear.

STOCKINGS   Sheer, seamless, two-way-stretch stockings, one size. Ultra sheer, 12 denier are worn for evening.

HATS   Small and neat, wide brims and shallow crowns are worn for summer – flowerpots, toques, turbans, domed and 'cake-tin' shapes are also worn. Bow and ribbon trimmings used to decorate the hats.

HAIR   Short bubble-cut with soft curls. Alice bands are worn to take the hair away from the face.

ACCESSORIES   Short cotton gloves are worn during the day, flared over the wrists, while long evening gloves are made in kid or fabric. Large handbags are favoured, with a basket-style in straw for summer. Other accessories include nylon umbrellas and stoles.

MAKE-UP   Similar to previous fashion.

DETAILS OF ILLUSTRATED PATTERN

An asymmetrical, full-length evening dress with a full skirt. The skirt consists of a circular overskirt of double tulle fabric over a semicircular foundation skirt of stiff lining fabric and tulle. The tightly fitting strapless bodice, with a shaped waist seam, is boned to the waistline and draped with tulle, which is arranged in narrow pleats diagonally. The draping extends into the overskirt and is gathered at the left side, front and back. A long piece of tulle is gathered over the left shoulder and may fall freely at the back or be wrapped around the shoulders to form a stole. The dress fastens to the left with a zip and hook-and-eye closure at the side seam. The bodice and right of the skirt are decorated with floral motifs embroidered with silver and green threads and beads.

FABRICS AND COLOURS   Sage green tulle and stiff artificial silk lining.

ACCESSORIES   Full-length kid gloves, worn wrinkled. A pearl choker and drop earrings complete the look.

NOTES ON CONSTRUCTION OF GARMENT

Construct the bodice of firm silk fabric and a double layer of tulle. The position of the boning is indicated by solid lines on the pattern. Leave an opening at the left side seam.

The semicircular foundation skirt consists of a layer of silk and tulle joined to the skirt and left open above the triangle at the left side seam, for the insertion of a 35cm (14in) zip fastener. The overskirt consists of two layers of tulle constructed as one, the upper layer decorated with floral motifs as illustrated on the sketch.

Left: 1950s evening dress with cape.

Right: Drawing of full-length evening dress (for the pattern see page 124).

Cut two strips of tulle to 134 x 122cm (53 x 48in). One long edge of each piece is joined to the overskirt between the hemline and points A and B. The two strips are then joined together to complete the skirt, for 85cm (33½in) from the lower edge. This enables the two strips to be taken either side of the zip opening in the left side seam. The overskirt is attached to the foundation over the shaped waist seam and each of the attached strips pleated and gathered between points A and C at front and B and C on the back bodice. The strips will extend above these points and are narrowly pleated across lower front and back, meeting at the right side seam where they are pleated between points D and E.

The two separate strips of tulle are pleated and attached to the bodice between points F and C, either side of the zip opening at the left side seam and draped across the front and back bodice. They meet at the right side seam where they are secured between points G and H. The upper line of draping on the bodice is indicated by dotted lines on the pattern.

Narrow pleating of the fabric over the bodice is secured with fine stitching lines to the foundation.

A long strip of tulle 220 x 134cm (86½ x 53in) is gathered on to the left front bodice between points J and K.

The full length is approximately 103cm (40½in) from natural waistline.

MEN

PREDOMINANT FASHION FEATURES

Lounge suits continue in the style of the early 1950s. Two-piece, single-breasted suits are the most popular style. Chesterfield and raglan-style overcoats are worn, loose-hanging with flap or patch pockets usual.

FABRICS   Houndstooth and herringbone tweeds, stripes and checks as well as worsteds are worn.

COLOURS   Greys, blues and browns are popular. Summer suits feature stone, natural and light tan shades. Slacks are natural, light tan and navy in colour, while shirts are white, light blue, natural, biscuit and grey. Bolder patterns and colours are also worn, such as paisley, spots and checks. Sports shirts are popular in checks of blue, green and grey.

UNDERGARMENTS   Cellular brief-style jockey trunks are worn with sleeveless singlets and short-sleeved vests.

SHOES   The toes are less rounded and Oxford-style lace shoes are worn in two-tone effects using reverse calf. Half-brogues are worn for town and sandals for summer.

SOCKS   These are made in variety of materials including wool, nylon, cotton lisle, Terylene, plain or fancy in shades of blue, beige, brown, mulberry, yellow or black. The toes and soles of wool socks are reinforced with nylon.

HATS   The importance of the hat continues to diminish. Bowler hats are worn for business, with small porkpie hats and felt trilby hats for general wear.

HAIR   Short-back-and-sides remains the correct style for business. The younger set wear Elvis Presley styles, which are longer, combed back and swept up in front to form quiff and greased with long sideburns.

ACCESSORIES   Patterned and plain scarves in brushed wool are worn, as are leather gloves covering the wrist with centre vents. Silk or wool, pastel, patterned or regimental stripe ties are favoured, while cigarette lighters and wrist watches complete the look.

DETAILS OF ILLUSTRATED PATTERNS

A semi-formal evening dress consisting of dinner jacket, cummerbund and dress trousers. The single-breasted jacket fastens with one button at the waistline, with a low-rolling shawl collar faced in ribbed black silk or satin fabric. Welt pockets retain the slimness over the hips, while the skirt is cut with little flare and is well rounded at the lower foreparts. Slanted welt pocket on the breast displays a handkerchief with double points. The jacket is cut with a shaped centre-back seam. Two-piece, set-in sleeves finish with a slit cuff and three-button fastening.

The dress trousers are cut on similar lines to day wear trends, with a single pleat into the waistband at fronts. A single row of silk braid may be present at the outer leg seams.

A pleated black silk or satin cummerbund is worn at the waistline. A plain or pleated white shirt with a soft front and a wing or turn-down collar and black tie completes the outfit.

FABRIC AND COLOURS   Wool worsted in midnight blue, charcoal grey or white is worn according to the occasion. Black silk or satin is used for the cummerbund and collar facing.

FOOTWEAR   Black patent-leather Oxford-style shoes with plain blue or black silk socks.

ACCESSORIES   A black silk tie is correct to wear with the dinner jacket. A white linen handkerchief is worn in the top jacket pocket and a second, for use, is tucked in the sleeve. Gold cuff links and a signet ring complete the outfit.

NOTES ON CONSTRUCTION OF GARMENTS

Fold a series of 1cm (⅜in) pleats across the cummerbund to reduce the width to 13cm (5in). The cummerbund meets at centre back with a hook-and-eye closure. Stiffen it with firm interfacing. For the trousers use the waistband pattern from 1947–1948.

Right: Drawing of man's dinner outfit (for the pattern see page 125).

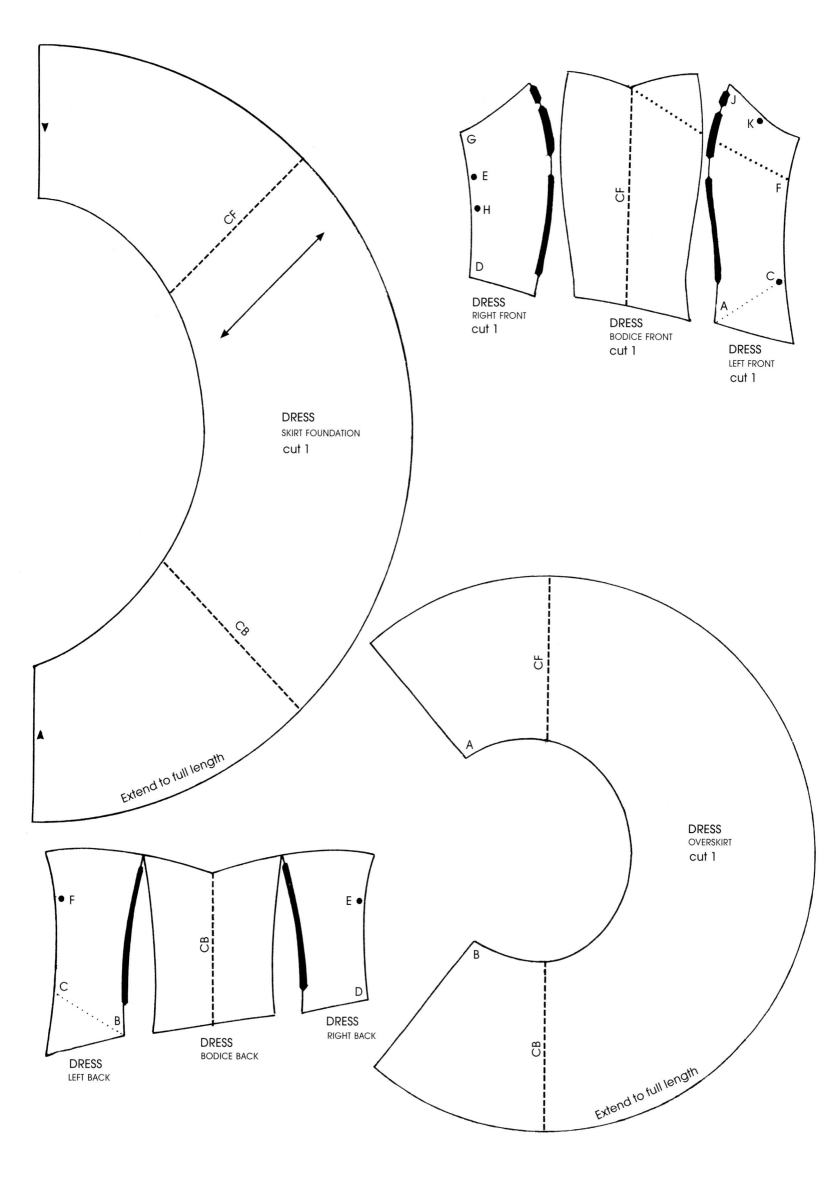

DRESS
RIGHT FRONT
cut 1

DRESS
BODICE FRONT
cut 1

DRESS
LEFT FRONT
cut 1

DRESS
SKIRT FOUNDATION
cut 1

CF

CB

Extend to full length

DRESS
OVERSKIRT
cut 1

CF

CB

Extend to full length

DRESS
LEFT BACK

DRESS
BODICE BACK

DRESS
RIGHT BACK

DINNER JACKET
BACK
cut 2

CB

DINNER JACKET
FRONT
cut 2

CB

TROUSERS
BACK cut 2
FRONT cut 2

DINNER JACKET
FRONT SLEEVE
cut 2

pleat

DINNER JACKET
BACK SLEEVE
cut 2

CB

CUMMERBUND
cut 1 on fold

CF fold

1956

WOMEN

PREDOMINANT FASHION FEATURES

Narrow and full silhouettes continue. Longer length skirts are worn tightened at the hem. Shorter jackets feature raised waists. Bulky soft coats are worn, as are capes, tapering towards the hem. Chanel's comfortable jersey cardigan suits and wrapover skirts are much copied.

Half-belts are worn on suits, coats and dresses. Casual wear includes slim pants and chunky sweaters ('Sloppy joes') and midriff blouses for summer.

Off-the-shoulder tops are worn with skirts, shorts, trousers and jeans. Pin-stripe denim skirts and knitted twin sets are also often worn.

Teddy girls wear button cardigans, scoop-neck blouses and full skirts over layers of petticoats.

Evening and summer dresses feature off-the-shoulder, sleeveless bodices, which are more fashionable than strapless.

FABRICS Fine wools and tweeds are worn, with uncrushable cottons for summer dresses. Thick, soft fabrics are used for coats. For evening, firm silks, *peau de soie*, brocade, faille, clouds of chiffon, flare-free net and non-tarnishing Lurex are all used.

COLOURS Black and white and reds predominate with pinks, pale blues and grey for evening.

DECORATION Contrast braiding is used on suits. Bright cotton prints, spots and stripes, huge coloured checks and larger floral patterns are also favoured. Bows in contrast or matching fabric are worn under the bust, at shoulders, openings and bodices. Bead and sequin embroidery and flowered jewels are also used for decoration.

UNDERGARMENTS Brightly coloured underwear in nylon and Terylene is worn. Bra-slips are in fashion, as are stiff felt or paper nylon petticoats, tiered on a slim-fitting hip yoke. Three-quarter and half-cup bras and strapless bandeau bras are worn. A waspie-belt – 10.25cm (4in) wide corset, laced at the back and worn over a girdle – is boned to exaggerate the hips and raise the waist. Corsets and girdles with zip fastenings are also worn.

SHOES High-heeled shoes with a narrow foot and pointed toe are worn. Bow decorations are popular, as are cut-out details. Lower, slim heels are worn for comfort.

STOCKINGS Sheer skin-tone nylons.

HATS Breton and turban styles are popular. Flowerpot, toque or brimmed styles with black veilings are worn, as are veiled cocktail hats.

HAIR Similar to previous fashion.

ACCESSORIES As previous fashion, with larger handbags and clutch bags.

MAKE-UP Eyes and lips are heavily outlined under veils. Pink lipstick and matching nail varnish are worn for evening.

DETAILS OF ILLUSTRATED PATTERNS

A teenage 'rock-and-roll' outfit consisting of a very full dirndl skirt and scoop-neck top. The skirt is worn over petticoats of taffeta or paper nylon, gathered on to a flat hip yoke. A narrow belt of matching fabric is worn at the waistline. The top, with wide V-neckline at front and back, extends over the natural shoulderline. The V-line is accentuated by seaming in the front bodice ending in small pleats over the bust. Darts at the waistline shape the bodice to the figure and give emphasis to the bustline.

FABRICS AND COLOURS A bold printed check cotton of red, black or blue on white ground. The top is white cotton.

Left: Teenage couple doing the Jitterbug in the living room.

Right: Drawing of a teenage 'rock n' roll' outfit (for the pattern see page 128).

FOOTWEAR Flat rubber-soled canvas pumps with an elasticated front gusset, worn with white ankle socks.

NOTES ON CONSTRUCTION OF GARMENTS

The front, back and sides of the skirt are cut to the same pattern. Make an opening of 20cm (8in) at left side. The total length of the skirt at the upper edge is gathered into the waistband. For the waistband cut a strip of fabric 68.5 x 5cm (27 x 2in) and add seam allowance to all edges.

Cut a second strip of fabric 78 x 5cm (30¾ x 2in) for the belt. Note: 5cm = twice finished width of waistband and belt.

The petticoat pattern is indicated by broken lines. Leave the left side of the yoke open. The petticoat is fastened with single button and loop at waistline.

For the top allow a 6mm (¼in) seam allowance between point B and pleat on top front.

MEN

PREDOMINANT FASHION FEATURES

The 'Italian Look' slims down men's fashions further – the cut is skimpy and close-fitting, with short jackets 15–18cm (6–7in) above the usual men's length; the effect is square and straight. The chest width and shoulders are less pronounced and the sleeves, collars and lapels are all narrowed. Trousers are skimpy and short, without turn-ups. Two-piece suits are more usual, adding to the lighter, slimmer look. This style remains popular during the latter half of the decade.

Teddy boys (Teds) wear thick, draped suits, featuring high-buttoning with a long skirt and one or two vents, step collars and drainpipe trousers. White shirts are worn with the collar turned up or with a bootlace tie. Fancy waistcoats of brocade complete the look.

Italian knitwear features V-neck sweaters in fine knit and chunky styles with fancy bulked stitches.

FABRICS Terylene and mixture suiting fabrics promote the lighter, slimmer look. Fine check fabrics are used for suits and linen, cotton and mixture fabrics for shirts.

COLOURS Business suits are worn in black or dark grey with light-coloured suiting fabrics in stone, tan and pale grey. Tweed sports jackets are worn in neutral tones. White and blue shirts are worn for summer.

SHIRTS AND UNDERGARMENTS Similar to previous fashion.

SHOES Slim and pointed Italian shoes – 'winklepickers' – extend well beyond the natural toeline.

SOCKS Socks are made in variety of materials – wool, nylon, cotton, lisle and Terylene – and are plain-ribbed or patterned. Plain brightly coloured socks are worn with Teddy-boy fashions.

HATS Bowler hats for business while porkpie or snap-brim-style hats with smaller brims are worn to balance narrow suits.

HAIR The 'Italian look' is short and neat, cut an even length all over and styled, in contrast to short-back-and-sides, which still remains popular among older men. Teddy boys wear their hair longer, greased and swept back at the sides and raised at the front, with long sideburns.

ACCESSORIES Narrow ties with squared ends. Narrow bootlace ties are worn with Teddy-boy suits. Other accessories include umbrellas, cuff links and scarves.

DETAILS OF ILLUSTRATED PATTERNS

This Teddy-boy outfit features a long drape coat with low-rolling shawl collar and one-button fastening at waistline. The coat is cut with broad shoulders and chest, with moderate waist shaping and only a slight flare in the skirt. Flap pockets are set low on the hips and slanted welt pocket on the breast displays a white or coloured handkerchief. Set-in sleeves finish with a shaped cuff, faced with velvet to match the collar. Many variations of the coat are possible including a higher-fastening step collar with velvet facings and pockets.

The drainpipe trousers are cut shorter than conventional trouser styles, and fit the figure closely.

An embroidered fabric waistcoat (single or double-breasted), white shirt and bootlace tie complete the outfit.

FABRIC AND COLOURS Wool twill tweed or woollen mixture fabric in black, grey or check is used for the coat. A lighter weight is used for the trousers, often of a darker cloth than the jacket.

FOOTWEAR Pointed winklepickers or thick crêpe-soled, lace-up casual shoes, worn with brightly coloured socks.

HAIR Worn fairly long, greased and swept back at the sides and raised at the front, with long sideburns.

NOTES ON CONSTRUCTION OF GARMENTS

Ease back to front at shoulder seams. The shoulders are well padded to give essential drape to the jacket. The collar and sleeve cuffs are faced with velvet; the pocket flaps and welt pocket on the breast may also be made up in velvet fabric.

The drainpipe trousers should fit the legs closely; adjust the pattern according to individual measurements.

Right: Drawing of Teddy-boy outfit (for the pattern see page 129).

gather

SKIRT
FRONT cut 1
BACK cut 1
SIDE PANELS cut 2

CB

PETTICOAT
SKIRT BACK
cut 2

gather

• A

PETTICOAT
SKIRT FRONT
cut 1 on fold

gather

CF fold

TOP
BACK
cut 1 on fold

CB fold

• B

B

pleat

TOP
FRONT
cut 1 on fold

CF fold

CB fold

PETTICOAT
YOKE BACK
cut 1 on fold

A

A

PETTICOAT
YOKE FRONT
cut 1 on fold

CF fold

DRAPE COAT
BACK
cut 2

CB

vent

DRAPE COAT
FRONT
cut 2

TROUSERS

······· BACK cut 2

——— FRONT cut 2

CB

CF

TROUSERS WAISTBAND

DRAPE COAT
FRONT SLEEVE
cut 2

DRAPE COAT
BACK SLEEVE
cut 2

1958

WOMEN

PREDOMINANT FASHION FEATURES

General characteristics of the fashion include skirts barely covering the knee and shoulders less sloped. Half-belts are worn at the sides, back or front, high or low, dipping or straight. The waist continues to fluctuate. Rounded 'eased-away' collars are worn instead of the previous stand-away necklines.

Yves St Laurent's 'Trapeze line' features flaring from the shoulders to a full, wide hem, giving a cape appearance, with three-quarter-length sleeves and the shortest skirts at knee level.

Coats are thick and soft with rounded shoulders. Three-quarter-length coats are worn over slim skirts.

Waistless shift and sack dresses are worn tapering to the knees. 'Chemise dresses are more popular than ever' (*Tailor and Cutter*, June 1958). Loose backs sometimes contrast with a front held in with a belt, drawstring or darting, giving a curved, concave line.

Chanel's jersey suits and blazer jackets continue to be much copied by ready-to-wear manufacturers. Brightly coloured blouses tone with suits, and the fabric is used to line the jacket.

Casual wear includes tapered jersey trousers with Italian sweaters and blouses. Easy-care Courtelle jumpers are worn in lemon, blue and pink pastel shades.

For evening dipping hemlines are worn, raised at the front. Chanel's tulip line features fullness billowing out from the waist and caught in at the bottom to a narrow hem. On similar lines 'cocoon', 'melon', 'puff-ball' and 'barrel' lines are used extensively for evening dresses.

FABRICS 'Wool takes on new textures' (*Harper's Bazaar*, January 1958) – mohair, corded weaves and bouclette are all used in plain, coloured and mottled designs. Basketweaves, dogtooth checks, herringbones, men's suiting fabrics, slub-weave silks and rayons are also used. Soft, thick, woollen fabrics are used for coats, as are wool velours and Melton cloth. Corduroy, jersey and denim is used for casual trousers, striped denim for skirts. Synthetic and cotton mixture fabrics are used for easy-care summer dresses. Uncrushable knitted cottons, crease-resistant cotton prints and check cotton tweeds with knitted look are also worn. For evening, taffeta, satin, brocades, nylon and silk chiffon and tulle are worn. 'Courtelle' is the first British acrylic fibre, produced commercially by Courtaulds.

COLOURS Tweeds are worn in muted colours, mixed with black, and knitted-look tweeds are also used. Pastels in ice blue and lemon are worn for the summer and all shades of green are popular. Brighter colours are worn in the evening. 'The colour spectrum breaks into five: the blues, the mineral greens, the browns, the marigolds and the sharp reds – all accented by bold black and white' (*Tailor and Cutter*, June 1958).

DECORATION 'Bows are everywhere.' Floral, paisley and bold, colourful prints are worn, as are spots of all sizes, prints resembling leopard skin, herringbone and knitted fabrics. Other decoration includes large and multi-coloured buttons, mink collars and scarves and contrast braiding on suits.

UNDERGARMENTS Similar to previous fashion.

SHOES Italian, remaining very narrow with squared-off points and fine stiletto heels. Contrasting toe-caps and cut-out styles are popular. Pumps are worn for low-heeled shoes.

STOCKINGS Tinted nylon stockings in very sheer, skin-tones. Ankle and knee-high socks for the younger set, worn with pumps.

HATS Small, perched over the forehead and worn square on the head in veiled flowerpot, cloche, toque and Breton styles. Straw is worn for summer, with feathered and veiled hats for evening. The beret is a very popular style 'worn in every size, at every angle' (*Harper's Bazaar*, January 1957).

Far left: Sleeveless square-necked slim dress with a boxy jacket.

Left: Model Cynthia Blackburn wearing a satin evening dress by Christian Dior.

Right: Drawing of slimline shift dress (for the pattern see page 132).

HAIR Women brush hair out rather than flatten it and wear it waved, not curly. Fringes are popular. For evening, additional hairpieces are worn swirled around the head.

ACCESSORIES Short, cotton or nylon gloves are worn for day, coloured to match the outfit. Washable suede and leather gloves are popular and are worn over the elbow for evening. Gigantic bags in clutch and strap styles complete the outfit.

MAKE-UP Eyes and lips are heavily outlined when worn with veiled hat styles. Emphasis is on the eyes, with blue-green eyeshadows, eye-pencil and mascara. Eyebrows are softly defined. Lips are outlined with lip-pencil then filled in with lipstick. Red and pink shades are used.

DETAILS OF ILLUSTRATED PATTERN

A slimline shift dress with a boat neckline, yoke and sleeves cut in one piece. The dress is gathered into the yoke at the front and caught on the hips with broad, buttoned tabs. The buttons are repeated on the short sleeves. The straight skirt narrows to the hemline, and is shorter than the previous fashion.

FABRIC AND COLOURS Dogtooth-check rayon, navy blue, red, black and white.

FOOTWEAR High stiletto court shoes in two colours with squared-off toes and cut-out vamp, buckle trim.

ACCESSORIES A very large black leather briefcase-style handbag. Above-the-wrist white cotton gloves, a choker-length necklace with triple string of pearls and matching clip earrings complete the outfit.

NOTES ON CONSTRUCTION OF GARMENT

Gather dress to yoke at the front and back as indicated on the pattern. Leave an opening in the left side seam for a 35cm (14in) zip fastener.

For the attached hip belts, cut four strips of fabric (top plus facing) to 6 x 22cm (8¾in x 2½in). Round the ends as shown by dotted lines on the pattern. Add a 1cm (⅜in) seam allowance to all belt edges.

The dress should fit closely over the hips; adjust the pattern as necessary to suit individual figures.

MEN

PREDOMINANT FASHION FEATURES

Similar to previous fashion. Single-breasted suits are worn with narrow lapels and flap and jetted pockets. Dinner jackets follow day trends, and are single-breasted with narrower lapels or shawl collar. The facings, cuffs, waistcoat lapels and collar trimming are of matching satin (usually dark blue) and often lined with contrast fabric, such as burgundy.

FABRIC AND COLOURS Similar to previous fashion. Wool worsteds and basketweaves are used, as are fancy checks – blue-and-tan or blue-and-grey combinations are popular.

HATS The 'hatless' mode continues. The trilby and snap-brim hat with narrow brim, and bowler worn with business suit, remain popular.

All other details similar to previous fashion.

DETAILS OF ILLUSTRATED PATTERNS

A single breasted two-piece lounge suit with narrow lapels and one-button fastening at waistline. The jetted pockets retain slimness over the hips and the welt pocket on the left breast displays a handkerchief with double points. The jacket is relatively short and close-fitting, with sloping shoulders and narrow, two-piece sleeves finished with a slit and single button. The back is cut with a centre-back seam and no vent.

The trousers are cut closer to the leg and shorter in length than previous styles. They are self-supporting, with a straight waistband and adjustable slide fasteners.

The outfit is worn with a button-through pastel-coloured shirt with an attached collar and a narrow, striped tie.

FABRICS AND COLOURS Lightweight linen-look Terylene and wool suiting fabric in grey, fawn or brown.

FOOTWEAR Slim-fitting lightweight laced shoes with squared-off toes and stitched upper. Short wool and nylon socks may be plain or fancy.

HAIR Cut short and neat, with more emphasis on 'styling'.

ACCESSORIES Jewellery worn includes cuff links, signet ring and tie pin.

NOTES ON CONSTRUCTION OF GARMENTS

Ease back to front at shoulder seams.

For the trouser waistband trace off the pattern from A to B for the right side with fly extension. Trace off band from A to C for the left side with front button extension. Add 1cm (⅜in) seam allowance to all edges of waistband.

The shirt back pattern is indicated by dotted lines. For a pleat at centre back, place the edge of the pleat line on fold of fabric.

Right: Drawing of two-piece lounge suit (for the pattern see pages 132–133).

CB

JACKET
BACK
cut 2

JACKET
FRONT
cut 2

CB fold

JACKET
COLLAR
cut 2 on fold

TROUSERS
BACK cut 2
FRONT cut 2

JACKET
FRONT SLEEVE
cut 2

A   B   C

CB   TROUSERS WAISTBAND cut 4   CF

JACKET
BACK SLEEVE
cut 2

WOMEN

PREDOMINANT FASHION FEATURES

'Skirts begin swinging' (*Harper's Bazaar*, October 1959) – they are shorter, barely covering the knee, and are wider at the hem.

Shorter jackets, some cropped to waist-length, are worn with wide belts and bulky cape collars with wrapover looks, dipping or folding over waist. Round necklines and a natural-looking waist are a feature.

Jackets are buttoned high with neat collars and revers. Coats or jackets with dresses are a popular combination.

There is a new silhouette – seaming moulds the dress or jacket to the figure under the bust, giving a corselet effect; at the hip-bone the seaming is released into tiny pleats.

Chanel's cardigan suits with weighted jacket hems are universally copied.

Coats are seven-eighths in length or shorter. The line may be straight or wide, but is always bulky. Heavier sleeves are set into rounded shoulders.

The Italian influence is seen on casual wear – chunky sweaters are worn with wider armholes, tapered trousers and sweater dresses. Knitted twin-sets and V-neck pullovers are specially dyed to match slim, pleated wool skirts. Knitwear is 'still easy and uncluttered, but without the bulky texture of earlier crops' (*Harper's Bazaar*, November 1959).

For evening, the 'cocoon' is worn – a full skirt caught in at narrow hem, similar to 1958.

FABRICS Worsted, barathea, jacquards, novelty suitings, jersey, velour and bouclé are all used, with rich lace, firm satins, brocades and velvets for evening.

Rough textures are used for coats and suits, such as soft, luxury mohair, loose tweeds and bouclé wool. Grey flannel is used for simple winter dresses and suits and dogtooth checks are also worn.

COLOURS All shades of green are worn, as well as pastel summer shades – peach, lemon, pinks, soft blues and white.

DECORATION Paisley prints, spots and bold checks are worn as are large buttons, embroidery and appliqué motifs. Pleats and pockets are used to give one-sided emphasis. Fabrics with the look of a fine knit are used to decorative effect and mink trimming is a fashion luxury.

UNDERGARMENTS As previous fashion.

SHOES High stiletto heels are worn, 10.25cm (4in) in height and 1cm (³⁄₈in) in diameter.

STOCKINGS As previous fashion.

HATS Taller hats are worn to balance higher hairstyles. The line is full and rounded, covering the whole head and hair, with narrow brims. With fuller hairstyles it is now permissible to go hatless.

HAIR Back-combed for extra fullness. Fringes, lacquered beehive styles, wigs and hairpieces (hair built up over wire frames) are also fashionable. For the young set, a short, curly style, is pulled back off the face with head bands.

ACCESSORIES Long kid gloves are ruched over the wrist for evening; short for day with flared wrists. Large handbags and bags with chain handles are carried. Other accessories include fabric-covered or metal head bands, wrist watches and inexpensive costume jewellery.

Left: Illustration of a woman dressed in leopard-print fur on the cover of *Tatler* magazine.

Left: A model wears a Chanel suit.

Right: Drawing of long coat with faux leopard-fur collar (for the pattern see pages 136–137).

MAKE-UP Heavy eyes and paler lips are in style. Eyeliner continues to flick up at outer corners and false eyelashes are shaped and applied to far corner of eyes. Pastel lip shades and nail varnish is worn in 'frosted pink' and 'strawberry vanilla'.

DETAILS OF ILLUSTRATED PATTERNS

A straight, seven-eighths-length coat with a wide faux leopard-fur collar. The coat is bulky and loose-fitting throughout with three-quarter-length split sleeves and shaped turn-back cuffs. A wide buckle and band trim of self-fabric are set well back from the front edges, which are cut with generous overlap, fastening with four gigantic buttons. Deep pockets are set in at the side seams.

The coat is worn over a matching sheath dress with a widened scoop neckline, narrow three-quarter-length sleeves, and a centre-back vent at the hemline. The dress fits closely to the figure – shaping is achieved by double darts at front and back. The skirt tapers slightly towards the hemline.

FABRICS AND COLOURS Loosely woven, textured tweed fabric in deep brown or tan.
FOOTWEAR Soft leather, high-heeled court shoe with a draped vamp, buttoned down the centre. Sheer, tinted, nylon stockings are also worn.
HAT A faux leopard-fur, flowerpot-style hat is worn with a turn-down brim and leather bow decoration.
ACCESSORIES The soft leather handbag, with metal frame and clasp and semicircular covered handles, matches the shoes. Over-the-wrist gloves of soft kid with hand-stitching and rolled effect at flared wrists.

NOTES ON CONSTRUCTION OF GARMENTS

The collar facing of faux leopard fur is cut without seam at neckline. Make small darts below the roll-line of the coat collar to ensure a stand-away effect at the neckline. The pockets may be set in at the side seams.

MEN

PREDOMINANT FASHION FEATURES

The Italian influence on clothes continues. Knee-length overcoats are worn with a 'flared skirt', and belted. Raglan styles are popular. Knitted sports shirts are worn with a turned-down attached collar, short sleeves and tunic-style front-button fastening, for casual wear.

FABRICS Terylene suiting fabrics are worn. Checked tweeds are used for sports jackets. Trousers are made in worsted flannel, Acrilan/wool or Terylene/wool.

COLOURS Striped fawns and blue. Suits are available in light and dark shades, stone, tan, navy and grey.
UNDERGARMENTS Underwear in 'Helanca' stretch nylon is easy-care and requires no ironing. Sleeveless vests and jockey shorts are worn, as are short-sleeved vests and poplin trunks, which are front-buttoning with elasticated tops.
SHOES AND SOCKS Similar to previous fashion. Slip-on casual shoes with elasticated side-gussets are worn.
HATS AND HAIR Similar to previous fashion. Beards begin to return to popularity.
ACCESSORIES Similar to previous fashion.

DETAILS OF ILLUSTRATED PATTERN

A short, double-breasted overcoat with four-button fastening, wide lapels and upper collar of fur. The coat is loose-fitting throughout and cut without shaping. The shoulders are sloped and sleeves are plain. Angled welt pockets are set fairly high on the foreparts. The flannel trousers are cut fairly narrow in the leg and are short in length. They are self-supporting, with a straight waistband and side-seam pockets.

FABRICS AND COLOURS Shetland wool dogtooth check top fabric in black and white, lined with tartan.
FOOTWEAR Slim-fitting lightweight laced shoes with squared-off toes and stitched upper. Short wool and nylon socks may be plain or fancy.
HATS Felt trilby hat with a narrower brim, to balance the slimmer line in men's fashions.
ACCESSORIES Long, tightly furled umbrella. Jewellery includes cuff links and a signet ring.

NOTES ON CONSTRUCTION OF GARMENT

Cut the upper collar of fur 6mm ($^1\!/_4$in) larger all round than the coat collar to allow for extra thickness of fabric. Topstitch the front and lapel edges 1cm ($^3\!/_8$in) from the outside edge. Use the trouser pattern from 1958.

Right: Drawing of double-breasted overcoat (for the pattern see page 137).

WOMAN'S COAT
BACK
cut 1 on fold

CB fold

WOMAN'S COAT
FRONT
cut 2

DRESS
FRONT
cut 1 on fold

CF fold

CB

DRESS
BACK
cut 2

vent

young ideas, young and daring fashions, new music and ways of life and unprecedented exposure of the legs. Continuing this comparison, the 1960s really only 'swung' towards the middle of the decade, in the same way that the characteristics most remembered of the 1920s took full effect in the central years.

With her slim, youthful figure and undeveloped torso, the young lady of the 1920s led the way in fashion. Fashion was dominated by the younger set, and this was again the case in the 1960s, but now the 'Bright Young Things' who led the revolution were no longer made up of the middle and upper classes; the more cosmopolitan 'teenager' was drawn from a far wider section of the population. From the baby boom after World War II the 1960s youth evolved, sentencing to death the old values. A feeling of battle rose to the surface, of tradition versus change, and of age versus youth – a reaction, perhaps, to the intense boredom of the early 1950s, a time still tainted with the austerity and seriousness of war. In addition, fresh influences created an atmosphere in which the youth prospered, and enjoyed a measure of social and economic emancipation. Between 1956 and 1966 the income of the average 16-year-old doubled, and without the financial pressures of adult life the prosperous youngster was able to buy records and magazines and take a new interest in fashion. Parents, too, benefited from the economic boom, as car sales doubled and an ever-increasing number of families could afford what had previously been luxuries such as televisions, fridges and washing machines.

Above: Twiggy epitomized the look and figure of the 1960s.

The profiteers of the 'youth explosion' were those best prepared to meet the demands of the new generation. Fashion was the first to exploit the new teenage market, and in doing so established the fashion industry firmly for youth. Mary Quant is the designer who stands out with most conviction at this time, fashion led by the young for the young. 'I always wanted young people to have a fashion of their own, absolutely 20th century fashion.' She met this challenge by opening her own dress shop, 'Bazaar', in the King's Road, Chelsea, during the mid-1950s. Frustated with the fashion available commercially, she ventured into the world of designing. In line with the needs of the new society, she presented youthful designs which could be easily adapted to the commercial market; uncluttered grey flannel pinafore dresses and soft blouses met with early success and established her quickly as a major leader in fashion. Evidence of her impact is perhaps denoted by her appearance in 'Long-Life' advertisements in *Vogue* magazine early in 1961, set in her Chelsea workroom. Royal recognition followed with an OBE for her services to fashion. Notably, she arrived at Buckingham Palace in a mini-skirt.

The mini-skirt is the most distinctive trend of the decade. At the extreme of the fashion the thighs became the new erogenous zone, a revolution in that this part of the female body had to date remained covered. Again, a parallel with the 1920s is evident, since both periods evinced a desire to shock and challenge and to take the skirt to its extreme.

The shortening of the skirt led inevitably to the replacement of the stocking by tights, which were worn universally from 1965. These might be thick and ribbed in winter or with lacy patterns or even Lurex for the evening.

Courrèges is another outstanding 1960s designer, remembered chiefly for his space-age fashions from 1964. Incorporating new and exciting materials, plastics, PVC and metallic vinyls, they demonstrated a worldly interest in the space programme and scientific advance. The progress of the first moon landing in 1969 was watched on the television all over the world. The hovercraft early in the decade, Concorde and computers, heralded the 1960s as the birth of the technological age.

Fashion became fun, and those unprepared to accept new fashion values fell quickly by the wayside. After the war the age of the fashionable woman had remained somewhere around 35, and many could not readjust fast enough to the younger market. Fashions of the 1960s were exclusively for the young, and unsuited to the mature figure. This is not to say that this section of the market was without designers, but their style of clothes became aloof from the frenzy and constant change of the fashion industry. The Chanel suit provided the most adaptable fashion, and with its capacity for successful imitation, kept its place firmly for at least the first half of the decade. Fashion for the young no longer echoed the lines of their parents; conversely, shorter skirts, new fabrics and simpler lines affected all women's wear in a less extreme form. Most women by the mid-1960s accepted a skirt well above the knee without protest.

The desired figure, idealized by models Twiggy and Jean Shrimpton, epitomized the half-starving 'little girl lost' look, a look which demands further comparison with the 1920s, when the schoolboy figure became the foundation of the mode. The bust and waist were of little importance; 'A' line dresses obliterated the waist, and jeans and chain belts sat at hip-level. The 1920s also witnessed the birth of unisex fashion, beginning with the knitted jumper. By 1966 it was often difficult to distinguish between the sexes from the back view; T-shirts, hipster jeans and wide belts with large buckles were worn interchangeably by men and women. The unisex feature was heightened by relaxing the law of fastening, demanded by mass-production, with jeans and skirts for women closing to the right. Skinny-rib jumpers with polo or V-necks also changed hands frequently and suited the skinny boyish male.

Exciting fashion was no longer exclusively the right of women, a trend already established in the 1950s. Men took an active interest in and experimented freely with new fabrics and styles alongside their partners. Trousers were narrow at the turn of the decade and flares and hipsters created an alternative silhouette by the mid-1960s. Men's clothes generally were slimmer-fitting by this time, with darts in shirts, shaped trouser legs and waisted jackets. Neckties widened and the kipper shape evolved, often brightly coloured, patterned or in knitted fabrics, matching or even clashing with the shirt. The car, too, exerted its own influence on fashion; overcoats became shorter, clothes generally lighter and the hatless mode triumphed. Among the young, short casual battle-dress-style jackets with chunky zips often incorporated the new fabrics: synthetic suedes and leathers, PVC and wet-look; man-made furs decorated collars, cuffs and linings, often brightly coloured for women's wear. With a more relaxed approach in evidence, a decline in the use of evening wear was inevitable. At the same time, however, evening clothes for men became more flamboyant, with coloured silk shirts with frills and jabots. Although it was worn only by the most extrovert, the influence of such clothing was felt, and many adopted turtle and polo-neck shirts as well as elaborate lace-front bands for dinner jackets. Morning

Below: Model Helga Berk photographed in a short mini dress.

suits remained the correct attire for weddings, most popularly in grey, although some youngsters challenged this convention. At his wedding in 1964 Mick Jagger wore a sweater and corduroy trousers. Patent-leather shoes were still correct for formal wear, but plain leather was worn, and by 1964 slip-ons with elastic side gussets became popular. The Chelsea boot, likewise, with Cuban heels and fine sole, was universally worn with slim-fitting trousers. 'Corfam', a new plastic, which claimed to breathe like leather, led to inexpensive footwear. For women knee-high boots, or synthetic leather pull-on socks, which created the impression of boots when worn with matching shoes, created the total look with the mini skirt.

The extreme of one male fashion was worn by the modernists or 'mods', a culture which exhibited extreme clothes-consciousness. Their major influence came from the cut of Italian suits; always in search of the totally new, they wore clothes not seen before, scouring specialist sports shops for cycling shirts or golf shirts and trousers, and parka anoraks. Some mods wore make-up and were characterized by their regular use of the latest cheap form of transport for youngsters – the scooter.

The major source of mod fashions was Carnaby Street, the hub of the teenage world, full of the new boutique-style shops. John Stevens acquired his first shop in 1963 at the age of twenty, and caught the imagination of the mods with hipsters and high collars. Boutiques sold the latest fashions at reasonable prices, and quickly extended from London to the provinces. The necessary high turnover demanded efficient mass-production, and ready-to-wear steadily replaced couture. Britain emerged as a fashion leader, as *Vogue* tells us in 1965: 'In New York it's the London Look, in Paris it's *Le Style Anglais*', 'Everyone wants to copy the way we look'. Mary Quant responded to the demands of her customers by setting up the Ginger Group in 1963. She extended her influence to America in a whistle-stop tour in 1965, where models in mini-skirts moved rhythmically to popular music, and in 1966 began to manufacture make-up to

Above: Girl in a 1960s sports car, wearing boldly patterned prints.

complete the total look. Another immediate success commercially was the Biba chain of stores from 1964, providing incredibly inexpensive fashion in dark, absolutely 1960s-style surroundings.

Fashion became a commodity available to the masses, a distant cry from its exclusive nature at the turn of the century. Commercialization was further advanced by the simultaneous growth of supporting industry, particularly the media and improved communications. Teenage magazines, such as *Honey* from 1966, captured the latest ideas with glossy photographs in exotic surroundings. They provided the essential link with the 'it' world; the fashions were up to the minute and available.

The concept of the boutique spread to other areas. Terence Conran, the 'Mary Quant of the furnishing world', opened Habitat in the Fulham Road, London, in May 1964, reconciling fashion and furnishings. He brought new products to the high street, fresh and fit for the purpose for which they were designed.

Britain led the way in the field of popular music as in fashion, the two interacting, and both entirely to do with being young. The pop scene was filled with British talent, and The Beatles as the centre of popular culture became idols, with the young keen to copy the style of their cheeky and confident Liverpool heroes. Sixty million singles were sold to the affluent teenager in 1963, although the pop-record boom had begun in the 1950s with stars such as Elvis Presley and Little Richard (notably American at this stage). The Beatles led the way with collarless jackets and shirts, Chelsea boots and above all the Beatle cut, with hair brushed forward to create a fringe. Men wore their hair generally longer in the 1960s.

Out of popular culture came 'pop art' and 'op art', although these never influenced the masses to the same extent as records and fashion. However, bright colours and new ideas epitomized the mood of the 1960s and influenced fashion to a degree, with 'op art' fabrics and psychedelic colours. 'Style' was all important, and it became cool for pop stars to appreciate art, encouraging a massive increase in Design and Art Schools, aided by the fact that grants were easy to come by. The art world was creative and forward-looking.

Many were quick to question the morality and behaviour of the teenagers with more leisure time and money, who constantly challenged and seemed keen to destroy the world their parents had fought for. Compulsory National Service was abolished in 1962, adding, in some people's eyes, to the lack of discipline among the young. The attack was launched largely through fashion, as it had been during the 1920s, and the scantiness of women's dress was cited as evidence of lack of morality. Nudity appeared to be the keynote, page three of the Sun was launched, and 1964 saw the first topless dress. A short-lived summer fashion with few followers, it was however the forerunner of the bare midriff, and of mesh and crochet dresses. Beneath these flesh-coloured body-stockings and tights heightened the impression of nudity.

The Pill hit the headlines in the 1960s, enabling women to take responsibility for their own fertility. 'Keep taking the tablets' became a national catchphrase, and married and unmarried women alike obtained supplies from the Family Planning Association, who were responsible for testing the new drug. The FPA had, in fact, been formed before the war, but had struggled to become reputable, since even as late as the mid-1950s the subject of contraceptives was taboo and they were difficult to obtain. The role of women was changing, too; although still tied to the home many women, in particular a growing number of married women, went out to work. The increasing sophistication of labour-saving devices, and the availability of fast convenience foods and easy-care man-made fibres – Orion, Courtelle, Terylene – took the drudgery out of housework and made this possible. However, women were still expected to perform two jobs equally well, and the conflict of the two roles led to discontent. The permissive society put perhaps even greater pressure on women, who were portrayed and exploited as sex symbols. Men dominated in industry and politics, and even where they did the same job, men's wages were higher. The women's liberation movement, from 1968 onwards, demanded equal pay and equal rights. The seeds of the movement were sown in the 1960s, although its influence is more directly associated with the seventies. It is interesting that both the 1920s and the 1960s were periods of female emancipation.

A new class had arisen without the traditional values. The aristocracy of fashion gave way to the 'popocracy', as a new young class emerged. There seemed to be a tremendous desire to wipe out the old world. 'Modern' and 'big' were beautiful words; reconstruction of bombed-out cities continued with high-rise blocks, clean lines and strong geometric shapes. 1960s planning was conceived in terms of the car, now a mass-produced commodity, and universal mobility. Large, centralized shopping precincts threatened the corner shops, and slum areas were demolished on a massive scale, breaking up the traditional patterns of the neighbourhood and community life. This trend was heightened by the insular effects of the television on family life. Belief in a scientific approach to planning lacked the personal touch, and redevelopment schemes were given further incentive through strong government promotion and subsidy. The 1960s saw the wholesale destruction of buildings, homes, shops and churches and, even more disheartening, the prefabrication systems of building were to prove unsuccessful, causing even greater housing and social problems in later years.

Motorways opened up the country, the M1, from 1959, providing a 'new deal for drivers' – the longest stretch of new road built in Britain since the Romans, 'in keeping with the bold, exciting and scientific age in which we live'. By the early seventies a fairly comprehensive motorway system had been completed across the country, with the M1 and M6 link in 1972. However, the grand plan was delayed, for the money ran out.

'Is it too good to be true, is it too good to last?' Macmillan had asked in 1959. Idealism evaporated at an alarming speed, and with increased competition from abroad Britain failed to capitalize on technological improvement and declined as a world power. Wage freezes and cuts in public spending in 1966, and devaluation of the pound in 1967, set inflation on its upward course. With the economy floundering the people showed less confidence and began to look for the 'alternative' society. The party was over, the year 1968 rife with revolution and rebellion – demonstrations against American involvement in Vietnam, and against nuclear war; violent student riots; revolution versus law, order and establishment. From America came the hippy cult, and with it hard drugs, heroin, LSD and the psychedelic flower-power fantasy world. Long hair and ethnic clothes were evidence of society's drop-outs, and fashion followed the new influence. Clothes became softer and more romantic, and colours faded. Make-up, which had for so long darkened the eyes and paled the lips, looked more natural. Hair was worn loose, plaited or in curly Afro cut, and embroidered afghan coats and long kaftans came on the scene. In 1968, the micro-skirt, the extreme of the mini, made a brief appearance, and in the same year the long, straight midi-skirt. By 1969 the battle of mini-midi-maxi was in full force; the lady with the mini-skirt, high boots and maxi-coat a common sight. The maxi-coat was the longest length seen since 1914, a fashionable expression of the demand for change.

The 1960s, then, closed with an air of discontent. It had been almost a freak era of prosperity and growth, an era in which everything had seemed possible. Britain was fashionable and confident, everyone had swung to British records, and British clothes and goods were topping the charts worldwide. The atmosphere of the

1960

WOMEN

PREDOMINANT FASHION FEATURES

The style of the late 1950s continues relatively unchanged, with skirts becoming shorter, especially for younger fashions. Skirt hems, whether full or slim, finish at the knee. Shirtwaister dresses with full skirts are popular.

Chanel's collarless suits in loosely woven tweeds and with contrast braiding are much copied by ready-to-wear manufacturers. The Italian influence continues with casual tapered trousers, bold prints for summer, and sweaters.

Twin sets, comprising a short-sleeved jumper and matching cardigan, are an essential item of women's wardrobes. Knitted suits and soft polo necks are also worn.

There is increasing interest in young fashions. Mary Quant's slim pinafore dresses of grey flannel are the look of the year, worn with long-sleeved soft blouses or polo-neck sweaters.

FABRICS 'Grey flannel – the newest, smartest basic for day' (*Vogue*, 1959). Other fabrics include black- or grey-and-white tweeds, checks, stripes and herringbones. Loose tweeds are worn as are linen and bold cotton prints for summer. Tricel, textured nylon, Bri-Nylon, Orion, Courtelle and Terylene fibres are extensively used. In 1961, ICI introduces 'Crimplene' and in 1962 Courtaulds' first Elastane (highly stretchable fibre) and Spanzelle went into production.

COLOURS Grey, black and white, in any combination, is always fashionable. Brighter colours are worn for summer and teenage dresses favour turquoise, French navy, red and yellow. Checks and stripes combining many colours are also worn, as are chunky sweaters in bright colours – lilac, yellow, gold and red, sometimes combined with metallic Lurex thread.

DECORATION Scarf necks on dresses, suits and coats are worn. Bows remain popular as are striped and checked fabrics in bold, bright colours.

UNDERGARMENTS Similar to late 1950s. Slim-fitting girdles are worn, with diagonal control panels for slim hips and tummy. Bras with pre-formed cups are worn for shape and uplift, and are circular-stitched and wired.

SHOES Remaining slim and pointed or with squared-off toes. High, narrow stiletto heels are worn, as are low, tapered heels for the young.

STOCKINGS Matt-finish stretch nylon stockings, seamless. Dark plaid knit stockings are worn for winter.

HATS Larger hats with tall crowns and wide brims; halo hats.

HAIR Hair remains full, back-combed and waved, with a long wispy fringe brushed over the forehead, or a half-fringe from the side-parting. 'A new shorter look is coming in for day' (*Harper's Bazaar*, May 1960). Cut short and close at the nape of the neck, with the side pieces long and curled forward; a smooth, sleek fringe comes halfway across forehead. The style retains width and fullness, curled outwards or under at the ends. Hair is worn high for evening with false hairpieces swirled on top of the crown. Wigs and hairpieces add fullness and height.

ACCESSORIES Accessories include short gloves for day, handbags with chain handles and watches with face inset in bracelet strap. Gloves and hats lose importance for young fashion.

MAKE-UP Eye make-up becomes darker as lips pale. Eyeliner is swept upwards at the outer corner, beyond the natural eyeline. Eyebrows are heavily emphasized, straighter, not arched.

DETAILS OF ILLUSTRATED PATTERN

A double-breasted coat-dress with a wide neckline, notched collar and detachable over-collar. The dress fastens with six large buttons and wide belt of self-fabric, the back bodice gathered into the waistline seam. The straight skirt is shaped to the waistline by means of two small pleats at either side of the front opening and darts at the back. The two-gore skirt back has a low pleat at the centre. The dress has plain, short, set-in sleeves.

FABRIC AND COLOURS Grey flannel with a white piqué collar.

FOOTWEAR Slim-fitting pointed leather court shoe with a lower shaped heel, worn with seamless stretch nylon stockings.

ACCESSORIES Short cotton gloves and a large leather handbag with metal frame and clasp.

Left: Beehive hairstyle.

Right: Drawing of coat-dress (for the pattern see page 144).

NOTES ON CONSTRUCTION OF GARMENT

Point S on collar patterns indicates the position of the shoulder seam. Make up a detachable collar and bind the raw neck edges. Hand stitch it into position when the dress is complete.

MEN

PREDOMINANT FASHION FEATURES

Single-breasted jackets and two-piece suits continue in popularity. Jackets fasten higher with three to four buttons instead of the usual one or two, are more fitted, are waisted and are longer. The trousers remain short and narrow, with or without turn-ups.

Overcoats begin to be replaced by shorter car coats, which finish above the knee, and anoraks. Longer overcoats are worn with business suits. Many have detachable, zipped-in warm lining. Unlined casual jackets with zip-up fronts are also worn.

Shirts are mostly coat-style – button-through, with attached pointed collars. Single cuffs and button fastenings are more usual than double cuffs. Chunky and lightweight sweaters are also worn.

Dinner jackets feature narrow shawl collars of ribbed silk. Wide silk cummerbunds are worn with plain white shirts and black tie.

FABRICS Lighter-weight suiting fabrics, wool combined with Terylene and nylon are all worn. Less bulky fabrics are used generally for overcoats, trousers and jackets, and checked tweed for sports jackets.

COLOURS Striped fawns and blues are popular and suits are available in light and dark shades – stone, tan, navy and grey.

UNDERGARMENTS Short-sleeved and sleeveless vests are worn with jockey shorts or trunks with elasticated tops.

SHOES Slim Italian shoes continue. Slip-on shoes or boots with higher heels and rounded toes are also worn. Patent leather is the correct evening wear.

HATS The importance of the hat is diminishing. Trilby-style hats with tapered crowns and narrower brims are worn in tweeds and corduroy, along with bowler hat for business wear.

HAIR Remaining short with more emphasis on style.

ACCESSORIES Driving gloves in perforated leather, or leather palms with fabric or string uppers, buttoning or elasticated at wrist. Narrow ties, knitted with squared ends, stripes or subtle patterns. Neatly furled umbrella with business suit.

DETAILS OF ILLUSTRATED PATTERNS

This two-piece lounge suit remains slim-fitting, with high-rolling narrow lapels and three-button fastening. Shoulders are more sloped and there is evidence of less ease across the chest and back. The foreparts are well rounded at the lower edges, with flap pockets at hip-level and a welt pocket on left breast. Narrow, two-piece sleeves finish with a slit cuff and three-button fastening to harmonize with fronts. The trousers are cut on the skimpy side, with narrow leg and short in length.

The suit is worn with a light-coloured shirt and narrow knitted tie with squared ends.

FABRICS AND COLOURS Lightweight suiting fabric of Terylene and wool in grey, fawn or brown.

FOOTWEAR Slim-fitting slip-on casual shoes with a low heel, elasticated side gussets and rounded toes.

NOTES ON CONSTRUCTION OF GARMENTS

Trace off the trouser waistband from A to B for right side, and A to C for left side, to allow for the button extension. Add a 1cm (³⁄₈in) seam allowance to all edges of the waistband. Add a vent to the centre back 24cm (9½in) long and 4cm (1½in) wide.

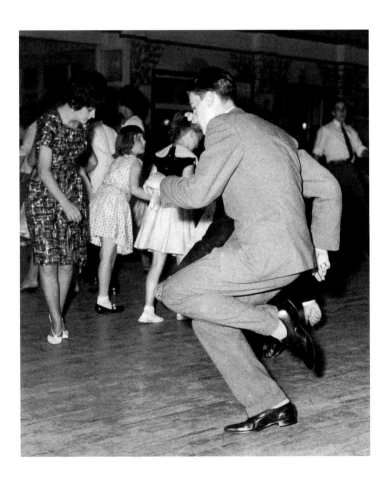

Left: Young man in a suit twists on the dancefloor.

Right: Drawing of two-piece lounge suit (for the pattern see page 145).

DRESS
BODICE BACK
cut 2

CB

S

DRESS
BODICE FRONT
cut 2

CF

DRESS
SLEEVE
cut 2

DRESS
COLLAR

CB fold

S

DRESS
SKIRT BACK
cut 2

CB

pleat

pleats

CF

DRESS
SKIRT FRONT
cut 2

DRESS
DETATCHABLE COLLAR
cut 2 on fold

CB fold

S

Bind this edge

CB

JACKET
BACK
cut 2

JACKET
FRONT
cut 2

TROUSERS
······ BACK cut 2
—— FRONT cut 2

JACKET
FRONT SLEEVE
cut 2

A   B   C

CB   TROUSERS WAISTBAND cut 4   CF

JACKET
BACK SLEEVE
cut 2

JACKET
COLLAR cut 2 on fold

CB fold

WOMEN

PREDOMINANT FASHION FEATURES

Fashion is dominated by the young – the mini evolves as skirts rise steadily, reaching mid-thigh. Simple, uncluttered lines dominate, devoid of pleats, slits and intricate seaming. Sleeves are set in, plain or gathered at sleevehead and flared out to the wrist. Cut-out sleeveless styles are worn for summer. Collars are pointed or rounded, all large and unstarched, often contrasting with the outfit. See-through dresses are made of crochet net or with open midriff. White on dark colours are predominant.

Trouser suits are worn with tailored or casual jackets. Tabards – sleeveless, hip-length tops tied at the sides – are worn with polo-neck jumpers and trousers.

Chunky, zip-fastening casual jackets feature synthetic fur trimming or lining. The coats just cover the skirt or finish above it, and feature wide floppy collars. 'Unisex' fashions include denim jeans, close-fitting trousers with no turn-ups made with zip fly front, hipsters, safari jackets (shirt-style with patch pockets), skinny-rib sweaters and polo-necks.

Mini-dresses or trouser-suits are dressed up for evening in metallic Lurex fabrics or satins. Long kaftans – loose-fitting unbelted robes in bright colours – are the first ethnic fashions.

FABRICS Jersey, crêpe, crocheted or open-work fabrics, PVC, synthetic suede and leather fabrics, vinyl, silver vinyl and plastics are all used. Fun-fur fabrics, such as synthetic nylon, Dynel, or Acrilan, are dyed in bright colours.

COLOURS Grey and black are always fashionable. White, shades of mauve, from lilac to deep purple, and bright colours, such as red, orange and purple, are combined with black. Paisley prints, op art fabrics and bold geometric prints are used. Real and fake fur trimming is worn.

UNDERWEAR Underwear becomes briefer with fashion trends. The short, tailored bra-slip combines a bra and petticoat. Flesh-coloured body stockings imply nudity under open-work dresses.

SHOES Zip-fastening knee-high boots are worn. Patent leather and synthetic materials are common.

TIGHTS Worn universally, as the shorter skirts make stockings impractical. Lace, fishnet and patterned tights are all worn, with Lurex for the evening and colourful ribbed tights for warmth in winter. Cream with dark colours predominates.

HATS Hats are worn less. Helmet styles and peaked Beatle caps are young unisex fashions.

HAIR Sleeker, losing the fullness and height of the early 1960s. Long hair is popular, with a side or centre parting and fringe. Some hair is cut in a very short, boyish style, cropped close to the head, heightening effect of unisex fashions.

ACCESSORIES There is an increasing use of synthetic materials for gloves, bags and jewellery. Other accessories include PVC gloves (keyhole types), large drop earrings of coloured plastic, coloured plastic bangles and chain belts. Wider belts are worn with hipster trousers.

MAKE-UP Lipsticks continue to pale down as eyes become heavier, achieved with heavy eyeliner, lash-building mascara and false eyelashes shaped and applied to the outer corners of eyes.

DETAILS OF ILLUSTRATED PATTERN

A bold, geometric, 'A' line mini-dress, with long sleeves of small chequerboard pattern complementing the large checked fabric at the lower edge of the dress. The length is approximately 15cm (6in) above the knee. The uncluttered, simple line of the dress uses contrast to create impact. The dress is relatively long in comparison with the very short skirts worn during this period. The mini skirt rapidly became briefer and briefer.

FABRIC AND COLOURS Crisp printed cotton or rayon crêpe in bold black and white.

FOOTWEAR Black patent T-bar shoes with low square heel and rounded toes, with a white contrast on toe cap and edges. The shoes are low-heeled and clumpy in appearance. Cream ribbed tights are also worn.

ACCESSORIES A white patent or plastic shoulder bag with optional handles and clasp opening. Drop earrings of black and white plastic discs and beads completes the outfit.

NOTES ON CONSTRUCTION OF GARMENT

Alter dress to length of mini required. Separate dress sections A, B and C at the back and front of dress – cut out each in a different fabric. When using a check fabric, the hemline is cut straight and not shaped, as on the pattern. For sleeve cuff, cut a strip of fabric 21.5 x 5cm (8½ x 2in), twice finished width. Add a seam allowance to all edges.

Left: Girl in shirt-style dress with a boy in a striped blazer and drainpipe trousers.

Right: Drawing of A-line mini dress (for the pattern see page 148).

MEN

PREDOMINANT FASHION FEATURES

Age groups dress differently. 'The young class produces most of the experiment, most of the good ideas, almost all the bad ideas, and is the basic pressure for change in appearance' (*Tailor and Cutter*).

Lounge suits feature natural shoulders, minimum padding, slim lapels rounded at notches, slanted flapped pockets and longer vents. When three-button, the jacket is buttoned high above the waist. Four-button jackets become increasingly popular, with high, slim lapels, long side vents and the centre two buttons only fastened. Double-breasted jackets button high, with little overlap. In multi-button styles the breast pocket is often omitted. Waistcoats remain in the minority. The plain polo-neck sweater is the most popular casual accessory.

Trousers add to the long line. They are straight and slim-fitting, following the shape of the leg, with low rise and vertical pockets. Few turn-ups appear. Hipster trousers sit well below the waist, flaring from the knees.

Overcoats continue to shorten to well above the knee – almost jacket length. Longer, narrow and close-fitting styles are worn by city gentlemen. Raglan styles are also popular as are zipped anorak styles. Collarless suits and jackets, popularized by the Beatles, are slim-fitting and high-fastening.

Young fashion cults, such as the mods, feature Italian hairstyles and jackets, suede chukka boots with crepe soles and narrow trousers. Rockers trends feature long hair, leather jackets, zip-up boots and drainpipe trousers.

FABRICS Pin- and chalk-stripes, hopsack and twill continue to lead in formal suits. For more casual suits, herringbone tweed and coloured overchecks on dark backgrounds are worn. Floral and op-art fabric prints are used for shirts.

COLOURS Suit colours remain conservative, in blues, greys and browns.

UNDERGARMENTS Vests are often dispensed with under tighter-fitting shirts. Jockey shorts are worn.

SHOES A long, flat silhouette is achieved, with buckles and brass decorations and leather and crepe soles. Slip-ons remain popular. High boots with elasticated sides, higher heels and rounded toes are worn. Chelsea boots are popularized by the Beatles. Squared toes and higher heels are worn with flared trousers. Mods wear flat, broad, square toes. Man-made materials are used for footwear.

SOCKS As previous fashion.

HATS Still not showing any signs of returning to popularity. Peaked Beatle caps are popular for the young.

HAIR Short and brushed back, with no parting. Longer hair is popular among the young. The Beatle cut is brushed forward into a fringe.

ACCESSORIES Ties tend to be either very plain, with either no pattern or a minimum of patterning on self-coloured silks, or very bold indeed. Fancy-knit woollen ties are worn in sober colours. For the more flamboyant, the wide kipper-shape tie is 12–15cm (5–6in) wide. Shirts and ties are made of matching fabrics. Belts, when worn, are wide, with large buckles. Cuff links are worn with evening wear.

DETAILS OF ILLUSTRATED PATTERNS

A young casual fashion consisting of hipster trousers, a black polo-neck sweater and a waistcoat. The waistcoat has contrast binding on the outside and armhole edges. It can also be used at the upper edge of the patch pocket if using (not supplied on pattern). It fastens with four gilt buttons at centre front.

The hipster trousers fit just over the hips and are close-fitting throughout, with cross pockets more common than those set in the side seams. It is also considered fashionable to tuck the trouser bottoms into the top of the calf-length boots.

FABRICS Cotton gabardine or cotton/polyester mixture fabric is used for the hipsters with loosely woven wool/Terylene used elsewhere.

FOOTWEAR Calf-length Chelsea boots with elasticated side gussets, pull-on side tabs and squared toes and heels.

ACCESSORIES A wide leather belt is worn at the trouser waistband. Signet rings and identity bracelets are also popular.

NOTES ON CONSTRUCTION OF GARMENTS

Bind the outside and armhole edges of the waistcoat as shown by the darker lines on the pattern. Trace off the trouser waistband from A to B for the right side and A to C for the left side to allow for a button extension. Add a 1cm (⅜in) seam allowance to all edges of waistband. Hipster trousers should fit closely over the seat and legs; adjust as necessary. Construct with cross pockets from lowered waistline as indicated on the pattern. The shirt pattern is provided as an alternative to the polo-neck illustrated. It is close-fitting, shaped into the waistline at the back and has a pointed, button-down collar.

Right: Drawing of hipster trousers worn with a polo neck and waistcoat (for the pattern see pages 148–149).

CB fold

DRESS
BACK
cut 1 on fold

A

B

C

CF fold

DRESS
FRONT
cut 1 on fold

A

B

C

DRESS
SLEEVE
cut 2

S

opening

CB fold

MAN'S SHIRT
COLLAR STAND
cut 2 on fold

• D

CB fold

MAN'S SHIRT
COLLAR
cut 2 on fold

D

MAN'S SHIRT
BACK
cut 2 on fold

CB

MAN'S SHIRT
FRONT
cut 2

CF

fold line

CB fold

MAN'S SHIRT
YOKE
cut 2

MAN'S SHIRT
CUFF
cut 4

WAISTCOAT
BACK
cut 1 on fold

CB fold

WAISTCOAT
FRONT
cut 2

TROUSERS
BACK
cut 2

SHIRT
SLEEVE
cut 2

S

opening

TROUSERS WAISTBAND cut 4

CB

A

B
C

TROUSERS
FRONT
cut 2

pocket line

1968

WOMEN

PREDOMINANT FASHION FEATURES

The mini reaches its extreme – the micro or 'pelmet' skirt, just covering the upper thigh. The year also witnesses the first signs of change towards a more feminine ideal. Mini-dresses become flounced and frilled. Bias-cut skirts give more flare. Simple, uncluttered jersey dresses are worn with long rounded or pointed collars, in white to contrast. Tunic dresses are worn with or without trousers. Mini-suits develop – short waist-length, double-breasted jackets, paired with short, pleated or plain skirts. Trouser suits and co-ordinated clothes develop – matching trousers, jackets, skirts worn with blouses and sweaters – making possible mix-and-match fashions.

Unisex fashions continue with hipster trousers, jeans, T-shirts, casual zip-fastening jackets and anoraks.

For evening, diverse styles are all equally fashionable, from dressed-up mini-dresses, velvet trouser suits and mini-skirts worn with more ornate blouses featuring frills and jabots to full-length, loose-fitting kaftans.

The flower power and hippy movement gives rise to psychedelic, paisley and boldly printed fabrics. Much use is made of leather and brocade for head bands and belts. Long beads, leather fringing, bells and tinsel contribute to an overall untidy and relaxed 'thrown-together' look. Ethnic fashions include afghan coats (sheepskin with silk and gold embroidery) and kaftans.

FABRICS Softer fabrics include crêpe, jersey, plain and textured velvets, synthetic suedes and leather and synthetic furs. Disposable paper is used for short-life garments.

COLOURS White, black and greys remain fashionable as well as softer colours, such as greys, purples and lilacs. Paisley prints, checks and tartans are used, as are bright psychedelic patterns.

DECORATION Ruffles, lace, ethnic embroidery, fur fabric trimmings, tassels, large chunky zips in bold colours and large buttons for coats and mini-suits all feature.

UNDERGARMENTS Mini-length bra-slips are worn, while softer bras give more natural bustline. Pantie-briefs are common. Stretch briefs in nylon and Spandex are worn over tights to prevent them slipping down – they are available in bright colours, since they might be visible under the very brief skirt.

SHOES Knee-high and over-the-knee boots with zip or front-lace fastening – white is a popular colour worn with the mini-skirt in vinyl and leather. Shoes are generally heavier, rounded or with square toes, and low squared heels. Wide strapped styles are worn, and chain and buckle decorations are a feature.

LEGWEAR Coloured and patterned tights are worn, with Lurex for evening, particularly cream tights with dark colours. White, patterned knee-high socks are also worn.

HATS Hats are worn less by all age groups. Head bands of leather, brocade and beads are popular among hippy groups.

HAIR Long, straight hair with a centre-parting and fringe, or an Afro – a very full, tightly curled style, frizzed outwards and following the line of the head.

ACCESSORIES Wide belts are worn with large buckles in PVC and embossed leather, sometimes with attached purse pouches. Chunky silver jewellery includes large rings and bracelets with semi-precious stones. Enamel pendants and long beads are also worn.

MAKE-UP Similar to previous fashion, with softer eye-shadows – browns, lilacs and mauves are used with more romantic fashions.

DETAILS OF ILLUSTRATED PATTERNS

A lady's edge-to-edge suit with contrast binding. It features a patent belt at the natural waistline, flap pockets at hip-level and two-piece set-in sleeves. An A-line mini-skirt is cut on the bias. The outfit is worn with a masculine shirt and kipper tie.

Far left: Girl wearing a pink shirt dress and Chelsea hat.

Left: Girl in a floral mini dress takes a photograph of Carnaby Street, London.

Right: Drawing of suit (for the pattern see page 152).

FABRICS Tartan medium-weight woollen fabric.

FOOTWEAR The white patent or plastic shoes have squared toes, low square heels and a gold chain decoration over flap. Textured cream tights are also worn.

HAT Large felt hat with a deep rounded crown and wide, shaped brim with patent band and buckle trim.

ACCESSORIES The black-and-white patent or plastic box-style handbag has a metal clasp fastening. Black patent wrist-length gloves are also worn.

NOTES ON CONSTRUCTION OF GARMENTS

Cut the skirt on the bias of fabric.

MEN

PREDOMINANT FASHION FEATURES

'The silhouette is still a slim line but it is becoming bolder and simpler with more emphasis on shape' (*Tailor and Cutter*, March). Coats have a natural shoulder line and fit closely over the chest; waist suppression is very marked and the bottoms of the coats are flared to stand away from the trouser legs.

Style detail follows this same trend towards boldness and simplicity. Lapels are broad. Pockets have deep flaps and clean lines and on some coats there is no outside breast pocket. Buttons are kept to a minimum.

Trousers are generally plain-fronted and slim-fitting, but there is a move away from the 'drainpipe' effect. From the knee down they are cut slightly wider, and there is a trend towards a return of the turn-up for town as well as country wear.

Hipster trousers and flared velvet trousers and jackets remain fashionable. The increasing fashion for unconnected trousers and jackets enables mix-and-match separates. Jerkins and tunics are worn with trousers, with or without belts, and polo-neck jumpers – unisex fashion. Casual jackets, knitted cuffs and waistband and chunky zip fastenings also feature.

Button-down, pointed collars on shirts are worn by men and women. Sports shirts are worn for casual wear.

A greater variety of clothes may be worn for evening – frilled shirts with fuller sleeves and ruffle fronts, pointed, rounded collars, and polo-necks, often worn with velvet dinner jackets. Shawl-collar dinner jackets are worn with dress shirts with a tucked or pleated front and frilled centre band, which might be separate from the shirt. Classic lounge suits and casual clothes are worn, such as jerkin outfits or trousers and shirts.

Hippy men wear brightly coloured shirts, leather jerkins, head bands and beads.

FABRICS Plain and textured velvets, stretch jersey, suede and leathers and synthetic imitations are all worn. Terylene and Crimplene fibres are used for easy-care clothes.

COLOURS Conservative colours are used for classic suits and bright floral prints for shirts. Black and white polo necks are most popular.

UNDERGARMENTS Similar to previous fashion.

FOOTWEAR Footwear includes Chelsea boots with elasticated sides, slip-on shoes with squared toes and higher heels with flared trousers. Buckle decorations are popular.

SOCKS Similar to previous fashion.

HATS The hatless mode continues. Bowler hat with curled brim is worn for business.

HAIR Long hair for the young and very long straight hair for hippies.

ACCESSORIES Scarves, cravats and wide kipper ties are popular. Shirts and ties often match, featuring flowers and bold stripes. Tightly furled long umbrellas, and white handkerchief visible in breast pocket with business suits. Other accessories include identity bracelets, wedding rings and neck chains.

DETAILS OF ILLUSTRATED PATTERNS

A close-fitting blazer jacket with moderately wide lapels and two-button fastening; large shaped patch pockets appear at hip-level with a slanted welt pocket on the left breast. Foreparts are cut away at lower edges and two-piece sleeves finish with a slit and single button.

The hipster trousers fit just over the hips and are close-fitting throughout, with cross pockets more common than those set in side seams.

The boldly striped silk shirt has a button-down pointed collar and matching tie and handkerchief.

FABRICS Wool and Terylene medium-weight flannel suiting fabric is used for the blazer; lighter weight for the trousers.

FOOTWEAR Slip-on shoes with leather vamp decoration and flap.

NOTES ON CONSTRUCTION OF GARMENTS

Trace off the trouser waistband from A to B for right front, and from A to C for left front to allow for a button extension. Add a 1cm (³⁄₈in) seam allowance to all edges of the waistband. The trousers should fit closely throughout – if necessary shape the leg seams. Adapt the shirt pattern from 1965–1966.

Right: Drawing of blazer with hipster trousers (for the pattern see page 153).

JACKET
BACK
cut 2

JACKET
SIDE FRONT
cut 2

JACKET
FRONT
cut 2

TROUSERS
BACK
cut 2

CB fold

JACKET
COLLAR
cut 2
on fold

JACKET
FRONT SLEEVE
cut 2

JACKET
BACK SLEEVE
cut 2

A

CB

TROUSERS WAISTBAND cut 4

CF

B

C

TROUSERS
FRONT
cut 2

pocket line

1969–1970

WOMEN

PREDOMINANT FASHION FEATURES

'In fashion the revolution is over. A new quiet reigns' (*Vogue*, 1969). Mini-skirts are still the predominant fashion, but lose the monopoly retained since the mid-1960s. The battle of mini/ midi/ maxi lengths begins – a full-length maxi-coat is often worn with mini-skirt and knee-high boots. Calf-length midi-skirts are slim-fitting and straight.

Coats, jackets and suits for men and women feature wide, floppy collars and revers. Trouser suits or trousers with tunic tops or jerkins remain popular. Unisex denim jeans and short-sleeved and collarless T-shirts are worn.

The layered look begins – long-sleeved shirts are worn with short-sleeved pullovers or sleeveless vests. The romantic look features blouses with jabots, frills and lace, long evening dresses and flared mini styles. The hippy style continues.

FABRICS Plain and crushed velvet is worn for day and evening. Suede and leather and synthetic imitations is used, as is the PVC 'wet-look' – crinkled vinyl for coats, jackets and accessories.

COLOURS Black, navy and grey for outdoor coats. Softer mauves, browns, greys are worn while paisley and floral prints remain popular.

DECORATION Buckles, dull metallic snap-fasteners, jabots, frills and lace.

UNDERWEAR The women's liberation movement stimulates the development of seamless bras, in Helanca stretch lace, and half- and quarter-cup bras, revealing the nipples. 'Don't let them know you wear a bra' (*Vogue*). Front-fastening styles are available. Pantie-briefs are also worn.

SHOES Thigh- or knee-length vinyl boots are worn in white and black. Full-length front lace-fastening are used for knee-high styles. Stretch vinyl leggings are worn with ordinary court shoes to give impression of boots. Shoes retain the rounded or squared toes and square heels. Buckle decoration is popular. Lace-up shoes fasten to the instep.

LEGWEAR Similar to previous fashion. Knee-socks are worn less frequently while black tights continue to be popular.

HATS When worn, hats have large, floppy brims or high square crowns and a stiffer brim. Pull-on crochet hats are also worn.

HAIR For a softer, Pre-Raphaelite look, hair is rippled by plaiting when wet and combed out, or is taken back from the face in a chignon, with curled tendrils of hair at the sides.

ACCESSORIES Accessories include vinyl and wet-look gloves, large belts and buckles, thick plastic bangles and long beads.

MAKE-UP More natural-looking than previous years. Eye make-up is available in many colours including browns and soft lilacs. Lips are less pale.

DETAILS OF ILLUSTRATED PATTERN

A full-length maxi-coat with shaped panels and four-button fastening. The pockets are set in the front panel seams at hip-level. The coat features a plain collar and two-piece set-in sleeves. It is worn with a simple, two-piece A-line mini-skirt and black polo-neck jumper.

FABRIC AND COLOURS Heavy wool flannel or similar mixture fabric is used for the coat, in black, grey or navy. Imitation suede is used for the mini-skirt in grey or navy (pattern not included).

LEGWEAR Knee-length stretch vinyl black boots with rounded toes and low squared heels are worn with black fishnet tights.

ACCESSORIES The grey or purple suede shoulder bag has outside flap pockets and zip fastening. A wide patent or plastic belt and plastic clip earrings complete the look.

NOTES ON CONSTRUCTION OF GARMENT

Leave an opening for pockets in the front seam as indicated on pattern.

Left: Girl wearing a black polo-neck mini dress and knee-high boots.

Right: Drawing of maxi-coat (for the pattern see page 156).

MEN

PREDOMINANT FASHION FEATURES

The jackets are cut higher, with flared skirts and longer lapels. Suit trousers begin to flare at the knees.

Overcoats are longer-waisted with a longer, flared skirt and large collars and lapels. Car coats become shorter.

Young unisex fashion includes denim suits and separates, hipster jeans and T-shirts. Hippy styles continue.

FABRICS Similar to previous fashion.

COLOURS Similar to previous fashion.

DECORATION Jacket collars might be faced in velvet.

UNDERGARMENTS Similar to previous fashion.

SHOES Moccasin-style shoes are worn for casual wear. Slip-on shoes have squared toes. Ankle boots featuring a buckle fastening or decoration are popular.

SOCKS Similar to previous fashion.

HATS Similar to previous fashion.

HAIR Longer hair and sideburns. Very long hair is popular among young students.

ACCESSORIES Large belts and buckles, cravats and scarves, wrist watches and cuff links with dinner jackets are all worn. Chunky jewellery such as identity bracelets, rings and neck chains are also common.

DETAILS OF ILLUSTRATED PATTERNS

This shirt-style casual jacket has a button-through strap front, top-stitching detail, patch pockets with flap, shirt-style sleeves, pointed collar with stand and box pleat at centre. The jacket back is cut with straight yoke.

The hipster trousers flare from the knees, remaining close-fitting over the seat and upper thighs.

The outfit is worn with an open-necked shirt with a button-down collar. This is a unisex style, worn by both men and women.

FABRICS Cotton gabardine, corduroy or denim for the jacket and trousers.

FOOTWEAR Casual suede laced Chelsea boot with crêpe sole.

NOTES ON CONSTRUCTION OF GARMENTS

A 1cm (⅜in) seam allowance is given on all edges, including the strap and front.

Separate the back yoke from the jacket pattern along line J–K. Add a seam allowance to both cut edges.

Separate the back sleeve pattern from the front sleeve between D–F and E–F. Add a seam allowance to cut edges. Construct placket at the sleeve opening, indicated by a small dot on the pattern.

Separate the jacket collar from the collar stand along line G–H. Add a seam allowance to cut edges.

Trace off the strap pattern from the jacket front to be applied to the left side of the jacket; the right side remains plain.

Trace off the trouser waistband from A–B for the right side and A–C for the left side to allow for a button extension. Add a 1cm (⅜in) seam allowance to all edges of the waistband.

Adapt the shirt pattern from 1965–1966.

Left: Fashion trio posing on a 1960s racing car.

Right: Drawing of jacket and hipster trousers (for the pattern see page 157).

CB

JACKET
BACK YOKE
cut 1 on fold

J   K

JACKET
BACK
cut 1 on fold

box
pleat

JACKET
FRONT
cut 2

strap

TROUSERS
.... BACK   cut 2
——— FRONT   cut 2

JACKET
CUFF
cut 4

S

F

JACKET
BACK SLEEVE
cut 2

JACKET
FRONT SLEEVE
cut 2

opening

opening

D   E

A   B   C

CB

TROUSERS   WAISTBAND   cut 4

CF

JACKET
COLLAR
cut 2 on fold

G   H

CB fold

COLLAR STAND
cut 2 on fold

CF

Glossary

ACCORDION PLEATS narrow knife pleats.

ALPACA fabric made from wool of alpaca animal – usually with black cotton warp and alpaca weft.

APPLIQUÉ fabrics applied to the garment for decoration.

ARROWHEAD triangular, hand-worked reinforcement for top of pleats.

ASCOT TIE knotted cravat secured with pin.

ASTRAKHAN skin of young Astrakan lamb, or a curled-pile fabric imitating this.

BARATHEA a soft fabric of fine worsted or worsted and silk yarns.

BATISTE a soft, fine, plain-woven fabric of flax or cotton.

BEDFORD cord fabric with prominent ribbed texture in the warp direction; worsted yarns used for suiting and woollen yarns for heavier fabrics.

BERET soft hat constructed from a circular piece of fabric gathered on to a band.

BIAS fabric cut diagonally across the warp and weft threads at an angle of 45 degrees. Bias-cut fabric has greater elasticity.

BIRETTA square-shaped hat, similar to that worn by clergy.

BOATER straw hat with flat crown and brim.

BOLERO short jacket, above waist-level.

BOUCLÉ a fabric with a rough texture produced by means of looped yarns.

BOWLER man's stiffened felt hat with bowl crown and narrow brim, curled upwards. For city or business wear.

BOX PLEATS composed of two knife pleats, the pleats facing each other with folds meeting at the back.

BRETON woman's hat with rounded crown and turned-up brim.

BRETON NET fine silk or cotton net originating in Brittany.

BROADCLOTH (COTTON) a lightweight fabric similar to poplin and suitable for shirtings.

BROADCLOTH (WOOL) a smooth cloth made in a twill weave from fine, woollen yarns, and given a dress face finish.

BROCADE a self-patterned fabric in which the pattern is developed during weaving; a heavy, silky fabric.

BUCKSKIN a soft leather made of deerskin or sheepskin.

BULKING synthetic yarns are naturally smooth and fine. Bulking is a process whereby the yarn is heat set, i.e. crimped, giving greater elasticity and softness of handle and appearance.

BULKED NYLON Crimplene.

CAMBRIC a lightweight, closely woven cloth with slight stiffening.

CAMI-BOCKERS combined camisole and *Directoire* knickers.

CAMI-KNICKERS combined petticoat and knickers.

CASHMERE fabric made with hair of the cashmere goat.

CAVALRY TWILL a firm, heavyweight fabric with steep, double twill lines, and sunken lines between. Originally applied to fabrics for making riding breeches for cavalry.

CELANESE lightweight silky fabric of artificial silk used for lingerie.

CHESTERFIELD gentleman's fitted overcoat.

CHIFFON light, sheer open-weave fabric.

CHIGNON fold or roll of hair worn at the back or nape of the neck.

CLOCHE a lady's close-fitting hat, bell-shaped, worn well down.

CORDUROY a ribbed pile fabric, the ribs formed in the warp direction.

COURT SHOE slip-on dress shoe.

COWL NECKLINE draped neckline where fabric falls in folds.

CRÊPE a plain-weave fabric with uneven, crinkled surface texture, made from highly twisted yarns.

CRÊPE DE CHINE a lightweight, plain-weave crêpe fabric.

CRIMPLENE bulked polyester jersey fabric with a patterned surface.

CUBAN HEEL a high, straight heel without curves.

CUMMERBUND a waist belt or sash.

DÉCOLLETAGE low-cut neckline.

DENIM a hardwearing, twill-weave fabric made from dyed cotton yarn.

DIAMANTÉ a sparkling decoration resembling diamonds.

DIMITY a fabric, usually of cotton, that is checked or striped by weaving two or more threads as one.

DIRNDL full skirt, gathered at the waist.

DONEGAL coarse woollen suiting fabric, characterized by brightly coloured flecks.

DOUBLE-BREASTED overlapping closure with double row of buttons.

DRILL a twill fabric, similar to denim, but usually dyed after weaving.

DUFFLE (DUFFEL) a heavy, low-grade fabric, brushed on both sides, made from woollen yarns for short coats known as duffle coats.

EMPIRE LINE high-waisted dress, as worn during the first French Empire.

EPAULETTE shoulder strap for decoration.

FACECLOTH cloth with finish given to one side of fabric only, e.g. in wool, façonne French word for figured, used to describe self-patterned fabrics.

FAILLE a fine, soft fabric, ribbed in the weft direction – see taffeta.

FAIR ISLE geometric designs used in knitwear, named from a Shetland island.

FLANNEL an all-wool fabric of plain or twill weave with soft handle. It may be slightly milled or raised.

FOREPART front parts of a garment.

FOULARD lightweight silk fabric, often printed.

FOUR-IN-HAND man's long tie, tied with a flat slip knot at neck.

GABARDINE (GABERDINE) a firmly woven twill fabric, used for outer wear.

GAITERS covering for ankles, fitting over shoe tops and secured with strap under the foot.

GAUNTLET gloves with wide extensions, covering the wrists.

GEORGETTE a fine, lightweight, open-mesh fabric, made from crêpe yarns.

GIGOT leg-of-mutton sleeve, tight at the cuff and full above.

GINGHAM a cotton fabric, woven from coloured yarns into stripes or checks.

GODET a triangular piece of fabric inserted in a skirt to make a flare.

GORE skirt panel, e.g. a four-gore skirt is a skirt with four panels.

GROSGRAIN a heavy ribbed silk used especially for ribbons and hat bands.

GROWN-ON cut in one with the garment, e.g. grown-on collar.

HAREM SKIRT divided skirt.

HERRINGBONE a twill-weave fabric in which the twill is reversed to produce stripes resembling herringbones.

HOBBLE SKIRT pre-World War I skirt which narrows towards the ankles, restricting the movements of the wearer to a hobble.

HOMBURG man's hat, of felt, with narrow brim and dented crown.

HOPSACK plain-weave fabric in which two or more warp or weft threads are used as one.

INSERTION LACE lace having two straight edges, used for inserting between the edges of two pieces of material.

INVERTED PLEATS two knife pleats facing each other, the folds of the fabric meeting at the front – the reverse of box pleats.

JABOT frill of lace at front of shirt or blouse.

JAP SILK (JAPPE) a fine, plain-weave silk fabric.

JERKIN a sleeveless jacket, usually collarless.

JERSEY a term applied to all knitted fabrics.

JETTED pockets piped or bound with self fabric.

KAFTAN (CAFTAN) a long-sleeved oriental garment, full-length.

KIMONO SLEEVE sleeve cut in one with the bodice.

KNICKERBOCKERS loose breeches gathered in at the knee.

KNIFE PLEAT single fold of fabric, sharply creased.

LAMÉ a general term for fabrics interwoven with metallic threads.

LASTEX a yarn produced from covered rubber, used extensively for 'stretch' undergarments and swimwear in the 1930s and 1940s.

LAWN originally a type of fine linen fabric, with the term extended to include cotton.

LISLE a highly twisted, good-quality cotton hosiery yarn.

LONGCLOTH plain-weave cotton shirting fabric, made in long pieces.

LOUIS HEEL high, curved heel.

LUSTRE a dress material with cotton warp and woollen weft, and highly finished surface.

LYCRA two-way-stretch elastic fibre introduced in early 1950s for underwear, sports garments, etc.

MAGYAR short kimono sleeves cut in one with the bodice.

MARCELLA a fancy or figured cotton fabric of piqué structure, used for dress shirt fronts.

MAROCAIN a dress material finished with a grain surface like morocco leather.

MARQUISETTE fine, open gauze fabric, usually of silk or cotton.

MEDICI COLLAR high-standing collar.

MELTON a strong heavyweight fabric for overcoats, finished by milling. The fibres are tightly matted, which gives the appearance of a felted material.

MERINO a fine dress fabric, originally made from the wool of merino sheep, later mixed with cotton.

MILLING the process of smoothing cloth.

MOIRÉ watermarked effect produced on lustrous ribbed or corded cloth, by means of heat and pressure.

MONK SHOE plain shoe with buckle fastening.

MOUSSELINE DE SOIE a French term describing muslin made from silk.

MUSLIN a general term for lightweight, open fabric of plain weave.

NAINSOOK a fine, light, plain-woven cotton cloth with a soft finish.

NAP a brushed appearance produced on a fabric surface.

NINON a fabric made from very fine highly twisted yarns.

NORFOLK JACKET a loose, pleated sports' coat with a waistband.

ORGANDIE a plain lightweight transparent cotton fabric, permanently stiff.

ORGANZA sheer, stiff plain-weave cloth of silk, rayon or nylon, not cotton. Often dyed, printed or embroidered.

OTTOMAN corded silk fabric.

OXFORD BAGS man's very wide trousers with turn-ups, popular during mid-1920s.

OXFORD SHIRTING a plain-weave shirting fabric made of good-quality yarn, usually cotton. Fancy weaves can be incorporated and dyed yarns used to form stripes.

OXFORD SHOES low-heeled, with lace ties.

PAISLEY a decorative pattern featuring an Indian cone or pine, used on fabrics.

PANAMA a hand-plaited straw hat made of plaited strips of the leaves of a South American plant.

PANNE VELVET velvet fabric with longer pile laid in one direction.

PAPER NYLON a crisp nylon fabric with a papery texture.

PAPER TAFFETA a fine, crisp fabric resembling taffeta, with a papery texture.

PEAU DE SOIE a French term, literally 'skin of silk', applied to fine, ribbed silk fabric.

PEPLUM a short, skirt-like section attached to the waistline of a dress, blouse or jacket.

PETER PAN COLLAR a flat, rounded collar.

PETERSHAM RIBBON (MILLINERY) a ribbed cotton ribbon.

PETERSHAM RIBBON (SKIRT) narrow fabric with lateral stiffness, often woven, with pockets to insert boning.

PILE a raised surface effect on a fabric formed by tufts or loops of yarn introduced into the fabric during weaving.

PILLBOX a small, round, brimless hat.

PIPING decorative edging composed of bias fabric strips, enclosing narrow cord.

PIQUÉ white cloth in light Bedford cord weave.

PLACKET form of opening made with additional band of self fabric. It may be visible on the right side of the garment or hidden beneath it.

PLISSÉ a French term meaning pleated fabric, with a puckered or crinkled effect.

PLUS FOURS baggy knickerbockers, the name derived from the four additional inches of cloth required beyond the knee.

POLYVINYL CHLORIDE (PVC) a vinyl plastic used to coat dress fabrics.

POPLIN plain-weave, medium-weight cotton fabric, with fine weft-way ribs.

PORKPIE man's hat, similar to trilby, with flatter, dented crown.

RAGLAN man's overcoat with raglan sleeves.

RAGLAN SLEEVE sleeve is cut in one piece with the shoulder.

RAISING brushed effect produced on surface of fabric.

REEFER short jacket, usually double-breasted.

REPP plain-weave fabric with prominent rib.

ROULEAU narrow tubes of fabric cut from bias strips, stitched and turned through (rouleau loops = rouleau used for button loops or decoration).

RUSSIAN BRAID (SOUTACHE) a narrow braid made with two covered cords in a continuous figure-of-eight pattern.

SADDLE-STITCHING hand-sewn running stitches of even length, worked in thicker threads for decoration on outside of garments.

SATEEN a glossy fabric of cotton or wool, resembling satin.

SATIN lustrous fabric with unbroken surface.

SCYE armhole.

SEERSUCKER fabric with surface puckered to form stripes or checks.

SELF-FABRIC in the same fabric as garment.

SERGE a twill-weave wool fabric, traditionally for suitings and outdoor wear.

SHANTUNG a plain-weave silk dress fabric with uneven surface resulting from the use of yarn spun from wild (tussah) silk.

SHAWL COLLAR smooth roll collar which is often cut in one with the front of the garment. There is only one seam, at the centre back.

SINGLE-BREASTED fastening with one row of buttons.

SNAP-BRIM hat with brim that turns down.

SNOOD hair covering of net or fabric.

SOUTACHE see Russian braid.

SPATS short ankle gaiters.

STETSON broad-brimmed felt hat.

STILETTO HEELS very narrow, tapered heels of covered steel.

STRAPPING a narrow strip of fabric or leather applied as a decoration.

TAFFETA a plain-weave, closely woven, smooth and crisp fabric with a fine, weft-way rib. (Taffeta, faille, and grosgrain are all weft-way rib cloths, listed in ascending order of prominence of rib.)

TAM O'SHANTER hat with flat, round top.

TOP-STITCHING rows of stitching on the outside of a garment for decoration.

TOQUE woman's brimless hat.

TRICORNE a three-cornered hat.

TRICOT knitted fabric of silk, cotton or rayon.

TRILBY man's soft felt hat with narrow brim and dented crown.

TROMPE L'OEIL (French) literally something that deceives the eye. Usually applied to sweaters or jumpers popular in the 1920s, with scarves, bows, or collars knitted into the design.

TULLE a fine, lightweight net with hexagonal mesh (woven); a very fine net fabric in plain weave from silk yarns.

TUSSAH a coarse silk produced by the wild silk worm.

TUSSORE a fabric woven from tussah.

TWEED coarse, rough-textured wool fabric for outer wear.

TWILL cloth woven in twill weave, giving diagonal lines on surface For a twill weave, weft threads are woven in steps across the warp threads, creating diagonally ribbed fabric.

ULSTER loose-fitting gentleman's overcoat.

UNISEX styles of clothes adopted by both men and women.

VEILING plain or ornamental nets used mainly for face veils or hat decoration.

VELOUR a heavy woollen fabric with surface raised to give velvet appearance.

VELVET a soft fabric with close, short warp pile – silk, nylon or cotton.

VELVETEEN cotton fabric with cut weft pile resembling velvet.

VICUNA cloth made of wool of vicuna animal.

VIYELLA trade name for lightweight fine wool- and-cotton-blend fabric.

WARP lengthwise threads of a woven fabric, interwoven by weft.

WEDGE HEELS shoes with continuous sole and heel, and no gap under instep.

WEFT crosswise threads of a fabric, woven into and crossing the warp.

WHIPCORD a fabric characterized by bold, steep warp twill, used for dresses, suitings and coatings.

WINKLEPICKERS shoes with elongated pointed toes.

WOOL TAFFETA plain-woven, lightweight fabric produced from worsted yarns.

WORSTED twisted yarn of long combed wool; closely woven fabric made from this.

ZEPHYR a fine cloth of plain weave used for dresses, blouses and shirtings, and made in various qualities. A typical zephyr has coloured stripes on a white ground and a cord effect made by the introduction of coarse threads at intervals.

Bibliography

FASHION AND TEXTILES

Arnold, J., *A Handbook of Costume*, Macmillan, 1973. *Patterns of Fashion: Englishwomen's Dresses and their Construction, vol. 2, 1860-1940*, Macmillan, 1973.

Beaton, C., *The Glass of Fashion*, Weidenfeld & Nicolson, 1954.

Bell, Q., *On Human Finery*, Hogarth Press, 1976.

Bond, D., *The Guinness Guide to 20th Century Fashion*, Guinness Superlatives Ltd, 1981.

Brooke, I., *Dress and Undress*, Methuen, 1958. *A History of English Costume*, Methuen, 1974.

Byrde, P., *The Male Image: Men's Fashion in England 1300–1970*, Batsford, 1979.

Carter, E., *The Changing World of Fashion*, Weidenfeld & Nicolson, 1977.

Cunnington, C.W., *English Women's Clothing in the Present Century*, Faber & Faber, 1952.

Cunnington, C.W. and P., *The History of Underclothes*, Faber & Faber, 1981.

Dorner, J., *Fashion in the 1920s and 1930s*, Ian Allen, 1973.

Ewing, E., *History of 20th Century Fashion*, Batsford, 1981.

Flugel, J.C., *The Psychology of Clothes*, Hogarth Press, 1930.

Garland, M., *Fashion*, Penguin, 1962.

Glynn, P., and Ginsburg, M., *In Fashion: Dress in the 20th Century*, Allen & Unwin, 1978.

Hall, C., *The 1920s in Vogue*, Octopus, 1983.

Hegan, A.J., Loasby, G., and Urquhart, R., *The Development of some Man-made Fibres*, The Textile Institute, 1952.

Hill, M.H., and Bucknell, P.A., *The Evolution of Fashion: Pattern and Cut from 1066 to 1930*, Batsford, 1983.

Laver, J., *Taste and Fashion*, Harrap, 1937. *Taste and Fashion*, 2nd edition, Harrap, 1945. *Women's Dress in the Jazz Age*, Hamish Hamilton, 1964. *A Concise History of Costume*, Thames & Hudson, 1969.

Lee-Potter, C., *Sportswear in Vogue Since 1910*, Thames & Hudson, 1984.

Mansfield, A., and Cunnington, P., *Handbook of English Costume in the 20th Century*, Faber, 1973.

Sichel, M., *Costume Reference 7: The Edwardians*, Batsford, 1978. *Costume Reference 8: 1918–1939*, Batsford, 1978. *Costume Reference 9: 1939–1950*, Batsford, 1978. *Costume Reference 10: 1950 to the Present Day*, Batsford, 1979.

Squire, G., *Dress, Art and Society 1950–1970*, Studio Vista, 1974.

Victoria & Albert Museum, *Fashion 1900–1939, A Scottish Arts Council Exhibition*. Exhibition catalogue, 1975.

Victoria & Albert Museum, *Four Hundred Years of Fashion*, Collins, 1984.

Wallbank, E. and M., *Pattern Making for Dressmaking and Needlework*, Pitman, 1952.

Waugh, N., *Corsets and Crinolines*, Batsford, 1954. *The Cut of Women's Clothes, 1600–1970*, Faber & Faber, 1968.

Wilcox, R. Turner, *The Mode in Hats and Headdress*, Charles Scribner's Sons, 1959.

Wray, M., *The Women's Outerwear Industry*, Faber, 1957.

Yarwood, D., *English Costume*, Batsford, 1969.

GENERAL

Banham, M., and Hillier, B. (edited), *A Tonic to the Nation – The Festival of Britain, 1951*, Thames and Hudson, 1976.

Blythe, R., *The Age of Illusion: England in the '20's' and '30's', 1919–1940*, Penguin, 1964.

Branson, N., *Britain in the 1920s*, Weidenfeld & Nicolson, 1971.

Branson, N., and Heinemann, M., *Britain in the 1930s*, Weidenfeld & Nicolson, 1972.

Briggs, A., *The History of Broadcasting in the United Kingdom, vol 1: The Birth of Broadcasting*, Oxford University Press, 1961. *The History of Broadcasting in the United Kingdom, vol 2: The Golden Age of Wireless*, Oxford University Press, 1965.

Cassin-Scott, J., and McBride, A., *Women at War 1939–1945*, Osprey, 1980.

Goldring, D., *The 1920s: A General Survey and Some Personal Memories*, Nicolson, 1945.

Graves, R., and Hodges, A., *The Long Weekend: A Social History of Great Britain 1918–1939*, Faber & Faber, 1940.

Hayward Gallery, *The 1930s, British Art and Design Before the War, Arts Council of Great Britain*, an exhibition catalogue, 1975.

International Council of Women, *Women in a Changing World: The International Council of Women since 1888*, Routledge & Kegan Paul, 1966.

Jackson, J., *Man and the Automobile – A 20th-Century Love Affair*, McGraw-Hill, Maidenhead, 1979.

Jeffreys, J.B.. *Retail Trading in Britain, 1850–1950*, Cambridge University Press, 1964.

Marsh, D., *The Changing Social Structure of England and Wales, 1871–1961*, Routledge & Kegan Paul, 1965.

Marwick, A., *The Explosion of British Society, 1914–1970*, Macmillan, 1963. *The Deluge*, Bodley Head, 1965. *Women at War 1914–1918*, Fontana in association with Imperial War Museum, 1977.

Mowat, C.L., *Great Britain since 1914: The Sources of History*, Hodder & Stoughton, 1970.

Nissel, M. (edited), *Social Trends: No.5, 1974*, Government Statistical Service, 1974.

Priestley, J.B., *English Journey*, Heinemann, 1934.

Pugh, M.D., *Woman's Suffrage in Britain 1866–1928*, Historical Association, 1980.

Rees, G., *St Michael – A History of Marks and Spencer, 2nd edition*, Pan Books, 1973.

Richardson, R.C., and Chaloner, W., *British Economic and Social History: A Bibliographical Guide*, Manchester University Press, 1976.

Stafford, M., and Middlemas, R.K., *British Furniture through the Ages*, Arthur Barker Ltd, 1966.

Tracey, H., *The British Press: A Survey, A Newspaper Directory, and a Who's Who in Journalism*, Europe Publications, 1929.

Wheen, F., *The 1960s*, Century Publishing, 1982.

White, C., *Women's Magazines 1693–1966*, Michael Joseph, 1966.

NEWSPAPERS AND MAGAZINES

Harper's Bazaar from 1929.
Ladies' Home Journal from 1890.
Tailor and Cutter from 1900.
Vogue from 1916.
Woman's Own from 1932.
Women's Wear from 1918–1925.
Woman's World from 1903–1958.
Daily Express from 1900.
Daily Herald from 1912.
Daily Mail from 1896.
Daily Sketch from 1909.